1993

THE NATURE OF MAN, OF BEING, OF GOD

HERE, in one volume, is the wisdom of the most spiritually harmonious age that Western man has known. In this age of belief, the period from the fifth to the fifteenth centuries, when religion and social institutions were closely related, philosophers discussed the nature of God, of Being, and of Man, with an intensity not known before or since.

In this remarkable book, Anne Fremantle, religious scholar and author, presents selections from the basic writings of such dominant philosophers of the medieval period as St. Augustine, St. Thomas Aquinas, Boethius, Erigena, Anselm, Abelard, Bonaventura, and Averroës, with an interpretation of their work woven throughout the texts.

ANNE FREMANTLE, an associate editor of Commonweal, *an editor of the Catholic Book Club, an associate professor at Fordham University, an editor-on-loan to the United Nations during the General Assembly, is also the author of numerous books, reviews, and articles, including* "The Papal Encyclicals in Their Historical Context."

THE AGE OF BELIEF

The Medieval Philosophers

SELECTED, WITH INTRODUCTION AND INTERPRETIVE COMMENTARY

by

ANNE FREMANTLE

A MERIDIAN BOOK

Published by the Penguin Group
Penguin Books USA Inc., 375 Hudson Street,
New York, New York 10014, U.S.A.
Penguin Books Ltd, 27 Wrights Lane,
London W8 5TZ, England
Penguin Books Australia Ltd, Ringwood,
Victoria, Australia
Penguin Books Canada Ltd, 10 Alcorn Ave.,
Toronto, Ontario, Canada M4V 3B2
Penguin Books (N.Z.) Ltd, 182-190 Wairau Road,
Auckland 10, New Zealand

Penguin Books Ltd, Registered Offices:
Harmondsworth, Middlesex, England

Published by Meridian, an imprint of New American Library,
a division of Penguin Books USA Inc.

COPYRIGHT, 1954, 1982 BY ANNE FREMANTLE

A clothbound edition of *The Age of Belief*
is published by Houghton Mifflin Company

Ⓜ REGISTERED TRADEMARK—MARCA REGISTRADA

First Meridian Printing, April, 1984

4 5 6 7 8 9 10 11 12

PRINTED IN CANADA

For A. J.
who will never read it

Acknowledgments

This book could never have existed but for the very great kindness of the following publishers who allowed me to include the vital parts—some large, some small, but all essential. I wish to thank each and every one of them: George Allen & Unwin, Ltd., D. Appleton-Century-Crofts, Inc., Benziger Brothers, Inc., Burns, Oates & Washbourne, Ltd., Cima Publishing Company, Columbia University Press, The Franciscan Institute, Harvard University Press, Longmans, Green & Company, Inc., The Macmillan Company, Marquette University Press, John Murray, Ltd., Open Court Publishing Company, Random House, Henry Regnery Company, Peter Reilly Company, Sheed & Ward, Inc., The University of Minnesota Press, and University of Pennsylvania Press.

I would like especially to thank Father Ivan Illich, Alistair Crombie, Esq., of All Souls, Oxford, and Mr. James John of the Institute for Advanced Study, Princeton, for vetting my manuscript, and for many valuable suggestions; also Etienne Gilson, for a few encouraging words at our only meeting, and for everything he has ever written, and Dr. Theodor von Mommsen for the kind loan of books.

Contents

How charming is divine philosophy
Not harsh and crabbéd as dull folks suppose
But musical as is Apollo's lute
And a perpetual feast of nectared sweets.

—*Comus*, JOHN MILTON

Introduction

"WE ARE LIKE DWARFS SEATED ON THE SHOULDERS OF GIANTS; we see more things than the ancients and things more distant, but this is due neither to the sharpness of our own sight, nor to the greatness of our own stature, but because we are raised and borne aloft on that giant mass."

So, in the twelfth century of our era, wrote Bernard of Chartres. This "giant mass" of "famous men and our fathers that begot us" is important to us not genetically and emotionally only. We get from our remote ancestors not just our faces and our frowns, the curve of an eyebrow and the trick of a likeness, but also all our history and our literature, our declarations of independence and our famous slogans. We get, too, our ideas and the very ways in which we think, together with the words we use to think with. Indeed "we have nothing that we are not given," nothing that has not been handed down and used again and again.

And the "giant mass" is made up of specific individuals. "Man" generically—if we admit that "man" exists apart from men, and one of the reasons for reading this book is to discover if we will admit "man" so to exist—has been defined by the "ancients" as "a rational animal capable of laughter." "Man," we know, invented the wheel, the pulley, the arch, the internal combustion engine, the airplane. He discovered electricity and split the atom. Yet who or what was this "man"? Very, very few men have invented or discovered anything; most men, through all the ages, and still today, are dwarfs who couldn't even figure how to set an egg up straight or how to light a fire by rubbing sticks together, unless borne aloft on the shoulders of the giants.

Now, between the "ancients" and ourselves, between the "glory that was Greece and the grandeur that was Rome"— the remote origin of all Western man—and the invention of gunpowder, we are apt to see with our mind's eye a dark, dismal patch, a sort of dull and dirty chunk of some ten centuries, wedged between the shining days of the golden Greeks, who "invented" everything (even flying, if we take the mythical Daedalus and Icarus seriously, even atoms, vitamins, and the way the planets circle the sun), and the brilliant galaxy of light given out jointly by those twin luminaries, the Renaissance and the Reformation.

These Dark Ages, which roughly cover all of time between

the Fall of Rome to the barbarians in the fifth century and the
fall of Byzantium (or Constantinople, or New Rome) to the
Turks in the fifteenth, have also been called the Ages of Faith
or, lumped together, the Age of Belief. They are often further
subdivided into the Dark Ages, from the fifth to the tenth century, and the Middle Ages, from the tenth to the fifteenth.

We in America are particularly apt to regard this Age of
Belief as a long way off, since our own history bears so little
physical relation to them. We do not, as Europeans do, worship in the very same buildings, buy and sell in the same
markets, count our money in the same countinghouses or ex-
changes, stay in the same hotels or inns, or live in the same
houses as these medieval ancestors of ours. But we still ask
the same questions, and each of us, as he or she matures,
passes through at least some of the same stages of the long intellectual process that is called civilization. We cannot fail to
meet the same problems as did our forefathers, and learning
their answers may help us to act upon them as intelligently as
they did, and may even, perhaps, teach us to avoid making always the same mistakes. And, as we become increasingly aware
of our own spiritual bankruptcy, we may look back with a certain appreciation—and even with a certain nostalgia—to those
spiritually solvent centuries, to that Age of Belief, which a
French poet, Paul Verlaine, called *"énorme et délicat."*

In this book, the Age of Belief is regarded in terms of its
philosophy; that is to say, in terms of the questions asked and
the answers given to the fundamental problems that the human
intellect asks in each generation about the nature of being, the
nature of man, the relationship of man to being—his own and
that of others. The questions will be pure philosophical ones,
and the people studied, philosophers. Sometimes the ideas will
sound religious, because of the terms in which they are stated,
but they will not be religious, nor political, nor historical, nor
economic, nor scientific. But they will be metaphysical, for
Western European philosophy during those thousand years
was based on Plato and Aristotle, two Greek metaphysicians
(*meta,* beyond, *physics,* what is discernible).

Plato (427-347 B.C.) introduced the art of thinking in concepts: he invented *ideas,* which he raised to a separate existence as metaphysical realities. His famous *Dialogues,* which
are more read today than ever before, insisted on some basic
premises, of which one was that: "all that is in the world is as
it is because it is best so, and it is only really conceived when it
is referred to the good as its final object."

Aristotle (384-322 B.C.) was a pupil of Plato, and became

the tutor of Alexander the Great (356-323 B.C.), of Macedon, one of the greatest conquerors the world has ever known. Aristotle preferred the deductive to the inductive method of reasoning (from things instead of toward things). He was an experimentalist instead of relying on intuitionalism. For Plato's self-moved mover of the universe, he substituted the unmoved mover. For Aristotle, the power and the act were parts of the metaphysical evolution, governed and perfected by formal, efficient and final causes.

All the ideas current during the whole of the Age of Belief stem from these two philosophers. Gilbert and Sullivan once wrote that every boy that is born alive is either a little liberal, or else a little conservative. For a thousand years of European history, everybody who thought at all was either a Platonist or an Aristotelian. St. Augustine, the first and one of the greatest of Christian philosophers, emerges as the greatest of the Platonists, and St. Thomas Aquinas, writing some eight hundred years later than St. Augustine, claims as his chief achievement to have brought the whole of Aristotle's thought within the orbit of the Christian faith.

But neither St. Augustine, nor St. Thomas, nor any other medieval philosopher, was content just to accept what Plato or Aristotle (or anyone else) had said. The essence of philosophy is that it must be fresh; it can never come out of a can; every philosopher has to ask the old questions anew and to produce fresh answers. Thus each new philosopher builds a new story onto the house he has inherited, the house that we all inhabit, the house of human wisdom.

For the purposes of this book, I have taken one of the most important questions raised by Aristotle in his *Categories,* that which the whole Middle Ages called the question of *Universals* (greenness, wetness, brightness, etc.), and have traced its history down the thousand years of the Age of Belief. I have given a clear statement of the problem first, as briefly written down by Porphyry who wrote in Greek, the language of Aristotle. Next, I have shown what Boethius thought of this problem, writing when Greek was falling out of fashion, and even Latin was threatened by the barbarian Goths, Vandals and Huns. I have shown the problem as argued by "realists" and "nominalists,"—realists being people who thought *Universals* really existed, and nominalists being people who thought they were only names, until at last William of Ockham finally dismissed *Universals* as only signs. The problem of *Universals* is very close to the problem of being, the whole idea of essence and

nunc fluens

of existence. We think this as keen as Kierkegaard and modern as Maritain, but it was wrestled with by Augustine and again by Aquinas. Augustine also had much to say about how we apprehend ideas, and where we find them, and his idea of memory crops up again and again in various forms. Also prominent is his idea of the relationship of time and of eternity —of the *nunc fluens,* the now flowing, of the one, and the *tota simul,* the absolute simultaneity, of the other (which he got from Plato via Plotinus).

Porphyry, Augustine, and Boethius form, as it were, the classical beginnings of Christian philosophy, with John Scotus Erigena making a bridge between them and such "new men" as Anselm, who has been called the second Augustine. The opposition raised its head with Roscelin and Abelard, and a whole new alignment of the problem of the relationship between reason and revelation came in with the Arab (Mohammedan) philosophers, and particularly with Averroës.

Etienne Gilson, the greatest medieval historian alive (and perhaps the greatest who has ever lived) wrote a whole brilliant book on the two kinds of medieval philosophers; those who believed that "since God has spoken to us it is no longer necessary for us to think," and the others who believed that "the divine law required man to seek God by the rational methods of philosophy" because it is man's first duty to use his God-given reason. These two types, the successors of Tertullian and those of St. Augustine, are both illustrated here.

The relationship between man's freedom and man's fate, between free-will and God's foreknowledge, was another of the questions that everyone struggled with during the Age of Belief and one that G. E. Moore, for example, has wrestled with in our time. St. Bernard had much that is worthwhile to say about that, as had St. Thomas Aquinas. St. Bonaventura and Duns Scotus both discussed at great length the possibility of the existence of a first principle, yet were as different in their approach and argument as it is possible for two men to be.

The questions and answers of these medieval men still constantly influence thinkers of today. I have tried to show in every case how the positions taken in the Age of Belief were followed by philosophers whose names are familiar; Kant, Hume and Hegel, Russell, Whitehead and Dewey. But the main purpose of this book is as a source book, with the emphasis on the original texts, many of which have not been hitherto available in translation, or are only available in a very few specialized libraries.

CHAPTER I

What Is Philosophy?

WHAT IS PHILOSOPHY? THE LITERAL MEANING IS EASY enough, for the English word stems from two Greek ones, *philo,* love, and *sophia*, wisdom. So philosophy is the love of wisdom, and a philosopher is a lover of wisdom. But wisdom is not an absolute; there is always more wisdom than any one person, or than all people together, can absorb. And, as Pythagoras, who lived in Greece in the sixth century before our era and was the first to call himself a philosopher, pointed out, since wisdom belongs only to God, a philosopher is a lover, not a possessor, of wisdom; boy seeks girl rather than gets girl. And the wisdom philosophy seeks above all things is the knowledge of being; what being is, and what is nonbeing; and, if there is any real difference between them, what that difference is.

All knowledge, all wisdom, is relative—relative to truth, —and the dictionaries, which define philosophy as the love of wisdom leading to the search for it, further explain that philosophy is the *knowledge* of general principles—that is, of what makes Tommy, and you and me and everyone and everything, tick. Philosophy is thus the knowledge of elements, causes and laws, as they explain facts and existences. But it is concerned primarily with being, with what really *is,* and the various types of philosophy vary in the positions they take up with regard to this problem of being. Some of the best known types of philosophy (in alphabetical order) are: association, critical, dogmatic, empirical, existential, inductive, metaphysical, mystical, positivistic, practical, speculative and transcendental.

According to Plato (427-347 B.C.), the first characteristic of the philosopher is that he must be prepared to

follow the answers wherever the argument goes, and Plato's
great pupil, Aristotle (384-322 B.C.), who was probably
the greatest philosopher who has ever lived, added: "Dear
is Plato, but dearer still the truth." St. Augustine, too (A.D.
354-430), said, some seven hundred years after Aristotle:
"Truth, wherever it may be found, *must* be avidly accepted."

The distinction between philosophy and science, which
also is a search after knowledge, is, basically, the distinction
between a point of view stemming from the general and
one stemming from the particular. Science deals with some
particular portion or aspect of reality arbitrarily abstracted
from the whole by the human mind. Philosophy is concerned with the whole problem of what being is, of whether
the universe is caused or is self-explanatory, and with the
totality of phenomena, in so far as they contribute to explain such fundamental problems.

There are obviously factors and events involving changes
from one type or state of existence to another; science certainly considers such to be within its province. But when
such changes involve a change from pure nonexistence to
mere existence, this obviously falls outside the province of
science, which assumes existence but does not claim to be
competent before questions involving its nature or its
modes. The scientist, while admitting he is incompetent,
may still deny that the philosopher is competent. But he
cannot deny the possibility of philosophical knowledge
without assuming its existence, for by and of itself science
has no way of concluding such knowledge is impossible,
nor even of proving that it does or does not exist.

Philosophy goes back to legendary times, and it was
probably a Greek, Dionysius of Halicarnassus, who defined
history itself as "philosophy teaching by examples."
Western philosophy, that is, European as distinct from
oriental, began with Thales, a Greek (640-546 B.C.)
whom Dante included in his carefully selected list of influential philosophers, headed by Aristotle, "the master of
those who know." Greek philosophy, which culminated in
Plato and Aristotle, is the basis of all later philosophy, for
the Greeks asked all the great questions, and suggested

most of the possible answers. After the Christian era began, St. Paul, speaking from the Areopagus in Athens (the hill of the god Ares), was the first to relate (around A.D. 40) the tenets of Christianity to the concepts of Greek philosophy. Later St. John, in the first chapter of his Gospel, laid the bases of Christian philosophy with his definition of Jesus Christ: "In the beginning was the Word . . . and the world was made by Him . . . and without Him was not anything made that was made."

But if Christianity early took cognizance of philosophy, the reverse was not true. The "sort of sickness," the "Jewish contagion," that the emperors feared would spread, and sought by persecution to stem, was not taken seriously by the Roman philosophers, who saw the Christians as either Jewish sectarians or oriental cultists. The rationalist historian William Lecky, in his *History of European Morals,* published in 1869, wrote:

[That the greatest religious change in the history of mankind should have taken place under the eyes of a brilliant galaxy of philosophers and historians, who were profoundly conscious of the decomposition around them, that all of these writers should have utterly failed to predict the issue of the movement they were observing, and that, during the space of three centuries, they should have treated as simply contemptible an agency which all men must now admit to have been, for good or for evil, the most powerful moral lever that has ever been applied to the affairs of man, are facts well worthy of meditation in every period of religious transition.]

FROM THE START, CHRISTIANITY COMPLICATED THE problems of philosophy, as it complicated the life of the philosopher, and it has continued to do so. In the London *Times* in 1928 a competent reviewer calmly asserted that Christianity was a good thing, and philosophy was a very good thing, but that Christian philosophy was a monstrous contradiction in terms. It is easy to see how the contradiction seems to arise. The Christian believes that not only does he search for wisdom, but wisdom also searches for him, and with more immediate success. God is not only that than which nothing greater can be imagined, but a person who, while declaring Himself to be wholly unimaginable, has yet revealed Himself and given Himself to man. There is a vast difference between arriving at a possible God at the extreme limit of man's reason, or as the First Cause of nature, and starting from a present God who gives Himself into man's heart. The process which may arrive at the former is philosophy; the study of the latter is called theology, and the response to its implications is religion.

In the first centuries of the Christian era, the Christians fought shy of the philosophers, either cold-shouldering them through fear of being worsted in argument—for the early Christians were apt to be simple, unintellectual characters—or from fear of being corrupted by pagan polytheistic and pantheistic ideas, because the oneness and the distinctness of God (that He is very different from all that is not God) were concepts which no Christian might compromise. Yet, even in the first centuries, there were a few Christians who wrote down arguments to be used against pagan philosophers and these included admitting all the basic truths that are common to all philosophies, such as, for example, that a thing cannot be and not be at the same time. By the time the Roman Empire became Christian, under the first Christian Emperor, Constantine the Great (A.D. 272-337), there was already a beginning of Christian philosophy. Christian philosophy is an intellectual inquiry into the nature of being, which accepts as a premise the possible existence of a Power outside man that is both the object and the instigator of man's search; or, as Christ put it, that He is Himself "the Way, the Truth and the Life."

The Greek philosophers finally civilized their Roman conquerors, and produced Cicero, the most completely civilized and cultured of the Romans, and Seneca, a pale copy of Socrates. In the second century A.D., Greek was the literary language in Rome (as French was in Moscow in the nineteenth century) but thereafter Greek gradually regressed, both as language and literature. Latin became the official language not only in Rome, but even in Constantinople, and soon the great Greek philosophers were only referred to and commented on, and after a time they came to be almost forgotten, and the manuscripts of their works got lost, or destroyed, when the cities and libraries where they were kept were destroyed. Thus, gradually the findings of Greek philosophy, the truths it had established, became handed on only by hearsay, or "as the Greeks say," and later still they had all to be puzzled out again.

While the unwieldy Roman Empire was falling apart, and a succession of generals was able more or less successfully to stem the flow of invading barbarians and to hold all or part of the huge Empire together, the silver ages of Latin culture produced a twilight struggle of pagans who could only repeat, at third hand and in translation, what their great philosophers had said, and of Christians not yet philosophically articulate. Such arguments as took place between Octavius and Cæcilius in Marcus Minucius Felix's *Octavius,* or between Symmachus (345-410) and the Spaniard Prudentius (348-410) can hardly be dignified with the name of philosophy, yet in them the outlines of the later Christian positions can already be traced.

The *Octavius* describes friends walking on the seashore near Ostia; one of these friends is an angry pagan who attacks the nasty Christians: Octavius defends them: "The bees have only one king, the flocks only one head, the herds only one leader. Can you believe that in heaven the supreme power is divided and that the entire majesty of that true, divine Authority is broken up? It is obvious that God, the Father of all, has neither beginning nor end; He who gives existence to all has given Himself eternal life; before the worlds were created He was a world in Himself. Whatsoever things there are He calls into being by His word, arranges them by His wisdom and perfects them by His might. He is invisible, for He is too bright for us to look upon. He is impalpable, for He is too pure for us to touch. He is incomprehensible, for He is beyond our ken—infinite, immense, and His real greatness is known to Himself alone. Our mind is too limited to understand Him, therefore we

can only form a just estimate of Him by calling Him
'inestimable.' Frankly, I will state that in my opinion the
man who thinks that he knows the greatness of God,
depreciates it; he who does not desire to depreciate it, is
ignorant of it. Nor need you seek a name for God: God is
His name. Names are only necessary where a large number
of persons have to be distinguished individually by special
marks and designations: for God, who is alone, the name
God is all sufficient." All the other walkers, at this argument's end (and it goes on to book-length) declare themselves convinced, indeed converted. Obviously here are
excellent apologetics. But here also is the beginning of a
feeling for philosophical argument: an attempt to approach
the opponent not with doctrinal bludgeons, but with metaphysical rapiers.

Prudentius' poem is very long. It is lovely poetry, just
on the edge of decadence, like a medlar or a perfect avo-
cado pear; but the argument is largely childish. Only just
sometimes does the Christian rise to the same dignified
heights as the objective and gentlemanly pagan, Symmachus.

From apostolic times on, there were two fairly well defined Christian positions: the deliberately, and aggressively,
anti-intellectual, whose supporters argued that since God
has spoken to us it is no longer necessary for us to think,
and a more orthodox, but minority, position that whatever
is true or good is ours. The leader of the anti-intellectuals
was Tertullian (?-?230), followed later by St. Jerome
(?340-420) who once, in a vision, had been scolded for
being a "Ciceronian rather than a Christian." It had ran-
kled, and he thereafter rejected philosophy as the fruit of
human pride, and even censured Origen (?185-?254), one
of the greatest Christian theologians and apologists, for
having used secular and even pagan doctrines in the interpretation of Scripture. Yet St. Jerome was one of the
few really great Greek scholars of his age, and his translation of the Hebrew and Greek Scriptures into Latin
(which is called the Vulgate) is still used today. Throughout the Middle Ages, these two positions were upheld, and
both by many saints—Saints Peter Damian and Bernard

of Clairvaux, for example, were on Tertullian's side, Saints
Bonaventura and Thomas Aquinas on the highbrow side,
which in the early ages had been upheld by such Christian writers as Manlius Theodorus, and Claudianus Ma-
mertus, and above all by St. Augustine (354-430). St.
Augustine was greatly influenced by two pagan philosophers, who both wrote in Greek. It was through the two
Neo-Platonists, Plotinus (205-270) and Porphyry (?232-
304), that St. Augustine became the inheritor and trans-
mitter of Greek philosophical thought. Though it is likely
that St. Augustine himself was not a Greek scholar, he
mentions and comments on these two Greek Neo-Platonist
philosophers with approval, and bases many of his positions
on theirs.

Porphyry was born at Tyr in 232 or 233 A.D., and at
the age of thirty he attached himself to Plotinus, who was
teaching in Rome, and from then on devoted himself to
disseminating Plotinus' ideas, and to helping him correct
and distribute his writings. In 270 Porphyry succeeded
Plotinus, published his master's collected works and
wrote his life. He also wrote a violent pamphlet in
fifteen volumes against the Christians. But his importance
as a philosopher stems from his commentaries on Aristotle's *Categories,* and above all, from his *Isagoge.* This
little treatise, later translated and commented on by Boethius, is the medium by which Aristotle's ideas were assimilated into Western thought as early as the fifth century, and
it is thanks to Porphyry, to St. Augustine whom he influenced and to Boethius, who translated him, that Christian
thought is related to, and was nourished by, Greek philosophy. The *Isagoge* is a study of the five denominations, or
predicables: genus, species, difference, property and accident, which are basic to Aristotle. But what Porphyry added
of his own was a positing, brief, but admirably clear, of the
problem of *Universals,* that was to become the most famous
and perplexing problem for the whole of the Middle Ages.
It is a problem that is clearly central to any philosophy, and
is still battled today to and fro between positivists, idealists, existentialists and neo-Thomists, as it was battled for

the thousand years from Porphyry to Aquinas between realists and nominalists.

This problem of Universals is: does whiteness, or fatness, or roundness, or anything that can be predicated of a number of things, really exist separately, apart from white things or fat things or round things? Or are the whiteness, the fatness, the roundness only in the things that are white and fat and round? Or are they only in our mind? Is whiteness merely a mental idea given us by all the white things we have ever known, and fatness the sum of all the fat things, and roundness the glomerate impression of all the round things we have perceived? If your reply is that whiteness exists, quite separately and substantially, then philosophically you are a realist; if you believe whiteness is only the mind's idea of the sum of things that are white, then in philosophy you are called a nominalist.

Here is Porphyry's statement, a brief and slim introduction to a tempestuous controversy that is not yet, and perhaps by its nature cannot be, resolved:

〔 Since it is necessary, Chrysaorios, in order to understand Aristotle's doctrine of Categories, to know what is genus, what difference, what species, what property and what accident, and that this knowledge is necessary also in order to make definitions, and, in general, for everything concerned with division and demonstration, whose theory is very useful, I will run over them briefly, and, as a sort of introduction, I will try to run over what the ancient philosophers said about them, while avoiding too abstruse enquiries and keeping even the simple ones within bounds. First of all, as to what concerns genus and species, the question is to know if they are realities subsisting in themselves, or are merely simple conceptions of the mind, and supposing them to be substantial realities, whether they are corporeal or incorporeal, and finally whether they exist separately or only in sensible things and with regard to them? I will avoid talking of this; it is a very profound problem, and it requires a deeper and more extensive research. I will try to show you here what the ancients, and among them, above all, the Peripatetics, have con-

ceived that is most reasonable on these last points and on
those which I propose to study.

Of Genus, it would seem that neither genus nor species
are simple terms. Genus, in fact, is used first of all of a
collection of individuals behaving in a certain way towards
a single being and in relation to each other. It is in this
way that the race of Heraclides is spoken of, because
their way of behaving is to spring from a common origin,
that is to say Hercules, and in the same way a number of
people who have a certain relationship towards each other
having come from a common ancestor are spoken of, and
the name they are given separates them radically from all
other races. Genus also has another meaning, it is the
point of origin of any thing, whether the generator himself is meant, or the place or thing engendered. Thus we
say that Orestes came from the race of Tantalus, or Plato
from the Athenian race, for the country is, also, a sort of
generating principle, like the father himself. Genus was
first the name for the point of departure or the origin of
any thing, and then, later, it came to include the multitude
of things which arise from a single principle. . . . There
is still another meaning to genus, and it is under this head
species is to be found, and this name doubtless accrued to
it from its resemblance to the preceding cases. Genus is,
in fact, a sort of principle for all the species which are
subordinate to it, and it seems also to contain the whole
multitude grouped under it. Thus genus is taken in three
meanings, and it is the third meaning which is the philosophical one, which is meant when genus is said to be the
essential attribute which can be applied to a plurality of
things specifically differing among themselves, as for example, animal. Indeed, so far as attributes go, some use
it of one being, such as an individual, for example, Socrates,
or this man here, that fellow there; others use it of several
people. And it is the case with genus, species, differences,
properties and accidents, that they share common char-
acteristics and ones that are not particularly applicable to
any individual. Genus, for example, animal; species, man;
difference, reasonable; property, the capacity to laugh;
accident, white, black, the being able to sit.

Thus genuses differ, on the one hand, from attributes applicable to one single individual, in that they are attributable to a plurality; they differ also, on the other hand, from attributes applicable to a plurality, that is to say from species, in that species, while being attributable to several individuals, are only attributable to individuals who do not differ amongst themselves specifically, but only numerically.

Thus *man,* which is a species, is attributed to Socrates and to Plato, who differ from each other, not in species, but in number; whereas *animal,* which is a genus, is attributed to man, ox and horse, which differ among themselves as species, not merely by number. Genus differs from property, in its turn, in that property is attributed to one species only, of which it is the property, and of the individuals comprising that species: for example, the capacity for laughter is the property only of man, and of men in particular, of men individually; genus, on the contrary, cannot be attributed to one species only, but to a multiplicity of terms differing in species.

Finally, genus differs from difference and from common accidents in that, although differences and common accidents are attributed specifically to multiple and differing terms, they are not attributed to multiple terms essentially. Indeed, if we ask what is the term to which difference and accident are attributed, we say that they are not attributed essentially qualificatively: for example, if one asks what man is like, we say he is a reasonable being; what a crow is like, we say it is black. In the first case reasonable is a difference; in the second, black is an accident. But if we are asked what is man, we reply that he is an animal, animal being the genus of man. Conclusion: to be affirmed of a plurality of terms is what distinguishes genus from individual predicates, which are only attributed to a single individual; to be affirmed of terms specifically different is what distinguishes genus from species or from property; finally, to be attributed essentially is what separates genus from differences and from common accidents which are attributed to subjects of which they are respectively the attributes, not in essence, but in quality or in some relation. This notion of genus, as we have just described it, errs neither by excess nor by default.*]

CHAPTER II

St. Augustine

AT THE VERY BEGINNING OF MEDIEVAL PHILOSOPHY STANDS St. Augustine, and, in a way, he stands also at its end. For as at the beginning is the bridge he made between Christian and classical ideas, so at the end is the rediscovery, by the Reformers, Martin Luther (1483-1546), Calvin (1509-1564), Zwingli (1484-1531), of Augustine's own emphasis on "conversation as consisting of two crossed monologues" and of the "fact of thought as an indication of the existence of God." To show how short the step from Augustine's "I think, therefore God is," to René Descartes' (1596-1650) "I think, therefore I am"—and how long—is one of the purposes of this book.

Augustine was born at Tagaste, in Roman Africa, near Tunis, in A.D. 354 and died as Bishop in Hippo, A.D. 430. His father was a pagan; his mother, Monica, a Christian. Augustine has left a most complete record of his childhood. He describes, in his *Confessions,* his child's joy in games, and his misery at school. And he analyzes a theft of pears made by him and a bunch of ragamuffin friends. They didn't even eat the pears, they raided the tree at night, just for sheer delight in doing what was forbidden. Whence came their delight was but one of the many questions he asked, and finally answered.

He was a brilliant child, and his parents sent him away from home to high school in Madaura, and later to Carthage. There he fell in love—"it is life that one loves in creatures, to love, and to be loved. And to love and to be

* Porphyry *Isagoge,* trans. J. Tricot, Paris, 1926.

loved was still more to me when I enjoyed the very body
of the beloved," he wrote. And there, too, he discovered
philosophy. It was the *Hortensius* of Cicero which showed
him another love, the love of wisdom, and at nineteen he
already felt the two loves tugging against each other. He
became, then, a Manichaean. The founder of this system
of thought was Manes, or Mani (?216-?276) a Persian
who taught that there were two eternally opposing substances, light and darkness. Man had a possibility, while
on earth, of becoming part of the kingdom of light; if he
did, then he would transcend his body. If he failed, he
would be reincarnated on an even lower plane, as animal
and even as insect, forever chained to the earth. This was
the Manichaean explanation of the problem of evil. Evil,
for the Christian, not being created by God, does not
really exist, *is* not, since all that is, is good. The Manichaeans believed that by eating no meat (which belonged
to darkness) but by eating quantities of vegetables (and
thus releasing their light into themselves) they would
hasten the kingdom of light. Unfortunately, this practice
led to many orgies, small children (particularly good con-
ductors of light) being stuffed until they died of windy
indigestion. The Manichaeans also condemned marriage
and procreation as evil, but allowed fornication, which led
to more orgies. Augustine began to see that this dualism, as
practiced, had disadvantages. Then, too, he began to find
flaws in the Manichaean system. He wrote at this time several books on the beautiful and the suitable, "two or three
books, I think," he mentions, but they somehow got lost.
When the Manichaeans held a public disputation and were
worsted, Augustine was really shaken. They persuaded him
to wait for Faustus, the chief interpreter of Manes' doctrine.
But Faustus could not answer Augustine's questions, and,
so, after nine years as a "Hearer," a Manichaean pupil, he
left them and went to Rome. Only physically, so far, for he
did not openly break with the Manichaeans, and, indeed,
after his arrival in Italy owed them his job as professor of
Rhetoric in Milan. For the prefect Symmachus, a pagan
and a personal opponent of St. Ambrose (the same Symmachus whom Prudentius attacked in his long argumenta-

tive poem), was delighted to nominate a young man known
to be a Manichaean, and therefore anathema to the Christians. (Manes had claimed that he held his authority directly from Jesus Christ, and that the Catholic teaching was
a perverted form of Christianity, so, for the Christians,
Manichaeans were a peculiarly nasty type of heretic.)
Augustine, therefore, at exactly the time when he lost his
Manichaean convictions, publicly became a Manichaean
appointee. Yet not long after in Milan he became a Christian, being baptized by St. Ambrose.

He has described, in some of the greatest prose passages
ever written, his mind's journey and what led him to baptism. He pursues truth down the nights and down the days,
and mourns everything that ever held him back.

[Too late loved I Thee, O Thou Beauty of ancient days,
yet ever new! too late I loved Thee! And behold, Thou wert
within, and I abroad, and there I searched for Thee; de-
formed I, plunging amid those fair forms which Thou hadst
made, Thou wert with me, but I was not with Thee. Things
held me far from Thee, which, unless they were in Thee,
were not at all. Thou calledst, and shoutedst and burstest
my deafness. Thou flashedst, shonest and scatteredst my
blindness . . . Thou did touch me, and I burned for Thy
peace.*]

FOR AUGUSTINE, HIS CONVERSION WAS THE BEGINNING OF
his life as a philosopher. He had thought a lot before, but
written little, and nothing that has remained. Now he was
to become one of the most prolific, as well as profound, of
philosophers. Many of his books have survived, and perhaps as many have disappeared during the fifteen hundred
years which separate him from us. He wrote on a variety of
subjects. Some of his books were to refute pagans or
heretics, like the Manichaeans, in whose teaching he once
had believed. But in all his argumentative treatises, in his
theology, history, and in his homilies, in his catechetical
instructions and even in his letters, can be found a philosophy. His lovely question *"quem colorem habet sapientia?"*

* The *Confessions of St. Augustine*, trans. Edward B. Pusey.

(tell me, what color has wisdom?) shows how intuitive
philosopher he was. And (although Augustine gratefull
admits his debt to Plotinus and to the other neo-Platonists
his philosophy is specifically Christian: "Not in the sel
same words," he relates, "but to the very same purpos
enforced by many and diverse reasons," he read in "certa
books of the Platonists, translated from Greek into Latir
that the Word was with God, and the Word was God. Bu
that the Word was made flesh and dwelt among us, that
read not there."

Among the problems that constantly recurred to him, a
much after his conversion as before, as they had occurre
to Aristotle, Plato and Plotinus, and as today they confror
J. P. Sartre, Bertrand Russell, Martin Heidegger, or an
other philosopher, alive or dead, were: What are things
Are they, at all? What is totally outside of time? What onl
inside of it? How can man's free will coexist with God
providence? The answers were, as has been said, more con
plicated after Europe became Christian, for thereafter o
the authority of divine revelation the full Catholic Fait
had *a priori* to be accepted: the Trinity, the Incarnatior
the Redemption, and all their consequences. Philosophy
function thereafter was to apply its method to the exac
interpretation of the data of revelation, and to procee
along the runway as far as the wheels of human reaso
could take the human machine, before it turned into th
wind, and was air-borne by faith.

Augustine's ideas on being and nonbeing, on the realit
of created things—"they are, and they are not, they are
because from God they derive existence; they are not, be
cause they only have being, they are not being"—ar
illustrated by the following passages from the *Confession*

[God made heaven and earth, and fills them, because b
filling them he created them. Thee none loseth but wh
leaveth. And who leaveth Thee, whither goeth or fleeth h
but from Thee well pleased to Thee displeased? . . . Fc
wheresoever the soul of man turns itself, unless towar
Thee, it is riveted upon sorrows, yea, though it is riveted o
things beautiful. And yet they, out of Thee, and out of th

soul, were not, unless they were from Thee. They rise, and
set; and by rising, they begin as it were to be; they grow,
that they may be perfected; and perfected, they wax old
and wither; and all grow not old, but all wither. So then
when they rise and tend to be, the more quickly they grow
that they may be, so much the more they haste not to be.
This is the law of them. Thus much hast Thou allotted them,
because they are portions of things, which exist not all at
once, but by passing away and succeeding, they together
complete that universe, whereof they are portions. . . .
But in these things is no place of repose; they abide not,
they flee; and who can follow them with the senses of the
flesh? yea, who can grasp them, when they are hard by? For
the sense of the flesh is slow, because it is the sense of the
flesh; and thereby is it bounded. It sufficeth for that it was
made for; but it sufficeth not to stay things running their
course from their appointed starting place to the end
appointed. . . .

The Word itself calleth thee to return: and there is the
place of rest imperturbable, where love is not forsaken, if
itself forsaketh not. Behold, these things pass away, that
others may replace them, and so this lower universe be
completed by all his parts.]

"IF GOD EXISTS, WHAT IS HE?" AUGUSTINE ASKS:

[What then do I love, when I love my God? who is He
above the head of my soul? By my very soul will I ascend
to Him. I will pass beyond that power whereby I am united
to my body, and fill its whole frame with life. Nor can I by
that power find my God; for so horse and mule that have
no understanding might find Him; seeing it is the same
power, whereby even their bodies live. But another power
there is, not that only whereby I animate, but that too
whereby I imbue with sense of my flesh, which the Lord
hath framed for me: commanding the eye not to hear, and
the ear not to see; but the eye, that through it I should see,
and the ear, that through it I should hear; and to the other
senses severally, what is to each their own peculiar seats
and offices; which, being divers, I the one mind, do through

them enact. I will pass beyond this power of mine also; for this also have the horse, and mule, for they also perceive through the body. . . .

I will pass then beyond this power of my nature also, rising by degrees unto Him Who made me. And I come to the fields and spacious palaces of my memory, where are the treasures of innumerable images, brought into it from things of all sorts perceived by the senses. There is stored up, whatsoever besides we think, either by enlarging or diminishing, or any other way varying those things which the sense hath come to; and whatever else hath been committed and laid up, which forgetfulness hath not yet swallowed up and buried. When I enter there, I require what I will to be brought forth, and something instantly comes; others must be longer sought after, which are fetched, as it were, out of some inner receptacle; others rush out in troops, and while one thing is desired and required, they start forth, as who should say "Is it perchance I?" These I drive away with the hand of my heart, from the face of my remembrance; until what I wish for be unveiled, and appear in sight, out of its secret place. Other things come up readily, in unbroken order, as they are called for; those in front making way for the following; and as they make way, they are hidden from sight, ready to come when I will. All which takes place when I repeat a thing by heart. . . .

These things do I within, in that vast court of my memory. For there are present with me, heaven, earth, sea, and whatever I could think on therein, besides what I have forgotten. There also meet I with myself, and recall myself, and when, where, and what I have done, and under what feelings. There be all which I remember, either on my own experience or other's credit. Out of the same store do I myself with the past continually combine fresh and fresh likenesses of things which I have experienced, or, from what I have experienced, have believed: and thence again infer future actions, events and hopes, and all these again I reflect on, as present. "I will do this or that," say I to my self, in that great receptacle of my mind, stored with the images of things so many and so great, "and this or that will follow." "O that this or that might be!" "God avert this

or that!" So speak I to myself: and when I speak the images
of all I speak of are present, out of the same treasury of
memory; nor would I speak of any thereof, were the images
wanting. . . .

Yet not these alone does the unmeasurable capacity of my
memory retain. Here also is all, learnt of the liberal sciences
and as yet unforgotten; removed as it were to some inner
place, which is yet no place: nor are they the images thereof, but the things themselves. For, what is literature, what
the art of disputing, how many kinds of questions there be,
whatsoever of these I know, in such manner exists in my
memory, as that I have not taken in the image, and left out
the thing, or that it should have sounded and passed away
like a voice fixed on the ear by that impress, whereby it
might be recalled, as if it sounded, when it no longer sounded; or as a smell while it passes and evaporates into air
affects the sense of smell, whence it conveys into the memory an image of itself, which remembering, we renew; or
as meat, which verily in the belly hath now no taste, and
yet in the memory still in a manner tasteth; or as any thing
which the body by touch perceiveth, and which when
removed from us, the memory still conceives. For those
things are not transmitted into the memory, but their images
only are with an admirable swiftness caught up, and stored
as it were in wondrous cabinets, and thence wonderfully
by the act of remembering, brought forth. . . .

Wherefore we find, that to learn these things whereof we
imbibe not the images by our senses, but perceive within
by themselves, without images, as they are, is nothing else,
but by conception, to receive, and by marking to take heed
that those things which the memory did before contain at
random and unarranged, be laid up at hand, as it were in
that same memory where before they lay unknown, scattered and neglected, and so readily occur to the mind
familiarised to them. And how many things of this kind
does my memory bear which have been already found out,
and as I said, placed as it were at hand, which we are said
to have learned and come to know which were I for some
short space of time to cease to call to mind, they are again
so buried, and glide back, as it were, into the deeper

recesses, that they must again, as if new, be thought out
thence, for other abode they have none: but they must be
drawn together again, that they may be known; that is to
say, they must as it were be collected together from their
dispersion: whence the word "cogitation" is derived. For
cogo (collect) and co-gito (recollect) have the same relation to each other as ago and agito, facio and factito. But
the mind hath appropriated to itself this word (cogitation),
so that, not what is "collected" anyhow, but what is
"re-collected," i.e., brought together, in the mind, is properly said to be cogitated, or thought upon.

The memory containeth also reasons and laws innumerable of numbers and dimensions, none of which hath any
bodily sense impressed; seeing they have neither colour,
nor sound, nor taste, nor smell, nor touch. I have heard the
sound of the words whereby when discussed they are de-
noted: but the sounds are other than the things. For the
sounds are other in Greek than in Latin; but the things are
neither Greek, nor Latin, nor any other language. I have
seen the lines of architects, the very finest, like a spider's
thread; but those are still different, they are not the images
of those lines which the eye of flesh showed me: he knoweth
them, whosoever without any conception whatsoever of a
body, recognises them within himself. . . .

All these things I remember, and how I learnt them I
remember. . . . And I perceive that the present discerning of these things is different from remembering that I
oftentimes discerned them, when I often thought upon
them. I both remember then to have often understood
these things; and what I now discern and understand, I lay
up in my memory, that hereafter I may remember that I
understand it now. So then I remember also to have remembered; as if hereafter I shall call to remembrance, that
I have now been able to remember these things, by the force
of memory shall I call it to remembrance.

The same memory also contains the affections of my
mind, not in the same manner that my mind itself contains
them, when it feels them; but far otherwise, according to
a power of its own. For without rejoicing I remember myself to have joyed; and without sorrow do I recollect my

past sorrow. And that I once feared, I review without
fear; and without desire call to mind a past desire.
Sometimes, on the contrary, with joy do I remember my
fore-past sorrow, and with sorrow, joy. Which is not
wonderful, as to the body; for mind is one thing, body
another. If I therefore with joy remember some past
pain of body, it is not so wonderful. But now seeing
this very memory itself is mind (for when we give a thing
in charge, to be kept in memory, we say, "See that you keep
it in mind"; and when we forget, we say, "It did not come
to my mind," and, "It slipped out of my mind," calling the
memory itself the mind); this being so, how is it that when
with joy I remember my past sorrow, the mind hath joy,
the memory hath sorrow; the mind upon the joyfulness
which is in it, is joyful, yet the memory upon the sadness
which is in it, is not sad? Does the memory perchance not
belong to the mind? Who will say so? The memory then is,
as it were, the belly of the mind, and joy and sadness, like
sweet and bitter food; which, when committed to the memory, are as it were, passed into the belly, where they may be
stowed, but cannot taste. Ridiculous it is to imagine these
to be alike; and yet are they not utterly unlike.

But behold, out of my memory I bring it, when I say
there be four perturbations of the mind, desire, joy, fear,
sorrow; and whatsoever I can dispute thereon, by dividing
each into its subordinate species, and by defining it, in my
memory find I what to say, and thence do I bring it: yet am
I not disturbed by any of these perturbations, when by
calling them to mind, I remember them; yea, and before
I recalled and brought them back, they were there; and
therefore could they, by recollection, thence be brought.
Perchance, then, as meat is by chewing the cud brought up
out of the belly, so by recollection these out of the memory.
Why then does not the disputer, thus recollecting, taste in
the mouth of his musing the sweetness of joy, or the bitter-
ness of sorrow? Is the comparison unlike in this, because
not in all respects like? For who would willingly speak
thereof, if so oft as we name grief or fear, we should be
compelled to be sad or fearful? And yet could we not speak
of them, did we not find in our memory, not only the

sounds of the names according to the images impressed by
the senses of the body, but notions of the very things themselves which we never received by any avenue of the body,
but which the mind itself perceiving by the experience of
its own passions, committed to the memory, or the memory
of itself retained, without being committed unto it.

But whether by images or no, who can readily say? Thus,
I name a stone, I name the sun, the things themselves not
being present to my senses, but their images to my memory.
I name a bodily pain, yet it is not present with me, when
nothing aches: yet unless its image were present to my
memory, I should not know what to say thereof, nor in
discoursing discern pain from pleasure. I name bodily
health; being sound in body, the thing itself is present with
me; yet, unless its image also were present in my memory,
I could by no means recall what the sound of this name
should signify. Nor would the sick, when health were
named, recognise what were spoken, unless the same image
were by the force of memory retained, although the thing
itself were absent from the body. I name numbers whereby
we number: and not their images, but themselves are present in my memory. I name the image of the sun, and that
image is present in my memory. For I recall not the image
of its image, but the image itself is present to me, calling it
to mind. I name memory, and I recognise what I name. And
where do I recognise it, but in the memory itself? Is it also
present to itself by its image, and not by itself?

What, when I name forgetfulness, and withal recognise
what I name? whence should I recognise it, did I not remember it? I speak not of the sound of the name, but of the
thing which it signifies: which if I had forgotten, I could
not recognise what that sound signifies. When then I remember memory, memory itself is, through itself, present
with itself: but when I remember forgetfulness, there are
present both memory and forgetfulness; memory whereby
I remember, forgetfulness which I remember. But what is
forgetfulness, but the privation of memory? How then is it
present that I remember it, since when present I cannot
remember? But if what we remember we hold it in memory,
yet, unless we did remember forgetfulness, we could never

at the hearing of the name recognise the thing thereby signified, then forgetfulness is retained by memory. Present
then it is, that we forget not, and being so, we forget. It is
to be understood from this that forgetfulness, when we
remember it, is not present to the memory by itself, but by
its image: because if it were present by itself, it would not
cause us to remember, but to forget.}

AUGUSTINE CONCLUDES THAT PAST AND FUTURE ARE ALL
measured, as is the present too, by memory; indeed all
reality, including God Himself, lurks there, in man's memory:

{ Thou hast given this honor to my memory, to reside in it;
but in what quarter of it Thou residest, that am I considering. For in thinking on Thee, I passed beyond such parts
of it as the beasts also have, for I found Thee not there
among the images of corporeal things: and I came to those
parts to which I committed the affections of my mind, nor
found Thee there. And I entered into the very seat of my
mind (which it hath in my memory, inasmuch as the mind
remembers itself also), neither wert Thou there: for as
Thou art not a corporeal image, nor the affection of a living
being (as when we rejoice, condole, desire, fear, remember,
forget, or the like); so neither art Thou the mind itself;
because Thou art the Lord God of the mind; and all these
are changed, but Thou remainest unchangeable over all,
and yet hast vouchsafed to dwell in my memory, since I
learnt Thee. And why seek I now in what place thereof
Thou dwellest, as if there were places therein? Sure I am
that in it Thou dwellest, since I have remembered Thee ever
since I learnt Thee, and there I find Thee, when I call Thee
to remembrance.

Where then did I find Thee, that I might learn Thee? For
in my memory Thou wert not, before I learned Thee.
Where then did I find Thee, that I might learn Thee, but in
Thee above me? Place there is none; we go backward and
forward, and there is no place. Every where, O Truth, dost
Thou give audience to all who ask counsel of Thee, and at
once answerest all, though on manifold matters they ask

Thy counsel. Clearly dost Thou answer, though all do not clearly hear. All consult Thee on what they will, though they hear not always what they will.]

HOW CAN A HUMAN BEING APPREHEND THINGS WITHOUT using the five senses, without sensory data? This is indeed another problem: how does the human mind know itself? Here, from his *On the Trinity*, Augustine tries to make at least one point clear.

[For the mind cannot love itself, except also it knows itself, for how can it love what it does not know? Or if anybody says that the mind, from either general or special knowledge, believes itself of such a character as it has by experience found others to be, and therefore loves itself, he speaks most foolishly. For whence does a mind know another mind, if it does not know itself? For the mind does not know other's minds and not know itself, as the eye of the body sees other eyes, and does not see itself; for we see bodies through the eyes of the body, and unless we are looking into a mirror, we cannot refract and reflect the rays into themselves which shine forth through those eyes and touch whatever we discern. But whatever is the nature of the power by which we discern through the eyes, certainly, whether it be rays or anything else, we cannot discern with the eyes that power itself, but we inquire into it with the mind, and if possible, understand even this with the mind. As the mind, then, itself gathers the knowledge of corporeal things through the senses of the body, so of incorporeal things through itself. Therefore it knows itself also through itself, since it is incorporeal, for if it does not know itself, it does not love itself.*]

AUGUSTINE'S APPROACH TO WHAT IS TODAY CALLED THE "space-time continuum," while it owes much to Plotinus (whose little treatise *Of Time and Eternity* deals with the same problems as Dr. W. T. Stace's book of the same name,

---

* Augustine, *On the Trinity*, Book IX, Chap. III from *Basic Writings of St. Augustine*, ed. Whitney Oates (Random House).

published in 1952), still has much that is his own. "I heard once from a learned man," Plotinus writes, "that the motions of the sun, moon and stars, constituted time, and I assented not. For why should not the motions of all bodies rather be times? Or, if the lights of heaven should cease, and a potter's wheel run round, should there be no time by which we might measure those whirlings? . . . Or, while we were saying this, should we not be speaking in time?"

Time, according to Dr. Einstein, can be treated, for the purposes of physics, *as if* it were a fourth dimension of a space-time continuum. Augustine says:

[Present of things past, memory; present of things present, sight; present of things future, expectation. I see three times, and I confess there are three. Let it be said too, "there be three times, past, present, and to come": in our incorrect way. . . .

I said then even now, we measure times as they pass, in order to be able to say, this time is twice so much as that one; or, this is just so much as that; and so of any other parts of time, which be measurable. Wherefore, as I said, we measure times as they pass. And if any should ask me, "How knowest thou?" I might answer, "I know, that we do not measure, nor can we measure things that are not; and things past and to come, are not." But time present how do we measure, seeing it hath no space? It is measured while passing, but when it shall have passed, it is not measured; for there will be nothing to be measured. But whence, by what way, and whither passes it while it is a-measuring? whence, but from the future? Which way, but through the present? whither, but into the past? From that therefore, which is not yet, through that, which hath no space, into that, which now is not. Yet what do we measure, if not time in some space? For we do not say, single, and double, and triple, and equal, or any other like way that we speak of time, except of spaces of times. In what space then do we measure time passing? In the future, whence it passeth through? But what is not yet, we measure not. Or in the present, by which it passes? but no space, we do not measure: or in the past, to which it passes? But neither do we measure that which now is not.

Does not my soul most truly confess unto Thee, that I do measure times? Do I then measure, O my God, and know not what I measure? I measure the motion of a body in time; and the time itself do I not measure? Or could I indeed measure the motion of a body how long it were, and in how long space it could come from this place to that, without measuring the time in which it is moved? This same time then, how do I measure? do we by a shorter time measure a longer, as by the space of a cubit, the space of a rood? for so indeed we seem by the space of a short syllable, to measure the space of a long syllable, and to say that this is double the other. Thus measure we the spaces of stanzas, by the spaces of the verses, and the spaces of the verses, by the spaces of the feet, and the spaces of the feet, by the spaces of the syllables, and the spaces of long, by the space of short syllables; not measuring by pages (for then we measure spaces, not times); but when we utter the words and they pass by, and we say it is a long stanza, because composed of so many verses; long verses, because consisting of so many feet; long feet, because prolonged by so many syllables; a long syllable because double to a short one. But neither do we this way obtain any certain measure of time; because it may be that a shorter verse, pronounced more fully, may take up more time than a longer, pronounced hurriedly. And so for a verse, a foot, a syllable. Whence it seemed to me that time is nothing else than protraction; but of what, I know not; and I marvel, if it be not of the mind itself? For what, I beseech Thee, O my God, do I measure when I say, either indefinitely this is a longer time than that, or definitely, this is double that? That I measure time, I know; and yet I measure not time to come, for it is not yet; nor present, because it is not protracted by any space; nor past, because it now is not. What then do I measure? Time passing, not past? It is in thee, my mind, that I measure times . . . the impression, which things as they pass cause in thee, remains even when they are gone. This it is, which still present, I measure, not the things which pass by to make this impression. This I measure, when I measure time . . . the past increasing by the diminution of the future, until by the consumption of the future all is past.

But how is that future diminished or consumed, which as yet is not? or how that past increased, which is now no longer, save that in the mind which enacteth this, there be three things done? For it expects, it considers, it remembers; that so that which it expecteth, through that which it considereth, passeth into that which it remembereth. Who therefore denieth, that things to come are not as yet? and yet, there is in the mind an expectation of things to come. And who denies past things to be now no longer? and yet is there still in the mind a memory of things past. And who denieth the present time hath no space, because it passeth away in a moment? and yet our consideration continueth, through which that which shall be present proceedeth to become absent. It is not then future time that is long, for as yet it is not: but a long future is "a long expectation of the future," nor is it time past, which now is not, that is long; but a long past, is "a long memory of the past."*]

THERE IS ANOTHER PHILOSOPHICAL PROBLEM WHICH exercised Augustine, as it very much exercises people today, and that is, whether we can apprehend meaning without words or signs? whether, as Augustine put it, "certain things can be taught without signs. Things themselves are not learned through words." This question has been tossed to and fro lately by thinkers such as the late A. H. Korzybski, the living Japanese Kagawa, Susanne Langer and I. A. Richards. The question whether there is a meaning prior to the sign has been discussed too in terms of their own disciplines by men such as J. Robert Oppenheimer, Jacques Maritain and Sir Herbert Read. Here are some of the things Augustine wrote about the problem:

[AUGUSTINE: Does it seem to you that anything which may be immediately done when one asks a question about

* *The Confessions of St. Augustine*, (*Op. cit.*).

it can be shown without a sign, or do you see some exception?

ADEODATUS [*aged 15—Augustine's son*]: Running through the items of this whole genus time and again, I do not indeed find anything in it which can be taught without some sign, except perhaps speaking and also possibly teaching. For I see that whatever I do after his question in order that he may learn, the questioner does not learn from the thing itself which he desires to have shown him. For if I am asked what walking is when I am still, or doing something else, and if I, by walking immediately, try to teach without a sign what has been asked—all of which has been discussed earlier—then how shall I avoid having the asker think that walking consists in walking only so far as I walked? And if he did think that he would be misinformed, for if someone walked not so far or farther than I did the questioner would think that this individual had not walked. And what I have said about this one word will be true of all the others which we thought could be shown without a sign, except the ones we excluded (talking and teaching).

AUG.: I accept that, in truth; but does it not seem to you that speaking is one thing and teaching another?

AD.: Surely it does, for if they were the same, none would teach without speaking, and since we teach many things by means of signs which are not words, who can doubt there is a difference?

AUG.: Are teaching and signifying the same or do they differ in some way?

AD.: I think that they are the same.

AUG.: What if it be said that we teach in order to signify? Is the assertion not easily refuted by the former statement?

AD.: That is so.

AUG.: If then we signify that we may teach and do not teach in order to signify, teaching is one thing, signifying another.

AD.: That is true, nor did I answer correctly that both are the same.

AUG.: Now tell me if he who teaches what teaching is does it by signifying or in some other way.

AD.: I do not see that there is any other way.

AUG.: Therefore, what you said awhile ago is false, namely, that when someone asks what teaching is the thing itself can be taught without signs, since we see that not even this can be done without signifying. For you have granted that signifying is one thing, teaching another. And if, as it seems, they are different, and teaching is only by means of signifying, then teaching is not shown through itself (per se), as you thought. Consequently, nothing has yet been found which can be shown through itself except speaking which also signifies itself as well as other things. Yet since this is a sign also it is still not entirely clear what things can be taught without the aid of signs.

AD.: I have no reason for disagreeing with you.

AUG.: It has been proved, therefore, that nothing is taught without signs, and that cognition itself should be clearer to us than the signs by means of which we cognize, although all things which are signified cannot be greater than their signs.

AD.: It seems so.

AUG.: Do you recall by what great circumlocutions we at length reached this slight point? For since we began this interchange of words which has occupied us for some time, we have labored to discover the following three points: 1. whether anything can be taught without signs, 2. whether certain signs ought to be preferred to the things which they signify, 3. whether the cognition of things is superior to their signs. But there is a fourth point which I wish to know briefly from you, namely, whether you think that these points are so clear and distinct that you cannot doubt them.

AD.: I wish indeed to have arrived at certainty after such great doubts and complications, but your question disturbs me, although I do not know why, and keeps me from agreeing. . . .

AUG.: I commend your hesitation. For it indicates a mind which is cautious and this is the greatest safeguard to equanimity. It is very difficult not to be perturbed when things we consider easily and readily provable are shaken by contrary arguments and, as it were, are wrenched from our hands. . . .

But come, let us consider more diligently whether you

think any of the points should be doubted. For consider, if someone unskilled in the art of bird-catching, which is done with reeds and bird-lime, should happen upon a fowler, carrying his instruments as he walked along though not fowling at the time, he would hasten to follow and in wonderment he would reflect and ask himself, as indeed he might, what the man's equipment meant. Now if the fowler, seeing himself watched, were to exhibit his art, and skillfully employ the reed, and then noting a little bird nearby, if he were to charm, approach, and capture it with his reed and hawk, would the fowler not teach his observer without the use of signification, but rather by means of the thing itself which the observer desired to know?

AD.: I fear this observer of bird-catching is like the man whom I referred to above, who inquires about walking; for it does not seem that in this case the entire art of fowling is exhibited.

AUG.: It is easy to free you from that worry. For I suggest that an observer might be intelligent enough to recognize the whole complexity of the art from what he saw. It is enough for our purpose if certain men can be taught without signs about some things, if indeed not about all things.

AD.: To that I can add that if the learner be very intelligent he will know what walking is fully when it has been shown by a few steps.

AUG.: That is agreeable. And I not only do not object, but I approve of your statement. For you see that the conclusion has been reached by both of us, namely, that some men can be taught certain things without signs, and that what we thought awhile back is false, that is, that there is nothing at all which can be shown without signs. For now of that sort, not one thing only or another, but thousands of things occur to the mind, which may be shown through themselves when no sign has been given. Why then do we hesitate, I pray you? For passing over the innumerable spectacles of men in every theater where things are shown through themselves without signs, surely the sun and this light bathing and clothing all things, the moon and the other stars, the lands and the seas, and all things which are generated in them without number, are all exhibited and shown through themselves by God and nature to those who perceive them.

If we consider this more carefully, then perhaps you may find that there is nothing which is learned by means of signs. For when a sign is given me, if it finds me not knowing of what thing it is a sign, it can teach me nothing, but if it finds me knowing the thing of which it is the sign, what do I learn from the sign?*]

HOW CAN MAN'S FREE WILL COEXIST WITH GOD'S ALL-knowing and all-willing Providence? This is a contemporary problem too. Can any man's will be free if there *is* an omniscient Creator, whose will sustains the worlds and all that in them is? Can there be any free will if there is *no* omniscient Creator? For if there is none, then Pavlov is right, who proved all man's actions are reflexes; or Freud, who saw man's will as compelled by unconscious drives, individual in his case, collective, if we believe his erstwhile disciple, C. G. Jung. Or, as Darwin claimed to prove, and the geneticists, as against Lysenko, it is the hereditary factors that condition man. Indeed, the problem of free will is as cogent today as in Augustine's time, and its relation to being has still to be thought through in the light of every new scientific discovery, as in the light of every new philosophic postulate.

Some of Augustine's ideas on this subject follow.

[And I sought "whence is evil," and sought in an evil way; and saw not the evil in my very search. I set now before the sight of my spirit the whole creation, whatsoever we can see therein (as sea, earth, air, stars, trees, mortal creatures); yea, and whatever in it we do not see, as the firmament of heaven, all angels moreover, and all the spiritual inhabitants thereof. But Thee, O Lord, I imagined on every part environing and penetrating it, though every way infinite: as if there were a sea, everywhere, and on every side, through unmeasured space, one only boundless sea, and it

* Augustine, *Concerning the Teacher*, trans. George G. Leckie Copyright, 1938, D. Appleton-Century Co., Inc. Reprinted by permission of the publishers, Appleton-Century-Crofts, Inc.

contained within it some sponge, huge, but bounded; that sponge must needs, in all its parts, be filled from that un-measurable sea: so conceived I Thy creation, itself finite, full of Thee, the Infinite; and I said, Behold God, and be-hold what God hath created; and God is good, yea, most mightily and incomparably better than all these: but yet He, the Good, created them good; and see how He en-vironeth and fulfils them. Where is evil then, and whence, and how crept it in hither? What is its root, and what its seed? Or hath it no being? Why then fear we and avoid what is not? Or if we fear it idly, then is that very fear evil, whereby the soul is thus idly goaded and racked. Yea, and so much a greater evil, as we have nothing to fear, and yet do fear. Therefore either is that evil which we fear, or else evil is, that we fear. Whence is it then? seeing God, the Good, hath created all these things good. He indeed, the greater and chiefest Good, hath created these lesser goods; still both Creator and created, all are good. Whence is evil? Or, was there some evil matter of which He made, and formed, and ordered it, yet left something in it which He did not convert into good? Why so then? Had He no might to turn and change the whole, so that no evil should remain in it, seeing He is All-mighty? Lastly, why would He make any thing at all of it, and not rather by the same All-mighti-ness cause it not to be at all? Or, could it then be against His will? Or if it were from eternity, why suffered He it so to be for infinite spaces of times past, and was pleased so long after to make something out of it? Or if He were suddenly pleased now to effect somewhat, this rather should the All-mighty have effected, that this evil matter should not be, and He alone be, the whole, true, sovereign, and infinite Good. Or if it was not good that He who was good should not also frame and create something that were good, then, that evil matter being taken away and brought to nothing, He might form good matter, whereof to create all things. For he should not be All-mighty, if He might not create something good without the aid of that matter which Himself had not created. These thoughts I revolved in my miserable heart, overcharged with most gnawing cares, lest I should die ere I had found the truth.]

AUGUSTINE SAW THAT THIS PROBLEM OF THE CO-
existence of man's free will and God's omniscience was
irrevocably linked with the problem of God's very existence. And he wrote a whole book *On the Free Choice
of the Will* from which these extracts are taken, to clarify
the subject in his own mind. In the following passage he
discusses with the Enquirer the possibility of arriving at a
certain knowledge of God's existence.

E. That one will I plainly acknowledge to be God, than
whom it is proved that nothing is superior.

A. That holds well. It will be enough for me then to show
that there is some such thing, which you will acknowledge
to be God; or, if there is one superior, you will grant that
that is God. Wherefore, whether it is higher or whether
it is not, when I shall have proved by God's assistance
what I promised, that what is above reason exists, it will
be proved that God exists.

E. Prove, then, what you are promising.

A. I shall do it: But first I ask whether the sense of my
body is the same as yours, or whether my sense is distinctly
mine, and your sense your own: which, if it were not so, I
would be unable to see through my eyes what you do not
see.

E. I grant that completely, though they (the senses) are
the same in kind, we yet have each one distinct sense
organs of seeing, of hearing, and all the others. For not only
can one man see and also hear what another hears not, but
someone may perceive by one of the senses what another
perceives not. Whence it is evident that your organic sense
is your own and my sense is mine.

A. That will be your answer too about that inner sense,
or is it otherwise?

E. Nothing other surely. For that sense, mine own, perceives my sense action, yours perceives your own. Therefore am I frequently asked by one who sees something
whether I also see it; because I perceive whether I see a
thing or see it not, he who asks does not perceive.

A. How about reason—Has not every one of us his own
reason? Since it may be that I understand something which

you understand not; and whether or not I understand you
can not know, but I know.

E. It is evident that individually we have each one his
own rational mind.

A. Can you say also that individually we have each a sun,
a moon, a lightbearing planet, and other such things which
we see, though each one sees by his own proper sense
organ?

E. I would not say that by any means.

A. We, many, therefore can see some one thing at the
same time, while our senses are individually our own, by
which simultaneously we perceive what we see all together;
so that while my sense is mine, and your sense is your own,
it can be that what we see is not, one thing mine, another
yours: but that one object may be present to both of us, and
may be seen at the same time by both.

E. That is very evident.

A. Come now, take note, and tell me whether anything
can be found that all men reasoning see in common, each
one by his own reason and his own mind, because that
which is seen is present to all; yet is not so changed into
the use of those to whom it is present as food and drink are
changed, but remains complete and entire, whether they
(present) see it or do not see it: or possibly you think
there is no such thing?

E. Even more—I see that there are many (such things),
of which it is enough to state one—(that is) the ratio and
the truth of numbers. They are present to all who reason,
so that every one takes account of them, each one, by his
own understanding, endeavors to comprehend; and one
may be able to do this easily, another with difficulty, another not at all: while yet it (the truth, the ratio of numbers) holds itself forth equally to all who are able to grasp
it. And yet, when any one grasps it, it is not changed nor
turned into the nourishment of the one who has perceived.
And when someone goes wrong in the computing of ratios,
it (the ratio itself) does not fail, but the computer fails so
much the more in error as he sees less perfectly the ratio.

A. Right truly:—But I see that you, not unskilled in these
things, have found readily what you would say. If yet

someone were to say to you that those numbers are impressed on the soul, not from any nature that is their own, but from those things we reach by the organic sense of the body as images of some visible things, what would you say? Or, would you think that too?

E. Not at all would I so think. For, if I did perceive numbers by a sense of the body, I could not therefore perceive by a sense of the body the ratios also of divisions of numbers and their united sums. By that light of the mind I refute him, whosoever, by adding or subtracting, has given a wrong answer as his solution.

And whatsoever I touch by a sense of the body as this air and this earth, and any other bodies I there perceive, I know not how long they will endure. But seven and three are ten, not now only, but forever; and by no means at any time have seven and three not been ten; nor at any future time will seven and three not be ten. This inviolable truth of number therefore I have declared to be common to me and to anyone at all who reasons.

A. I oppose nothing to you answering things very true and very certain. But that numbers are not drawn from the senses of the body you see easily if you think how a number is called so many times as it has one—For example, if a number has twice one, it is called two; three times one, three, and, if ten times one, it will be called ten. And any number at all, so many times as it has one, thence has it its name, and by that it is called number.

But whosoever thinks over *one* accurately finds by consequence that it cannot be perceived by the senses of the body. For whatsoever is perceived by such a sense is proved to be, not one, but many; for it is a body, and therefore has parts innumerable; but in order not to pursue parts minute and too disjointed, however small that corpuscle may be, it surely has one side right, another left, and an upper and a lower, a far side and a near side. It has limits and the limits have a center. For we must confess that these (dimensions) are inherent in a body how small soever it may be. We grant therefore that no body is truly and simply one. In which yet so many elements could not be enumerated but by a discerning cognition of one.

When, therefore, I search for *one* in a body, and I am sure that I find it not there, I know indeed what I search there, and I know that I will not find it there, and that it cannot be found or rather that it does not there exist at all.

When therefore I have known that a body is not *one* (simple), there I have known what *one* is. For, if I did not know *one*, I could not enumerate things plural in a body. But, wheresoever I have known *one*, I have not known it surely through a sense organ of the body. Because through a sense (organ) of the body I have known only body, which we prove to be not truly and simply one.

Moreover, if we have not perceived *one* by a sense organ of the body, we have perceived by that sense no number of those numbers which we discern by intelligence only. For there is not one of them that is not named so many times as it has counted one, the perception of which (one) is not by the sense of the body.

For the half of any corpuscle consists in two parts which equal the whole. It too has its own half. So, therefore, are these two parts in a body that the two are not unrelated.

But that number which is called two, because it has twice that which is simply one, the half of it, that is, that thing which simply is one, cannot in turn have (be) a half or a third, or any other fraction, because it is a simple, truly *one* (integral).

Then again, because holding the order of numbers, we see two after one, which is found to be the number added, double one. Double two is not added in the order of sequence, but, the number three being interposed, four follows, which is double two. And through all the other numbers, by a fixed and changeless law this order is held firm. So that after one, that is, after the first of all numbers, the first is that which holds the double of one, that is, two follows one. After two the first is number three, the second number four—double two. After the third, that is, number three, itself excepted, the third is made the double of it (three): For after the third, that is, after number three, the first is number four, the second number five, the third number six, which is the double of three. So also, after the fourth, the fourth number, itself excepted, is the double of

four. For after the fourth, that is number four, the first is
five, the second six, the third seven, the fourth eight, which
is double four. And so, through all the other numbers, you
will find what is paired in the first two, that is, what is
proved in one and two; so that, as many times as any
number is removed from the beginning, so many times
after it, is its double.

That therefore which we see through all numbers to be
immutable, fixed, and inviolate, whence do we see it? No
one by any sense of the body reaches all numbers, because
they (numbers) are unlimited. Whence therefore have we
known, that this is so over all (numbers); or by means of
what phantasy or phantasm is the truth so fixed of number
over things unnumbered, so confidently seen, but by that
light interior, which the corporeal sense knows not?

By these and by many such like arguments are men
forced to acknowledge—man to whom, thinking, God has
given mental keenness, and whom stubbornness does not
blind—that the ratio and the truth of numbers belong not
to the senses of the body: and that they stand unchangeable
and genuine; and this is a common truth, a thing to be seen
by all those who use reason.

Wherefore, since many other things could be suggested
that are present in common, and, in a manner public, to
those who use reason, and by them are seen through the
mind and reason of every individual discerning, and these
things (objective) remain inviolate and changeless—(while
this is so)—I yet not unwillingly have taken the fact that
this ratio and the truth of number occurred to you in the
first place, when you wanted to give an answer to that which
I had asked.

However, I ask, what, think you, ought to be the right
judgment on wisdom itself? Do you think that individual
men have each one his own wisdom, or think you that
wisdom is one, common to all, of which whosoever is par-
taker more completely, by that fact is he also the more
wise?

E. I know not what you call wisdom: I see indeed that
what is said or done wisely is regarded variously by men:
For they who are engaged in warfare seem to themselves

to be acting wisely; and they who, disinclined to war, devote care and energy on tilling the soil, praise that more, and attribute it to wisdom; and they who are shrewd in making plans to acquire money seem to themselves to be wise; they again who disregard all these things and put aside all such things temporal and make it their whole study to investigate truth, so that they may know themselves and know God, judge that this is the important work of wisdom; and they who are unwilling to give themselves to this leisure for the study and contemplating of truth, but rather by laboring and by cares and official duties, work for the welfare of men and engage themselves in the equitable ruling and governing of human conditions think themselves to be wise.

Wherefore, since we are studying this problem between ourselves, so that the answer to be given should not be what we believe, but what we hold by clear understanding, I will be unable to answer what you have asked until I know by contemplating and by a discerning reason that which by believing I hold wisdom to be.

A. Do you think that wisdom is other than truth in which the highest good is discerned and held?—For all those whom you have enumerated, pursuing different things, seek good and shun evil: but for this reason they follow different ways, that good appears one thing to one, other to another. Whosoever, therefore, seeks what is not to be sought, even though he would not seek it unless it appeared good, is in error. For he is not in error who seeks nothing; nor is he in error who seeks what he ought to seek.

In so far, then, as all men seek a happy life they are not in error. But in so far as anyone holds not the way of life which leads to happiness, while he may say and insist that he aims to reach no other thing but happiness, yet is he in error. For it is error to follow anything that brings us not to that which we have the will to attain. And so far as one errs the more in the way of life so much the less is he wise; because he is so much the more remote from the truth, in which the highest good is discerned and held. But it is by the attaining and the holding of the highest good that one is made happy, which, beyond controversy, is the aim of us all.

As it is established therefore that we all aim to be happy, so is it proved that we have the will to be wise, because no one is happy but by reason of the highest good, which is discerned and held in that truth which we call wisdom. As, therefore, before we are happy (contented) the notion of happiness is impressed on our minds: (For by that we know assuredly and without hesitation we say that we wish to be happy): So also, before we are wise, knowing, we have the notion of (knowing) impressed on the mind, by reason of which every one of us, if he is asked whether he wants to know, answers, without clouding the issue or doubt, that he does.

If, therefore, it is agreed between us now what wisdom is (knowing), which possibly you could not express in words (for if in no way you discerned it in mind, you would in no way know that you have the will to know, and that you ought to have this will, which, I think, you will not deny), I want you to tell me now whether you think that wisdom too (objective knowledge), like the ratio of numbers and truth, exhibits itself to all who use reason; or (because there are as many minds as there are men; and I see nothing of your mind) whether you think therefore that there are as many wisdoms as there are wise men.

E. If the highest good is one for all, it must be that the truth, in which the highest good is discerned and held, that is, wisdom, is one common to all.

A. But have you any doubt that the highest good, whatever that is, is one (the same) for all men?

E. Indeed, I am not sure, for I see different men rejoicing in different things as their highest good.

A. I, then, would have no one in doubt about the highest good just so as no one doubts that man can be happy only by attaining to the highest good. But, because the question is important, and possibly needs a long explanation, let us suppose that the highest goods are as many as are the diverse objects, which by different men are sought as their highest good. Does it then follow that wisdom also is not common to all, because those goods, which men discern and which they choose in wisdom, are many and different? For, if you so think, you may doubt also about the light of the sun, whether it is (physically) one, because the things which we discern by it are many and different. Of which many things each one chooses, according to his own will, what he enjoys through the sense of the eyes. And one looks upon the height of some mountain freely, and he rejoices in that sight; another looks over the level plane of a field, another regards the curving lines of valleys, another the greenness of forests, another the moving level of the sea, another compares all these beautiful things, or some of them at once, for the delight of seeing them.

As therefore these things are many and diverse which men see and choose to enjoy in the light of the sun, the light yet itself is one, in which the sight of each one beholding sees and holds what delights; so too there may be many things good, and also different (aims of life), from which each one may choose what he will, and by seeing it and holding it, fix it as the highest good to be enjoyed by himself rightly and truly; and yet it may be that that light of wisdom, in which these things can be seen, is one, common to all wise men (knowing).

E. I confess, it may be so, and nothing stands in the way; so that there may be one wisdom common to all men, even if the highest aims be many and diverse. But I would like to know whether this is so. For when we grant (in theory) that a thing may be so, we admit not that (actually) it is so.

A. For the present we hold that wisdom is (knowledge, objective truth); but whether it is one common to all, or whether men individually have wisdom, each one his own, as each one has his own soul or his own mind, that we do not yet hold.

E. So it is.

A. Now, that which we do hold, that wisdom (objective truth) is, and that there are men who know, and that all men desire to be happy—where do we see that? For that you do see it, and see it to be true I cannot doubt at all. This *true,* therefore do you so see as you see your own thought, which, if you make not known to me, I know not; or do you see, that you understand that this *true* can be

seen by me also, though (what you understand) is not
declared to me by you?

E. Aye, more, so (do I see) that, even independent of
my will, I doubt not that it can be seen by you too.

A. That one *true objective,* therefore, which we both see
by our individual minds, is not that same common to each
one of us?

E. Evidently it is.

A. Again, I believe that you deny not that we must aim
at wisdom (knowledge); also that you grant that to be true.

E. I have no doubt at all.

A. Can we, then, deny that this likewise is true and that
it is one; and, for all who know it, to be seen in common,
though every individual one beholds it, not by means of my
mind or your mind, but by his own mind, while that which
is beheld is present in common to all who behold?

E. By no means (can we deny).

A. Again, will you not acknowledge that it is most true
that we ought to live justly; that things less excellent are
to be subordinate to things more excellent; that like things
are to be compared to like; that to every one is to be given
what belongs to him (or her or it): and that the evidence of
the foregoing is common to me and to you and to all who
see it?

E. I am agreed.

A. How then, will you be able to deny that the unspoiled
is better than the spoiled; the eternal better than the temporal; the inviolable better than the violable?

E. Who can deny it?

A. Can any man, therefore, say that this *true* is his own;
while it is present immutably to all to be contemplated by
all who have the power to contemplate?

E. No one could say truly that it is his own, while it is as
much one and common to all as it is true.

A. Wherefore you can in no way deny that there is an
immutable truth, containing all those things that are immutably true, which (truth) you cannot say to be your own
or mine, nor can you say that it belongs to any man; but
that it is present, and in wonderful ways exhibits itself in
common as an unseen and universal light to all that discern

things immutably true. But who would say that all that is present in common to all reasoning and intelligent beings, belongs exclusively to the nature of any one of them?

You remember, surely, I think, what was said just a little time ago about the senses of the body—that those objects which we reach in common by the sense of the eyes and the ears, as are colors and sounds, which you and I see or hear simultaneously, do not belong to the nature of our eyes or our ears, but that they are physical qualities to be perceived by us in common.

So therefore you would not say that those (objective truths) which you and I in common perceive, each one by his own individual mind, pertain to the nature of the mind of either one of us. For you can not say that that which the eyes of two men see at the same time is (identified with) the eyes of one or the other; but it is some third objective, to which the sight of each one is directed.

E. That is very evident and very true.

A. Think you now, therefore, that this truth, about which we are talking much, and in which one soul we examine so many things—think you that it is more excellent than our mind is, or is it equal to our minds (on the same plane); or, again, is it less excellent?

But if it were less excellent we would judge, not according to it, but about it, as we judge of bodies (things corporeal), because they are inferior, and generally we say, not only that they are so or not so; but we say how a thing ought to be: So too of our soul, we know, not only that it is so (disposed or affected), but we know how it ought to be disposed.

Of bodies then, we so judge when we say: It is not so bright as it ought to be, or it is not four-squared, and many things in like manner. About souls, however, (we say): It is not apt as it ought to be; it is not gentle or not forceful, as the reason of our morals shall have reported.

All these things we judge according to those inner rules of truth which we discern in common. But upon the rules themselves no one passes judgment. For when one says that eternal things are preferred to things temporal, or seven and three are ten, no one says: so it ought to be; but, knowing that it is so, he corrects not as an examiner, but as an inventor [discoverer] he is pleased.

But, if this truth were on the same plane with our minds, it too would be changeable. For our minds at one time see more clearly, at another time less: and from this they show that they are changeable. While it (truth) is neither more true when it is seen by us, nor less true when we see it not: but entire and inviolate, it delights those who are turned to it by its lights, and those who are turned away it punishes by blindness.

How then about the fact that upon our minds we form judgments in accordance with this (truth); while upon the truth itself we can not pass a judgment? For we say that one understands less clearly than he ought, or, he understands as well as he ought. So much, indeed, ought the mind to understand (proportionately) as it can be brought to adhere more closely to the immutable truth. Wherefore, if (truth objective) is neither inferior nor on the same plane, it follows that it is superior and more excellent (than our minds).

But I had promised, if you remember, that I would show you that there is something that is higher than our mind and our reason. Behold, you have it—truth itself. Embrace it if you can, enjoy it, and be glad in the Lord.*]

CHAPTER III

Boethius

AUGUSTINE WAS MUCH INFLUENCED BY PLOTINUS, AND, in his turn, Augustine influenced Anicius Manlius Boethius (?480-524) who was born about half a century after Augustine died. Rome had fallen to the Goths, and effective authority in Italy was administered by the Gothic king

* Augustine, On the Free Choice of the Will, trans. Francis Tourscher (Peter Reilly Co.).

Theodoric, who was an Arian. The Arians were Christian
heretics who believed that God is one and all alone, and
that Christ was not begotten, but created, out of nothing,
before all else. Though He assumed a human body, He was
filled, not with a human soul, but, rather, with the Divine
Word. Thus, though all other things were made by and
through Christ, He neither shared the human soul's condition, nor, through His martyrdom, raised it to the plane
of the immortal. The Arians were more powerful and
numerous than the Catholics throughout the fourth and a
great part of the fifth century, and the Arian heresy lasted
for a full four hundred years. Theodoric, who employed
Boethius as one of the chief officials of his court, grew
alarmed when a Catholic became emperor at Constantinople, and thought his own subjects would waver in their
allegiance. So he first imprisoned Boethius at Pavia,
and then had him executed, in 524. Boethius had intended
to translate all of Plato's and Aristotle's works into Latin,
and to write commentaries on them. He only completed
translating the logical works of Aristotle, writing some theological treatises of his own, and the famous *Consolation
of Philosophy,* one of the two steady best sellers throughout
the Middle Ages. (The other was the *Treatise on the
Divine Names* of someone who called himself Dionysius
the Areopagite, but whoever he was, he was certainly not
St. Paul's convert, being born some centuries later.) Boethius
continues many of the arguments Augustine began, and his
light, lively style and the clarity of his mind make him still
most readable.

It was while he was in prison, between his condemnation and his death, that Boethius wrote the *Consolation
of Philosophy,* which even after the Reformation enjoyed
a great vogue, being many times translated into all the
European languages.

It is a dialogue between "my nurse Philosophy" as
Boethius calls her "in whose house I had remained since
my youth" and Boethius, weeping in his misery and banish-
ment. Their arguments are interspersed with verses, and
Philosophy, after many lovely statements "that what is, is
good," states that:

⟨ "Reason doth in such sort demonstrate God to be good
that it convinceth Him to be perfectly good. For unless
He were so, He could not be the chief of all things. For
there would be something better than He, having perfect
goodness, which could seem to be of greater antiquity and
eminence than He. For it is already manifest that perfect
things were before the imperfect. Wherefore, lest our reasoning should have no end, we must confess that the
Sovereign God is most full of sovereign and perfect goodness. But we have concluded that perfect goodness is true
happiness, wherefore true blessedness must necessarily be
placed in the most high God." "I agree," quoth I, "neither
can this be any way contradicted." "But I pray thee," quoth
she, "see how boldly and inviolably thou approvest that
which we said, that the Sovereign God is most full of sovereign goodness." "How?" quoth I. "That thou presumest
not that this Father of all things hath either received from
others that sovereign good with which He is said to be
replenished, or hath it naturally in such sort that thou
shouldst think that the substance of the blessedness which
is had, and of God who hath it, were diverse. For if thou
thinkest that He had it from others, thou mayest also infer
that he who gave was better than the receiver. But we most
worthily confess that He is the most excellent of all things.
Finally, that which is different from anything, is not that
from which it is understood to differ. Wherefore that which
is naturally different from the sovereign good, is not the
sovereign good itself. Which it were impious to think of
God, than whom, we know certainly, nothing is better.
For doubtless the nature of nothing can be better than the
beginning of it. Wherefore I may most truly conclude that
which is the beginning of all things to be also in His own
substance the chiefest good." "Most rightly," quoth I. "But
it is granted that the chiefest good is blessedness?" "It is,"
quoth I. "Wherefore," quoth she, "we must needs confess
that blessedness itself is God." "I can neither contradict,"
quoth I, "thy former propositions, and I see this illation
followeth from them."

"Consider," saith she, "if the same be not more firmly
proved hence, because there cannot be two chief goods,

the one different from the other. For it is manifest that of those goods which differ, the one is not the other, wherefore neither of them can be perfect, wanting the other. But manifestly that which is not perfect, is not the chiefest, wherefore the chief goods cannot be diverse. Now we have proved that both blessedness and God are the chiefest good, wherefore that must needs be the highest blessedness which is the highest divinity." "There can be nothing," quoth I, "concluded more truly than this, nor more firmly in arguing, nor more worthy God himself."]

IN HER EFFORTS TO CONVINCE BOETHIUS, PHILOSOPHY CONTINUES:

["generation of all things, and all the proceedings of mutable natures, and whatsoever is moved in any sort, take their causes, order and forms from the stability of the divine mind. This, placed in the castle of its own simplicity, hath determined manifold ways for doing things, which ways, being considered in the purity of God's understanding, are named Providence, but being referred to those things which He moveth and disposeth, they are by the ancients called Fate. Providence is the very Divine reason itself, seated in the highest Prince, which disposeth of all things. But Fate is a disposition inherent in changeable things, by which Providence connecteth all things in their due order. Perceivest thou now what followeth?" she asked. "What?" said I. "That" quoth she "all manner of fortune is good."]

PHILOSOPHY THEN PROVES THAT NOTHING HAPPENS BY CHANCE:

["if any define chance to be an event produced by a confused motion, and without connection of cause, I affirm that there is no real thing. For what place can confusion have, since He disposeth all things in due order? For it is a true sentence that of nothing cometh nothing, which none of the ancients denied, though they held not that principle of the efficient cause, but of the material subject." "I acknowledge it to be as thou sayest" admits Boethius; "in this rank of coherent cause, have we any free will or doth the fatal chain fasten also the motions of men's minds?" "We have," quoth she, "for there can be no reasonable nature, unless it be endued with free-will. For that which naturally hath the use of reason hath also judgment by which it can discern of everything by itself. Therefore they which have reason in themselves have freedom to will and nill. But yet I consider not this equal at all. For the minds of men must needs be more free when they conserve themselves in the contemplation of God, and less when they come to their bodies, and still less when they are bound with earthly fetters. But their greatest bondage is when, giving themselves to vice they lose possession of their own reason." Then I complained that I was now in a greater confusion and more doubtful difficulty than before. "What is that?" quoth she. "It seemeth," quoth I, "to be altogether impossible and repugnant that God foreseeth all things, and that there should be any free-will. For if God beholdeth all things and cannot be deceived, that must of necessity follow which His providence foreseeth to be to come. Even though things be foreseen because they shall be, yet they do not come to pass because they are foreseen. What else is it to think that God doth therefore foresee future things, because they are to happen, then to affirm that those things which happened long since, are the cause of that sovereign providence? Also, as when I know anything to be it must needs be so, so when I know that anything shall be, it must needs be to come. And so it follows that the event of a thing foreknown cannot be avoided." "This" she said "is an ancient complaint against Providence. I wonder why you think solution insufficient, who think that free-will is not hindered by foreknowledge, because they suppose that foreknowledge is not the cause of any necessity in things to come? I suppose no one will say that those things which are now done were not to come before they were done. So, as the knowledge of things present causeth no necessity in things which are in doing, so neither does the foreknowledge of things to come . . .

"Likewise those things which God hath present, will have

doubtless a being, but some of them proceed from the necessity of things, others from the power of the doers. And therefore we said not without cause that these, if they be referred to God's knowledge, are necessary; and if they be considered by themselves, they are free from the bonds of necessity. As whatsoever is manifest to senses, if thou referrest it to reason, is universal; if thou considerest the things themselves, it is singular or particular. But thou wilt say, 'If it is in my power to change my purpose, shall I frustrate providence if I chance to alter those things which she foreknoweth?' I answer that thou mayest indeed change thy purpose but because the truth of providence, being present, seeth that thou canst do so, and whether thou wilt do so or no, and what thou purposest anew, thou canst not avoid the divine foreknowledge, even as thou canst not avoid the sight of an eye which is present, although thou turnest thyself to divers actions by thy free-will.

"But yet thou wilt inquire whether God's knowledge shall be changed by thy disposition, so that when thou wilt now one thing, and now another, it should also seem to have divers knowledges. No. For God's sight anticipateth all that is to come and recalleth and draweth it to the presence of His own knowledge; neither doth He vary, as thou imaginest, now knowing one thing and now another, but in one instant without moving anticipateth and comprehendeth thy mutations. Which presence of comprehending and seeing all things, God hath not by the event of future things but by His own simplicity.

"God's knowledge also surpassing all motions of time, remaineth in the simplicity of His presence, and comprehending the infinite spaces of that which is past and to come, considereth all things in His simple knowledge as though they were now in doing.

"For which cause it is not called praevidence or foresight, but rather providence, because, placed far from inferior things, it overlooketh all things, as it were, from the highest top of things. Why, therefore, wilt thou have those things necessary which are illustrated by the divine light, since that not even men make not those things necessary which they see? For doth thy sight impose any necessity upon those things which thou seest present?

"No. But the present instant of men may well be compared to that of God in this: that as you see some things in your temporal instant, so He beholdeth all things in His eternal present. Wherefore this divine foreknowledge doth not change the nature and propriety of things, and it beholdeth them such in His presence as they will after come to be, neither doth He confound the judgment of things, and with one sight of His mind He discerneth as well those things which shall happen necessarily as otherwise. As you, when at one time you see a man walking upon the earth and the sun rising in heaven, although they be both seen at once, yet you discern and judge that the one is voluntary, and the other necessary, so likewise the divine sight beholding all things disturbeth not the quality of things which to Him are present, but in respect of time are yet to come. And so this is not an opinion but rather a knowledge grounded upon truth, when He knoweth that such a thing shall be, which likewise He is not ignorant that it hath no necessity of being. Here if thou sayest that cannot choose but happen which God seeth shall happen, and that which cannot choose but happen, must be of necessity, and so tiest me to this name of necessity, I will grant that it is a most solid truth, but whereof scarce any but a contemplator of divinity is capable. For I will answer that the same thing is necessary when it is referred to the Divine knowledge; but when it is weighed in its own nature that it seemeth altogether free and absolute. For there be two necessities: the one simple, as that it is necessary for all men to be mortal; the other conditional, as if thou knowest that any man walketh, he must needs walk. For what a man knoweth cannot be otherwise than it is known. But this conditional draweth not with it that simple or absolute necessity. For this is not caused by the nature of the thing, but by the adding of a condition. For no necessity maketh him to go that goeth of his own accord, although it be necessary that he goeth while he goeth. In like manner, if providence seeth anything present, that must needs be, although it hath no necessity of nature. But God beholdeth those future things, which proceed from free-will, present. These things, therefore, being referred to the divine sight are necessary by the condition of the divine knowledge, and, considered by themselves, they lose not absolute freedom of their own nature. Wherefore doubtless all those things come to pass which God foreknoweth shall come, but some of them proceed from free-will, which though they come to pass, yet do not, by coming into being, lose, since before they come to pass, they might also not have happened.

"Let us be then lifted up as much as we can to that height of the highest mind, for there reason shall see that which she cannot behold of herself. And that is, how a certain and definite foreknowledge seeth even those things which have no certain issue, and this is no opinion, but rather the simplicity of the highest knowledge enclosed within no bounds. For it is the common judgment of all that live by reason that God is everlasting, and therefore let us consider what eternity is.

"Eternity therefore is a perfect possession altogether of an endless life, which is more manifest by the comparison of temporal things, for whatsoever liveth in time, that being present proceedeth from times past to times to come, and there is nothing placed in time which can embrace all the space of its life at once. But it hath not yet attained tomorrow and hath lost yesterday. And you live no more in this day's life than in that movable and transitory moment. Wherefore, whatsoever suffereth the condition of time, although, as Aristotle thought of the world, it never began nor were ever to end, and its life did endure with infinite time, yet it is not such that it ought to be called everlasting. For it doth not comprehend and embrace all the space of its life together, though that life be infinite, but it hath not the future time which is yet to come. That then which comprehendeth and possesseth the whole fullness of an endless life together, to which neither any part to come is absent, nor of that which is past hath escaped, is worthy to be accounted everlasting, and this is necessary, that being no possession in itself, it may always be present to itself, and have an infinity of movable time present to it. Wherefore they are deceived who, hearing that Plato thought that this world had neither beginning of time nor should ever have any end, think that by this means the created world should be coeternal with the Creator. For it is one thing to be carried through an endless life, which Plato attributed to the world, another thing to embrace the whole presence of an endless life together, which is manifestly proper to the divine mind. Neither ought God to seem more ancient than the things created, by the quantity of time, but rather by the simplicity of His divine nature. For that infinite motion of temporal things imitateth the present state of the unmovable life, and since it cannot express nor equal it, it falleth from immobility to motion, and from the simplicity of presence, it decreaseth to an infinite quantity of future and past, and since it cannot possess together all the fullness of its life, by never leaving to be in some sort, it seemeth to emulate in part that which it cannot fully obtain and express, tying itself to this small presence of this short and swift moment, which because it carrieth a certain image of that abiding presence, whosoever hath it, seemeth to be. But because it could not stay it undertook an infinite journey of time, and so it came to pass that it continued that life by going whose plenitude it could not comprehend by staying. Wherefore, if we will give things their right names, following Plato, let us say that God is everlasting and the world perpetual."*]

BOETHIUS IN FIVE BRIEF TREATISES DEFENDED THE CATHolic position against the Arians, and in one of these, "a letter to John the Deacon," Boethius proved how "substances can be good in virtue of their existence without being absolute goods."

[I have [he wrote] therefore followed the example of the mathematical and cognate sciences and laid down bounds and rules according to which I shall develop all that follows.

I. A common conception is a statement generally ac-

* Boethius, *De Consolatione Philosophiae*, trans. Rev. H. F. Stewart (Loeb Classical Library, G. P. Putnam's Sons, 1926).

cepted as soon as it is made. Of these there are two kinds.
One is universally intelligible; as, for instance, "if equals
be taken from equals the remainders are equal." Nobody
who grasps that proposition will deny it. The other kind is
intelligible only to the learned, but it is derived from the
same class of common conceptions; as "Incorporeals cannot occupy space," and the like. This is obvious to the
learned but not to the common herd.

II. Being and a concrete thing are different. Simple Being awaits manifestation, but a thing is and exists as soon
as it has received the form which gives it Being.

III. A concrete thing can participate in something else;
but absolute Being can in no wise participate in anything.
For participation is effected when a thing already is; but
it is something after it has acquired Being.

IV. That which exists can possess something besides
itself. But absolute Being has no admixture of aught besides Itself.

V. Merely to be something and to be something absolutely are different; the former implies accidents, the latter
connotes a substance.

VI. Everything that is participates in absolute Being
through the fact that it exists. In order to be something
it participates in something else. Hence that which exists
participates in absolute Being through the fact that it exists,
but it exists in order to participate in something else.

VII. Every simple thing possesses as a unity its absolute
and its particular Being.

VIII. In every composite thing absolute and individual
Being are not one and the same.

IX. Diversity repels; likeness attracts. That which seeks
something outside itself is demonstrably of the same nature
as that which it seeks.

These preliminaries are enough then for our purpose.
The intelligent interpreter of the discussion will supply the
arguments appropriate to each point.

Now the problem is this. Things which are, are good.
For all the learned are agreed that every existing thing
tends to good and everything tends to its like. Therefore
things which tend to good are good. We must, however,

inquire how they are good—by participation or by substance. If by participation, they are in no wise good in themselves; for a thing which is white by participation in whiteness is not white in itself by virtue of absolute Being. So with all other qualities. If then they are good by participation, they are not good in themselves; therefore they do not tend to good. But we have agreed that they do. Therefore they are good not by participation but by substance. But those things whose substance is good are substantially good. But they owe their actual Being to absolute Being. Their absolute Being therefore is good; therefore the absolute Being of all things is good. But if their Being is good, things which exist are good through the fact that they exist and their absolute Being is the same as that of the Good. Therefore they are substantial goods, since they do not merely participate in goodness. But if their absolute Being is good, there is no doubt but that, since they are substantial goods, they are like the First Good and therefore they will have to be that Good. For nothing is like It save Itself. Hence all things that are, are God—an impious assertion. Wherefore things are not substantial goods, and so the essence of the Good does not reside in them. Therefore they are not good through the fact that they exist. But neither do they receive good by participation, for they would in no wise tend to good. Therefore they are in no wise good.

This problem admits of the following solution. There are many things which can be separated by a mental process, though they cannot be separated in fact. No one, for instance, can actually separate a triangle or other mathematical figure from the underlying matter; but mentally one can consider a triangle and its properties apart from matter. Let us, therefore, remove from our minds for a moment the presence of the Prime Good, whose Being is admitted by the universal consensus of learned and unlearned opinion and can be deduced from the religious beliefs of savage races. The Prime Good having been thus for a moment put aside, let us postulate as good all things that are, and let us consider how they could possibly be good if they did not derive from the Prime Good. This process leads me to

perceive that their Goodness and their existence are two
different things. For let me suppose that one and the same
substance is good, white, heavy, and round. Then it must
be admitted that its substance, roundness, color, and goodness are all different things. For if each of these qualities
were the same as its substance, weight would be the same
thing as color or goodness, and goodness would be the same
as color; which is contrary to nature. Their Being then in
that case would be one thing, their quality another, and
they would be good, but they would not have their absolute Being good. Therefore if they really existed at all, they
would not be from good nor good, they would not be the
same as good, but Being and Goodness would be for them
two different things. But if they were nothing else but good
substances, and were neither heavy, nor colored, and
possessed neither spatial dimension nor quality, beyond
that of goodness, they (or rather it) would seem to be not
things but the principle of things. For there is one thing
alone that is by nature good to the exclusion of every other
quality. But since they are not simple, they could not even
exist at all unless that which is the one sole Good willed
them to be. They are called good simply because their
Being is derived from the Will of the Good. For the Prime
Good is essentially good in virtue of Being; the secondary
good is in its turn good because it derives from the good
whose absolute Being is good. But the absolute Being of all
things derives from the Prime Good which is such that of
It Being and Goodness are rightly predicated as identical.
Their absolute Being therefore is good; for thereby it resides in Him.

   Thereby the problem is solved. For though things be
good through the fact that they exist, they are not like the
Prime Good, for the simple reason that their absolute
Being is not good under all circumstances, but that things
can have no absolute Being unless it derive from the Prime
Being, that is, the Prime Good; their substance, therefore,
is good, and yet it is not like that from which it comes. For
the Prime Good is good through the fact that it exists,
irrespective of all conditions, for it is nothing else than good;

but the second good if it derived from any other source might be good, but could not be good through the fact that it exists. For in that case it might possibly participate in good, but their substantial Being, not deriving from the Prime Good, could not have the element of good. Therefore when we have put out of mind the Prime Good, these things, though they might be good, would not be good through the fact that they exist, and since they could not actually exist unless the true good had produced them, therefore their Being is good, and yet that which springs from the substantial Good is not like its source which produces it. And unless they had derived from it, though they were good yet they could not be good through the fact that they exist because they were apart from good and not derived from good, since that very good is the Prime Good and is substantial Being and substantial Good and essential Goodness. But we need not say that white things are white through the fact that they exist; for they drew their existence from the will of God, but not their whiteness. For to be is one thing; to be white is another; and that because He who gave them Being is good, but not white. It is therefore in accordance with the will of the Good that they should be good through the fact that they exist; but it is not in accordance with the will of one who is not white that a thing have a certain property making it white in virtue of its Being; for it was not the will of One who is white that gave them Being. And so they are white simply because One who was not white willed them to be white; but they are good through the fact that they exist because one who was good willed them to be good. Ought, then, by parity of reason, all things to be just because He is just who willed them to be? That is not so either. For to be good involves Being, to be just involves an act. For Him being and action are identical; to be good and to be just are one and the same for Him. But being and action are not identical for us, for we are not simple. For us, then, goodness is not the same thing as justice, but we all have the same sort of Being in virtue of our existence. Therefore all things are good, but all things are not just. Finally, good is a general, but just is a species, and this

species does not apply to all. Wherefore some things are
just, others are something else, but all things are good.*]

THE MOST INFLUENTIAL OF BOETHIUS' WORKS, HOWEVER,
was his *Commentary on the Isagoge of Porphyry*. One C.
Marius Victorinus, called Afer, a native of Africa (died
circa 370), had already translated Porphyry, and Boethius
used this translation. Since Porphyry's *Isagoge* was already
a commentary on Aristotle's *Categories,* Boethius was already commenting at one remove; by the end of the Middle
Ages, the ripples caused by the stones Aristotle threw had
reached the edge of the pond—the limits of possible speculation—and all the answers were known; today, as has been
remarked, "we know all the answers, it is the questions
that we do not know."

The following are some extracts from Boethius' Dialogues on the *Isagoge.*

[When winter blows upon the Aurelian mountains, and
the east wind in those parts has broken the peace of the
night and disturbed its quiet, then is a time to go over in
the mind what the wisest men have illuminated with the
sharp sword of their intellect, piercing the darkness. Fabius
did just this, when he came to me as I lay in bed, thinking
and meditating on such things, and as we freely talked, all
domestic noises being hushed, he asked me to explain to
him what Victorinus the orator, a very wise man in his time,
had translated from Porphyry's *Isagoge,* that is, his introduction to the *Categories* of Aristotle, and what are the
preliminary devices of commentators used to prepare the
minds of their readers. I replied, "they always first explain
the intention, the utility, the genuineness, the originality
and the division of philosophy."

"What then," asked Fabius, "is the intention, into which
this work falls?" And I replied, "Philosophy is a genus, and
there are two species, one called theoretic and that is
speculative, and the other practical, and that is active. And
Aristotle, who himself is our bridge and the introduction to

* Boethius, *Quomodo substantiae,* trans. Rev. H. F. Stewart
  (Loeb Classical Library, G. P. Putnam's, 1926).

philosophy, could not see that any arguments could be understood unless we were prepared to understand the very
things about which we were to dispute. Then Porphyry seeing that in all things there was a first nature, from which
all others arose as from a fountain, considered those things
which were first to be subsistents and called them by the
name of genus. But nothing could be a genus unless certain
other things were contained within it, and these he called
species, but no genus could be the genus of only one species
but must be of several. Yet many species could not be
multiplied unless some distinction separated them. For
were there nothing dissimilar among them, there would
seem to be but one species, not many. These divisions and
dissimilarities of species are called by the name of difference, and it follows from this that every difference appears
first in the seed and occurs also in the substance, so that
neither can there be accident without substance nor substance without accident. For no accident can exist without
a foundation of substance, and substance cannot be perceived unless by means of accident. In order that color,
which is an accident, exist, it must be in a body which is a
substance. So also, when you see a body that is a substance,
you see this accident of color. Thus it is that neither is there
a substance beyond accident, nor can there be an accident
abandoned by substance. . . . Porphyry speculated about
these things, that is, accident and substance, genus, species,
property and accident and difference, and what genus is of
and by itself, and what difference plainly is. And he began
principally to deal with genus, species, difference, property
and accident. Now the knowledge of these five things is for
us a sort of root and many-sided source which flows into
all parts of philosophy. For in order to define a thing, you
must first give its genus. In order to define what is man, you
must first say man is an animal. Then, when you define man
as an animal, the genus animal and man, a species of animal, is defined by you, but it does not suffice only to give its
genus. For if you merely say man is an animal, do you
define a man any more than a horse, a cow or a donkey? . . .

"Let this be a definition of man. Man is an animal, that is
his genus, but man is a species, reasoning, that is the dif-

ference, capable of laughter, that is his property. So far in this definition no use has been made of accidents. But there is no doubt that accident adds nothing to definitions. For a definition seeks to describe substance, and accident does not describe substance, so accident is useless in a definition. Much has been written and argued by the ancients on these subjects, but they are only briefly touched upon in this further problem which now arises . . ." "Which is that?" asked Fabius. "This," I replied, "which can be asked of any and all genera and species: whether they really exist, or are merely perceived by the intellect alone and the mind, whether they are corporeal or incorporeal and whether once separated, they can be attached to sensible objects. This, then is the first question, whether genera and species are true, or whether they are but naked and empty figments of the imagination. This question can be phrased thus. Because man has a many-sided intelligence, he apprehends the quality of sensory objects subjected to his senses, and from these, having obtained some sort of an idea, he has thus provided himself with a way to the understanding of incorporeal objects. I, when I see individual men, and know that they seem men, and that they are men, I believe that I understand myself. Then my intelligence, having brought me so far, lifts itself higher, and is carried to this idea of a species of man, which has been posited under the genus animal, and understands that incorporeal thing that it was before it assumed particular bodies in individual sentient and intelligible men. Then there is this analogous question, whether certain things are wholly incorporeal, which never suffer from bodies, such as the soul or God, or whether such cannot exist with bodies, as for example, a primary limitless incorporeality.

"Once it has been established that genus truly exists, then there is no doubt another question will arise, whether it is corporeal or incorporeal. But this would be a frivolous or an absurd question, whether genus is corporeal or incorporeal, unless its existence had first been established. But this essential question can be disposed of in this fashion. No one doubts that incorporeal things can exist, although they are not apprehended by any of the senses, for men's

minds make clear what they are by thought. Now because
the first nature of these things is incorporeal (i.e., thoughts
in the mind) it may be that the incorporeal is the parent
of the corporeal. Genus, actually, is of itself neither corporeal nor incorporeal, but can become one or the other,
but species are, some corporeal, some incorporeal. Genus,
as 'animal,' species, as 'man,' difference, as 'reasoning,'
property as 'can laugh,' accident, as 'white': this is a brief
and succinct division. . . .

"But although genus is one, it can produce many species.
Thus it embraces many things just as it is divided into many
species. For man, crow and horse, which are species, when
it comes to animal, are equally animal. Thus the name of
animal is shared by all the species among themselves. But
species are a division of genus in some fashion, and are
multiplied, for when you divide genus into species, you
accept the same species for only as many as heretofore you
accepted as one. For the infinite variety of individuals can
be named under one generic term. Thus all individual men
belong to the species man, are one mankind. Yet the same
species in us is broken up into us all. So that everything
which is single and individual is divided from what it was
born, and everything that is not single or individual, but
can be divided, does not divide itself otherwise than to the
same extent that it can be brought together. For you can
say that every man is an animal, and it is true. But if you
say that every animal is a man, that is false . . .

"So in one way it is possible to know whether the name
of this, whose division we wish to make, is equivocal,
whether genus means that which is signified, or whether
genera and species and such others are grasped only by
understanding . . .

"Genera and species either exist and subsist or are
formed by the intellect and thought alone, but genera and
species can also not exist. This can be seen from the following. Anything that is simultaneously common to many
cannot at the same time be at one with itself. For whatever
is shared by man, and wholly possessed in common by
many things at the same time, is manifold. However many
species there are, there is the same genus in them all, not

that the separate species divide the genus into so many parts, but that every one of the species is in possession at the same time of the whole. From this it arises that the whole genus, present simultaneously in many individuals, cannot be one, for since it is totally in so many simultaneously it can not itself be one. But if this is so, and genus cannot possibly be one, then it follows that it cannot be; for whatever is, is because it is one, otherwise it is nothing. And the same may be correctly said about species . . ."

[Boethius goes on to say that if genus and species are multiple in number, there will be an infinite regression and so reason must proceed for ever, since no end of the breaking-down process occurs.] "But when the intellect receives from the senses things confused and mixed up with bodies, it distinguishes between them with its own strength and thought. For thus sense brings to us incorporeal things which have their existence through these same bodies, and the intellect which has the power to unite the disjointed and to disjoin the composite among all the things brought to it by the sense, so distinguishes the incorporeal nature in itself without bodies that where it is concrete it looks and sees the incorporeal nature in itself . . ."]

BOETHIUS ASKED "WHAT IS THE RELATION OF UNIVERSALS to the individual material things that exemplify them, and to the human mind that knows them?" The whole of medieval philosophy concerns itself, one way and another, with answering this question.

It was Martianus Capella, an African writing about the year 430, who first listed the seven liberal arts which were to form the basic curriculum of medieval students. He listed them in Books III to IX of an allegory, quite unreadable today, *The Marriage of Mercury and Philology*. This also contains (in Book IV) a list of the five predicables (genus, species, difference, property, and accident) and the ten categories. Also he lists oppositions, propositions and syllogisms—all more or less cribbed from Aristotle, and all a bit garbled in the cribbing.

Cassiodorus (c.490-585) lived in the Ostrogothic kingdom of Theodoric too, but, unlike Boethius, he survived.

Born in Calabria, Italy, he became private secretary to
Theodoric when only twenty, and later governor and sena-
tor. In 540 he retired to the monastery of Vivarium, which
he had founded on his estates, and died at the age of ninety-
five. He urged his monks to read, and made a library
list for them, which included Dionysius, Ptolemy, and
Porphyry.

St. Isidore of Seville (?560-636) fled from one Spanish
province to another. His fatherland was destroyed by the
Goths. Isidore was a brother of St. Leander, whom he
succeeded as Bishop of Seville, and was the last of the
Fathers of the West. He was "above all a compiler, perhaps
the greatest compiler who there has ever been." He com-
piled a summary of all human knowledge, and bequeathed
to the Middle Ages a sort of encyclopedia of all pagan and
Christian writings available at his time. He also wrote at
least eight books, of which a history and a defense of the
Catholic Church against the Jews are the best known. His
only contribution to philosophy is that he listed the pagan
philosophers and summarized their theories. With him the
last echoes of the ancient voices died in the West.

The classical sunset had all but faded by now; in a
broken Europe, cut up into many barbarian kingdoms,
Christianity was fighting for its life, and had little time or
energy to try to save classical culture too. But at least
it did not push classical culture off the raft to which both
clung: the raft of a common language (Latin) and of a
common law. Christianity and classical culture were linked
by their shared survival, were to remain bracketed thereafter. The Greco-Judeo-Christian tradition, that anoma-
lous, composite concept, had begun its joint fight for survival—which still continues today, although as Christopher
Dawson says, the "history of the early Middle Ages is
remarkable for its discontinuous character: indeed, it
seems at first sight to consist of a series of false starts."

CHAPTER IV

John Scotus Erigena

"THE MIDDLE AGES" IS A SOMEWHAT ELASTIC TERM covering more or less the ten centuries between the Fall of Rome to the barbarians in the fifth century of the Christian era and the Fall of Constantinople to the Turks in the fifteenth—a thousand years of European history which divide the Classical Ancient World of Greece and Rome from the Modern. These medieval ages have often been called the Dark Ages, both by the Humanists, the people for whom the classical world of *Litterae Humaniores,* or humane letters, is the best, and by those for whom Modern Times alone are civilized. A French historian, Michelet, for example, gloomed about "a thousand years without a bath," whereas another French historian, Etienne Gilson, speaks glowingly of "a thousand years of abstract speculation." The Humanists, Christopher Dawson tells us, regard the Middle Ages as a dark age of Gothic barbarity, while to the Reformers they were ages of spiritual darkness, and both parties wanted to wipe the whole thousand years clean off the slate and start again from classical antiquity. The modern-age enthusiasts want to start with the Reformation or the Renaissance, when they don't want to start still later with the French Revolution.

But there they are, those Middle Ages, a thousand years, straddling across human history. They "saw the making of Europe and the birth and rebirth of Western culture: they also witnessed the creation of that socio-religious unity that we call Christendom, and the gradual penetration of our culture by Christian beliefs and Christian moral and intellectual standards." It is with the last two words of Christopher Dawson that this book has to deal, with the "intellectual standards," or, rather, with the philosophical.

With Christian cultural standards too as they relate to philosophy. Not, however, with medieval political, psychological, artistic, literary, mystical or devotional standards. All medieval ideas were religious, since in the Middle Ages religion and civilization were so closely united that "religious institutions were the main organs of culture and almost every form of social activity possessed a religious sanction."

Like Gaul, and unlike God, the Middle Ages can be divided into three parts. The first, or Patristic period, is the transition, when the glow of the classical sunset dies into the stormy barbarian dawn. The real Dark Ages follow, during which the barbarians overran Europe, and then, painfully and gradually, were coaxed into the Christian fold. The Dark Ages culminate in the glorious twelfth century renaissance, which lasted for nearly two hundred years. Then it was that Christian culture produced such a feast of learning and literature, of law and art, as made it one of the glorious golden ages of man.

Christopher Dawson has described three ways in which religion may enter and become part of a culture. It may grow up "as it were naturally, with the life of the people, so as to seem inseparable from it." That was the case in Egypt, China, India, Greece and Rome. Or it may enter as a conqueror, as Buddhism entered China, or Islam Persia in the seventh, or Turkey in the fourteenth, century. Or it may enter a culture at the formative stage, and become part of, and be modified by, the new culture that is growing up. "The history of medieval Christianity is a classic example of the third process."

What is difficult for people of the Modern Age to understand (and it is just as hard for Christians as for agnostics) is that the Middle Ages were totally unaware of nationalism. From Iceland to Sicily there was one faith, one culture: as from Poland to Portugal. And from the point of view of ideas, whether a man came from Prester John's central Asiatic kingdom or the Church of Malabar in India, from the deserts of Egypt or the snows of Lapland, mattered not at all. Climaxing the Middle Ages is the thirteenth century, which, like the age of the Greek Pericles, or the Roman Augustus, that of Akbar the Indian or of the English Elizabeth I, is one of the "classical" ages, when human civilization, that slow, thorny cactus, suddenly flowers, and, as Voltaire said, "compensates the historian for the barren prospect of a thousand years of stupidity and barbarism."

The "stupidity and barbarism" were but a part, the growing-pains part, of an organization of society that was complete and perfect in its way. Resting on the uniformity of the faith professed, and on the absolute universality of the Church, undisputed by any sectarian body, there was, in the early Middle Ages, as Dr. Waldemar Gurian puts it, "no fundamental divergence of view as to the reciprocal concordance, and the repartition of rights, between the spiritual and temporal power. The medieval formula on the basic relation between the spiritual and the secular order presupposed a spiritual unity which was the signal feature of medieval society and was unique in history." Because of these broad agreements, disagreements could exist in many subsidiary areas, and a freedom of divergence was possible which was astonishing and has remained unique. The "freedom of the faith" was an astonishment even to Lecky, whose opinion of religion was that on the whole it had been detrimental to the pursuit of truth. But of the Middle Ages he wrote, in his *History of the Rise and Influence of Rationalism in Europe* (Longmans, 1865):

[Catholicism was then perfectly in accordance with the intellectual wants of Europe. It was not a tyranny, for the intellectual latitude it permitted was fully commensurate with the wants of the people. It was not a sect or an isolated influence acting in the midst of Europe and forming one weight in the balance of power, but rather an all-pervasive energy animating and vivifying the whole social system. A certain unity of type was then manifested, which has never been restored. The corporations, the guilds, the feudal system, the monarchy, the social habits of the people, their laws, their studies, their very amusements,

all grew out of ecclesiastical teaching, embodied ecclesiastical modes of thought, exhibited the same general ten-
dencies, and presented countless points of contact or of
analogy. All of them were strictly congruous. The Church
was the very heart of Christendom, and the spirit that
radiated from her penetrated into all the relations of life,
and colored the institutions it did not create. In such a
condition of society, heresies were almost impossible. For
while the particular form that a heresy assumes may be
dependent upon circumstances that are peculiar to the
heresiarch, the existence and success of heretical teaching
always proves that the tone of thought or measure of probability prevailing at the time has begun to diverge from the
tone of thought or measure of probability of orthodoxy.
As long as a church is so powerful as to form the intellectual condition of the age, to supply the standing-point
from which every question is viewed . . . it will realize
so perfectly the general conceptions of the peoples, that
no difficulties of detail will seriously disturb it. This ascend-
ancy was gained by medieval Catholicity more completely
than by any system before or since, and the stage of civilization that resulted from it was one of the most important
in the evolutions of society.]

MEDIEVAL PHILOSOPHY THUS OWED ITS CONTENT TO TWO
sources: on the one hand, to the religious background,
Jewish, Patristic, or later, as will be seen, also Muslim;
and, on the other, to the philosophy of the Greeks. The
development of religion and the assimilation of Greek
thought were two parallel and interactionary movements,
which culminated in a repeated attempt to reconcile
philosophy and religion by separating their spheres. And
the more complete the separation, the more satisfactory
and lasting the reconciliation, as will be seen.

As the barbarian pressure increased, the Roman legions
were not withdrawn; neither were they replaced. It was not
that "some people went away," but, rather, that others
failed to come: reinforcements did not come. Britain, Gaul,
Spain, Austria, Illyria were left to fend for themselves,
after the Roman garrisons, outnumbered, had been mas-

sacred, often to a man—as at Shrewsbury, as in Brittany, and elsewhere.

The waves of conquerors had come from the East, over the low Ural Mountains, the "not very high hills" which, as Hitler pointed out, are all that separate Europe from Asia; Goths and Vandals, Franks and Huns, in varying degrees and in different places, kept coming for some four hundred years; then they more or less settled down. The process took a long time, and was gradual; little pockets of Roman culture and civilization survived, in monasteries, around cathedrals, in corners of countries or on islands, such as the Ile de Lérins, in the south of France, or at Lindisfarne, off the North Sea coast of England, or in Ireland, or on Iona. From these islands and outposts gradually, too, the monks ventured back onto the mainland; sometimes they were successful and remained beside the conquerors to chivvy and Christianize, as did St. Columbanus, or St. Willibrod. Sometimes they were murdered, like St. Boniface, but something of what they had brought remained. The monks alone tried to conquer the conquerors, for generally the subject peoples hated them too greatly, and treasured their relics of *Romanitas,* or Roman being, and feeling, too dear. Indeed the long delay in the Christianization of the invaders owes much to the bitter hatred of the subject peoples, who once had been Roman. The Celts, for example, so hated the Saxons that they refused to try and convert them, lest they succeed, and the Saxons be saved. They *wanted* them eternally damned. On the other hand, there were Romans who welcomed the barbarians, as being less corrupt and evil than they. Such pessimistic Christians as Salvian, whose long life covered most of the fifth century, wrote in bitter melancholy of the wickedness of Christians at home in Rome contrasted to the virtues of the nice, healthy pagans. In his *The Governance of God* Salvian complains:

[I have made sufficient mention of how great are the vices of the Romans, vices with which the barbarians are not befouled . . . The vices of our bad lives alone have conquered us . . .

But what can be said of the present-day situation? The old abundances have gone from us. The resources of former times have gone. . . . With us, therefore, the causes of corruption are not in enticements, as with other men, but in our hearts. Our wickedness is in our mind, so that the loss of our wealth does not move us to amend our ways of life. We proceed to sin through love for evil things.*]

OTHERS OF THE CLERGY WERE MORE CHARITABLE—OR more provident. Gregory of Tours, for example, who came from a whole family of Saints (as today someone might come from a legal or medical family), tried hard to soothe the savage Frankish breast. His chronicles of court life are tragic, desperate accounts of superhuman efforts to contend with revolting savages—no missionaries in cannibal islands ever had more unpleasing characters with whom to deal. Gregory's problem, as Harmon Grisewood said, "was not endurance and resistance. His was acceptance and inclusion. He was not called to defend Troyes as did St. Loup, or to die in his cathedral, as St. Nicaise at Rheims, or to arm the city as St. Aignan at Orleans. His was a complex task. The conquerors were already baptized into eternity. They now had to be Christianized in the world. The danger was not that the Franks, Goths, etc., would destroy the Church, but that they would dominate it."

And so long as that danger was daily present, and until the relation of Church and State settled down into the dichotomy that was to be routine for the Middle Ages, there was no time for philosophy. Even sanctity had to be active, a "divinely guided improvisation" facing daily human grossness, greed, concupiscence; facing murder, poisoning, slaughters, and their resultant suffering, with firm compassion, and without any amazement.

In Rome, St. Gregory the Great (?540-604), one of the greatest of all Popes, by sending to England St. Augustine of Canterbury (who had been trained, as St. Patrick also, in the south of France), renewed the direct contacts

* Salvian, *The Governance of God*, from *The Writings of Salvian*, trans. Jeremiah O'Sullivan (Cima Publishing Co., 1947).

between Rome and the far parts of Europe and made possible the Carolingian Renaissance that began two hundred
years later. For it was from the outposts, from Ireland, the
only country in Europe where the monks still knew Greek,
from Iona and York, that learning and philosophic thinking came back to the mainland. Alcuin of York (735-804)
towards the end of his life wrote, "in the morning, when
my years and my studies were in full flower, I sowed in
England; now my blood chills, it is almost evening, but I
never cease sowing." Summoned by Charlemagne, the first
Holy Roman Emperor (crowned in St. Peter's, Rome, on
Christmas Day, 800), Alcuin was tutor to this great Frankish king and conqueror, and followed his court wherever
it moved. For Charlemagne's court was where he was, not
in any fixed place. Alcuin laid the foundations of what he
thought would be a new Athens, a France taught by both
Plato and Christ. He wrote a little book, a sort of cate-
chism, for his royal pupil (although it is not certain that
Charlemagne ever read it—or, indeed, ever learned to
read) to instruct him in the virtues. Alcuin planned the
complete curriculum of studies, too, for the whole Middle
Ages. His sevenfold division of the arts and sciences was
taken from Martianus Capella. Grammar, dialectic, rhetoric (these formed the *trivium*); arithmetic, geometry, astronomy and music (the *quadrivium*). Later these seven
formed the requirements for the Master of Arts degree all
over Europe, and are still, essentially, the basis of the
Litterae Humaniores or Greats' "School" at Oxford. Taken
in medieval times as a seven-year course, the mastery of
these liberal arts qualified a student to be considered cultured. And into this sevenfold scheme, and through it,
philosophy crept back into the Western World, taking a
modest place as a part of logic.

"And the philosophers?" Alcuin's pupil asked him.
"They knew that virtue, wisdom and truth were inherent
in human nature, and they sought them diligently," came
Alcuin's answer. "But then what difference is there between such philosophers and Christians?" asked Charlemagne rhetorically. "Faith only, and baptism," replied Alcuin.

Alcuin was a schoolmaster, not a philosopher. His successor, John Scotus Erigena, born in Ireland, and a great Greek scholar, was one of the most original thinkers of the whole Middle Ages. He reached the court of the Frankish king Charles the Bald about 840, and translated from Greek into Latin the works of Denys, the pseudo-Areopagite, and those of another early mystic, Maximus the Confessor, which had been sent to the king of France by the emperor of Constantinople, Michael the Stammerer. But John Scotus Erigena was much more than a translator, and he won great renown from King Charles the Bald, as a master of argument and dialectic.

A monk, Gottschalk, had insisted there was a double predestination, the righteous predestined to go to heaven, the sinners to hell. Predestination means that God—or destiny—has predetermined a man's fate, so that whether he is saved or damned is all arranged before he is even born. One of the great Christian problems was (and is) how to reconcile God's absolute foreknowledge with man's equally absolute free-will, without positing some form of predestination. Actually, as many medieval philosophers pointed out, to know is not necessarily the same thing as to will: God knows we will sin, but here in time His will is not our law unless *we* will it, and God no more prevents what He foresees, than a wise mother prevents a child spending its allowance on candy which will she knows make it both sick and sorry. Hrabanus Maurus, another monk, and Hincmar, bishop of Rheims, both saw the dangers for the Church in Gottschalk's position, which is a denial of the intrinsic value of all good works. Hincmar asked John Scotus to reply to Gottschalk. John Scotus Erigena, who had succeeded Alcuin as head of the Palace School, brilliantly proved that there can be predestination only to good—in that we are all called to be saints.

John Scotus Erigena's greatest work, *The Division of Nature,* "synthesizes the philosophical accomplishments of fifteen centuries, and appears as the final achievement of ancient philosophy."* Like Alcuin's little book, it is

* George Burch, *Early Medieval Philosophy* (Kings Crown Press, 1951).

in the form of a dialogue between Master and Pupil. Where reason is, faith has no place, declared John Scotus, anticipating Thomas Aquinas' statement that one cannot know and believe a thing at the same time. But the function of reason is to understand revelation, and interpret it. "Authority is the source of knowledge, but our own reason remains the norm by which all authority must be judged." And he defines faith as "a certain beginning by which knowledge of the Creator begins to be produced in the rational nature." He could not even imagine a faith which was opposed to reason.

In *The Division of Nature* John Scotus pointed out that to divide nature into Creator and creature is not enough. For him there are four divisions: God, Who is nature which creates and is not created; the intelligible world, which is nature, which is created and creates; the world of experience, nature which is created and does not create; and nature which neither creates nor is created—this last the return of the two that are not God to the divine unity. In the first and fourth, God is both beginning and end; He creates and is not created, and He neither creates nor is created. In the second and third John Scotus Erigena is speaking of ideas and existences, both being created, but not in the same sense. From God, via creation, back to Him, this process of exodus and return is at the heart of Erigena's philosophy.

But John Scotus, although he said that no one gets into heaven except by philosophy, was also a theologian; in all things, he said, see God only, for everything comes from Him, and to Him is the return. At the world's end, all nature, corporeal or incorporeal, will be deified, as fused iron is molten, as air is invisible when irradiated by light. Only the integrity of the natures will remain; for God, Who is our beginning and our end, still is our Creator, and the whole of human history, as the whole of natural science, is the total rhythm of procession and return, from the Creator and back to Him. Only, because of the Fall, in history the process is irreversible, whereas in nature it is continuous, circular, eternal. All things are resolved into the same unity from which they are derived:

❬ The end of all motion is its beginning; for it terminates at no other end save its own beginning from which it begins to be moved and to which it tends ever to return, in order to cease and rest in it.

In the intelligible world this law is the fundamental principle of all the sciences, that is of the seven liberal arts. Grammar begins with the letter, from which all writing is derived and into which it is all resolved. Rhetoric begins with a definite question, from which the whole argument is derived and to which it returns. Dialectic begins with essence, from which the whole argument is derived and to which it returns. Arithmetic begins with unity, from which all numbers are developed and into which they are resolved. Geometry begins with the point from which all figures are developed and into which they are resolved. Astronomy begins with the moment from which all motion is developed and into which it is resolved. Metaphysics begins and ends with God. In nature as a whole, division is creation, by which all things emanate, by successive states, from the divine unity. Analytic is called return, because all things return, through the same stages, to the same unity. All things flow constantly from God as water flows from a spring, and tend ever to return to Him as water tends ever to return to its level. God alone is without motion because, being the beginning and end of all things, he has himself neither beginning nor end. The flux of all things is not a motion in time, because all time is comprehended within one part of the process. It is not a cycle which repeats itself, but an eternal cycle, and the two aspects of the process are simultaneously eternal. Nature is eternal, but not static. It is eternally dynamic, moving by the dialectical process of division and return.

We do not know what God is . . . because He is infinite and therefore objectively unknowable. God Himself does not know what He is because He is not anything. Therefore, nothing can be predicated of God literally or affirmatively. Literally God *is not,* because He transcends being.

Although we do not know *what* God is, we infer from the existence of the world *that* He is, not that He is as any

intelligible essence, but merely that He exists as the cause
of all things. This inference is threefold. We observe that
things are, and infer that their cause is. We observe the
order of the universe, and infer that their cause is wise.
We observe that things are in constant motion, being alive,
and infer that their cause is life. Thus God, considered not
in Himself but as the cause of all things, has three aspects:
He is, He is wise, and He lives. His being is called the
Father, His wisdom is called the Son, His life is called the
Holy Ghost, words which denote not the three aspects
themselves, but their relation to each other. God's being is
His essence, what He is. His wisdom is His power, what He
can do. His life is His operation, what He does. Essence,
power and operation, in God or in anything, are not three
parts which compose the substance, but a simple and inseparable unity. Although the Son and the Holy Ghost are
in a certain sense derived from the Father, so that only the
Father is without any source, they are in no wise created
by Him, but are coeternal and coessential with Him. God,
therefore, in all three persons, constitutes nature which
creates and is not created.

All things created by God are created in the image of
God, and are therefore trinities consisting of essence, power and operation. These three are the substance of the
thing, all else is accident. As in the Trinity of God these
three are an inseparable unity, but they are distinct aspects
of that unity. In a tree these aspects are for it to be, to be
able to grow, and actually to grow. The essence is the unknowable being of the thing; the power is its specific character; the operation is its particular movement. All things
subsist in these three ways. Therefore, there is a threefold
creation of things . . . and there are three stages in the
division of nature; nature is divided into nonbeing and being; essence is divided into genera and species; species are
divided into individuals. These divisions are accomplished,
respectively, by the three persons of the Trinity; the Father
wills, the Son makes, and the Holy Ghost perfects. The
Father wills. This act of God is His essence; the creation
of the universe is not in God by accident, but by a certain
ineffable law that effects subsist eternally in their cause.

God does not know things because they are: they are because He knows them, and His knowledge of them is their
essence. The Son makes. That is, He divides the created
essence into the eternal ideas, which are called the primordial causes, because they cause and create all things. They
are the forms of things, not the visible qualitative forms,
but the intelligible substantial forms, by participation in
which all things subsist, that is, have their separate and special properties or powers. A tree grows because it participates in life. These ideas, existing in the mind of God,
contain the substances of all things: man, for example, is
most correctly defined as a certain intellectual notion
eternally made in the divine mind. The Holy Ghost perfects. That is, God, in His infinite activity, leads forth the
primordial causes into their effects, dividing the eternal
ideas into the particular things, both intelligible and visible,
which participate in them. These effects are related to the
primordial causes as words are related to the voice which
speaks them; they are subsequent not in time but in order
of causality. Unlike the eternal causes, they form genera
and species, they come into being through generation, they
move in time and space, and they are subject to accidents.
They include all essences (which in this aspect are more
properly called natures), all qualities, all quantities, and all
things comprised in the other categories. Separately, that
is, apart from their combinations, they are incorporeal, in-
corruptible, and indivisible. A combination of a certain
quality and a certain quantity produces matter, which is
not a new thing but a result of the combination, just as the
combination of light and an opaque body produces a
shadow, without in any way affecting either the light or the
body itself. Matter itself (apart from the forms it receives)
is likewise invisible and even indefinable. It is merely a
formlessness or mutability capable of receiving forms.
When, at a certain time, matter is joined to a certain form,
a visible body is produced. Thus, bodies are composed of
incorporeal things, qualities, quantities, forms and times.
They are not substances, being composed only of accidents,
and are therefore corruptible, for they can be resolved into
the accidents which compose them; when these are taken

away, nothing remains. All these accidents are accidents of
an essence and substantial form, but not of the body;
rather, the body is an accident of the accidents. In everybody, therefore, three aspects are considered: the matter,
that is, quality and quantity, of which it is made; the qualitative form which makes it a solid and visible body, and
the eternal essence or substantial form of which these are
the accidents.

The substance of every creature is threefold; there is the
essence of the thing, that is, God's knowledge of it, by
which it is made to be; there is the eternal form of the
thing, established among the primordial causes in the
Word, by which it is defined to be what it is; and there is
the particular thing, moving in time and subject to accidents, by which it is manifested.

All things always *were,* in the Word of God, causally,
in force and potency, beyond all places and times, beyond
generations made in place and time, beyond all forms and
species known by sense and understanding, beyond all
quality and quantity and other accidents by which the substance of any creature is understood to be, but not what it
is.

But also, all things *were not* always, for before they
flowed forth by generation into forms and species, places
and times, and into all the accidents which happen to their
eternal substance, immutably established in the Word of
God, they were not in generation, they were not in space
nor in time, nor in the proper forms and species to which
accidents happen.*]

DR. BURCH, WHO MADE THE MAGNIFICENT TRANSLATION
of Erigena quoted above, discusses at length whether
Erigena was a pantheist or not. Every Christian philosophe:
has continually to steer clear of the three great denials
of natural truth (that is, truth attainable by reason, as
against revealed truth). These denials are all sins against
or breakings of, the first commandment of the Christian, as

---

* John Scotus Erigena, *Patrologia Latina,* CXXII, ed. Jacques
Paul Migne, trans. George Bosworth Burch in *Early Medieval
Philosophy.* (Kings Crown Press, 1951.)

of the preceding Jewish, and the succeeding Islamic, faiths. This commandment is: "Thou shalt have none other Gods but Me," or "the Lord thy God is one," or "there is no God but God." The three denials of it are polytheism, pantheism and prometheanism. They mottle medieval philosophy as they mottle pre-Christian thought and the thought of post-Christian thinkers.

Polytheism is the commonest, the simplest, and the most elementary of the three. Subtle thinkers, like John Scotus, never fall into it. The Manichaeans were polytheists. Prometheanism is named for the Greek myth of Prometheus, who stole his father Zeus' fire from heaven, instead of waiting for the god to give it to him. Adam, too, was promethean when he took what he should have waited to be given, and man is promethean whenever he uses magic, whenever he seeks for God as power, or seeks God for His gifts; for example, when he tries by asceticism to capture higher states of consciousness, or to enter them by means of drugs or arts, or even when he tries to put himself into them, instead of waiting to be brought into them by God. Prometheanism is, at bottom, a mixture of conceit and cupboard love, and Aldous Huxley has brilliantly described it in his *Grey Eminence* only to fall into it in his the *Doors of Perception*.

Pantheism is far more plausible. Like polytheism, it constrains God to our own image, and whittles Him down to our size: it takes as its premise that God *is* all things, and that there is nothing which is *not* God. It may seem a paradox that pantheism is a denial of the unity: if created and creator are one, as they are for the true monist (and a pantheist must be a monist, since he insists on one, all-embracing Reality), and not two, as they are for the pluralist, surely the monist is affirming the unity, and it is the pluralist who is fractioning it? In reality, the reverse is true. For by denying his own createdness, the creature denies the Creator's omnipotence. If I am part of God, if the Self at its core IS God, then I cannot deny Him, nor He deny me, and there is no relationship, for He is as constrained by His being as I, and He is not the only necessary being, for I am necessary too, and He exists by my will as much as I do by His; then too, He is made in my image and likeness, not I in His. This monism or pantheism was skirted by John Scotus Erigena, though some think he came perilously close. Others think he escaped by a fairly wide margin, for he insisted that to return to God we must come forth from Him, while for the true pantheist we could not leave Him any more than He could leave us and there can be neither procession, nor return. The Rig-Veda, the greatest of the Hindu Scriptures, put it thus, *tat tuam asi,* i.e., God, thou art also. For the Christian, as for the Muslim and the Jew, there is always enough identity given to the creature for his "I" to say "Thou": for the Hindu there is no one who can say "I" except God, and God cannot separate anything from Himself.

Dr. Burch quotes rather a compromising passage of Erigena:

[God Himself is the maker of all things, and is made in all things; when He is sought above all things, He is not found in any essence, for He is not yet being, but when he is understood in all things, nothing subsists in some save him alone. Nor is He one thing and not another thing, but He is all things. [But then Erigena goes on to say that] man is the unity of all creatures. He is intellect, reason, sense, life and body, and there is no other nature besides these except God. All things are made in the divine mind, but they may be made in other minds also. You and I, when we argue, are made in each other. For when I understand what you understand, I become your understanding, and am made in you, in a certain ineffable way. . . .

As all things are derived originally from God, by various intermediate steps, so all things are resolved ultimately into God by the same intermediate steps. Thus God is the beginning, the middle and the end of all things, beginning because all things are from him by participation in his essence, middle because all things live and move and have their being in him, end because all things have their perfection and the end of their motion in him. Diffusion is goodness: reunion is love. God as cause of things is supreme goodness, and as end of all things is supreme love.

Love is the end and quiet cessation of the natural motion of all moving things, beyond which no motion continues; it is the connection and bond by which the universe of all things is joined together in an insoluble unity and an ineffable sympathy. God as goodness and God as love, the first cause of all things and final end of all things, are the same. The fact that they are identical is the fundamental law of nature.]

IN DESCRIBING THE FINAL END OF THE CREATED UNIVERSE, Erigena uses a simile many other mystics subsequently used:

[Just as the air appears to be all light, and the molten iron to be all fiery, nay, fire itself, their substances nevertheless remaining, so it is understood by the intellect that after the end of this world every nature, whether corporeal or incorporeal, will seem to be only God, the integrity of the nature remaining, so that God, who is in himself incomprehensible, will be somehow comprehended in the creature.]

JOHN SCOTUS DISAPPEARED FROM VIEW ABOUT 877, AND the next medieval thinkers of any importance were Bérenger, professor at the monastic school of Tours, who insisted that we only attain truth by reason and that it cannot be given by revelation, and St. Peter Damian, who said the opposite, agreeing with Tertullian that since God has spoken to us it is no longer necessary for us to think. St. Peter Damian was prior of Fonte Avellana and later Cardinal-Bishop of Ostia; he died in 1072. Lanfranc (1005-1089), another Italian, who was prior of Bec in Normandy, insisted, like St. Peter Damian, on the priority of faith, but refused to deny the validity of reason. His pupil and successor, St. Anselm, born at Aosta in Italy in 1033, became abbot of Bec in 1078, and Archbishop of Canterbury in 1093. His solution of the problem of the relationship of truth to reason, although only temporary, was one of the landmarks of medieval thought.

CHAPTER V

St. Anselm

ST. ANSELM HAS BEEN CALLED "THE SECOND AUGUSTINE."
He believed that faith precedes all understanding, and that
the wisdom philosophy seeks is given before it can be
apprehended. Unbelievers, he taught, strive to understand
but never can because they do not believe, for in religion
"faith plays the part played by experience in the understanding of the things of the world." Anselm sought a conclusive proof of the existence of God. As a biographer
wrote: "mere affirmation did not satisfy him, he demanded
proofs. This thought was continually before his mind. It
caused him to forget his meals, and pursued him even during his worship. After a night spent in meditation he at last
found what he had been seeking for years." What he found,
the famous "ontological" proof of the existence of God, was
denied by St. Thomas Aquinas (1225-1274), was re-
phrased by Duns Scotus (1265-1308), reaffirmed by René
Descartes (1596-1650), modified by Gottfried Leibniz
(1646-1716), and refuted by Immanuel Kant (1724-
1804), only to be revamped and reaffirmed by George
Hegel (1770-1831).

"I do not seek to understand that I may believe, but I
believe in order to understand. For this also I believe, that
unless I believed, I should not understand." Thus Anselm
begins his argument with the hypothetical fool, who, as is
stated in Psalm 53, verse 1, "says in his heart, 'There is no
God.' " Anselm insists that even the fool

[. . . is convinced that something exists in the understanding, at least, than which nothing greater can be conceived.
For when he hears of this he understands it. And whatever

is understood exists in the understanding. And assuredly that than which nothing greater can be conceived, cannot exist in the understanding alone. For suppose it exists in the understanding alone: then it can be conceived to exist in reality, which is greater.

Therefore, if that than which nothing greater can be conceived, exists in the understanding alone, the very being than which nothing greater can be conceived, is one than which a greater can be conceived. But obviously this is impossible. Hence, there is no doubt that there exists a being than which nothing greater can be conceived, and it exists both in the understanding and in reality.

And it assuredly exists so truly that it cannot be conceived not to exist. For it is possible to conceive of a being which cannot be conceived not to exist; and this is greater than one which can be conceived not to exist. Hence, if that than which nothing greater can be conceived, can be conceived not to exist, it is not that than which nothing greater can be conceived. But this is an irreconcilable contradiction. There is, then, so truly a being than which nothing greater can be conceived to exist, that it cannot even be conceived not to exist; and this being thou art, O Lord, our God.

But how has the fool said in his heart what he could not conceive; or how is it that he could not conceive what he said in his heart? since it is the same to say in the heart, and to conceive.

But, if really, nay, since really, he both conceived, because he said in his heart; and did not say in his heart, because he could not conceive; there is more than one way in which a thing is said in the heart or conceived. For, in one sense, an object is conceived, when the word signifying it is conceived; and in another, when the very entity which the object is, is understood.

In the former sense, then, God can be conceived not to exist; but in the latter, not at all. For no one who understands what fire and water are can conceive fire to be water, in accordance with the nature of the facts themselves, although this is possible according to the words. So, then, no

one who understands what God is can conceive that God
does not exist; although he says these words in his heart,
either without any, or with some foreign, signification. For
God is that than which a greater cannot be conceived. And
he who thoroughly understands this, assuredly understands
that this being so truly exists, that not even in concept can
it be nonexistent. Therefore, he who understands that God
so exists, cannot conceive that he does not exist.

It is certain, then, that the supreme Nature is not identical with what has been created. But no rational mind can
doubt that all creatures live and continue to exist, so long
as they do exist, by the sustenance afforded by that very
Being through whose creative act they are endowed with
the existence that they have. For, by a like course of reasoning to that by which it has been gathered that all existing
beings exist through some one being, hence that being alone
exists through itself, and others through another than themselves—by a like course of reasoning, I say, it can be
proved that whatever things live, live through some one
being; hence that being alone lives through itself, and
others through another than themselves.

But, since it cannot but be that those things which have
been created live through another, and that by which they
have been created lives through itself, necessarily, just as
nothing has been created except through the creative,
present Being, so nothing lives except through its preserv-
ing presence.

But if this is true—rather, since this must be true—it
follows that, where this Being is not, nothing is. It is, then,
everywhere, and throughout all things.]

BUT THE HYPOTHETICAL FOOL FOUND AN UNEXPECTED
defender: Gaunilo, a monk of Marmoutier, near Tours,
made a reply "on behalf of the fool." Gaunilo argued:

[The fool might make this reply:
    This being is said to be in my understanding already,
only because I understand what is said. Now could it not
with equal justice be said that I have in my understanding
all manner of unreal objects, having absolutely no existence

in themselves, because I understand these things if one speaks of them, whatever they may be?

Unless indeed it is shown that this being is of such a character that it cannot be held in concept like all unreal objects, or objects whose existence is uncertain: and hence I am not able to conceive of it when I hear of it, or to hold it in concept; but I must understand it and have it in my understanding; because, it seems, I cannot conceive of it in any other way than by understanding it, that is, by comprehending in my knowledge its existence in reality.

But if this is the case, in the first place there will be no distinction between what has precedence in time—namely, the having of an object in the understanding—and what is subsequent in time—namely, the understanding that an object exists; as in the example of the picture, which exists first in the mind of the painter, and afterwards in his work.

Moreover, the following assertion can hardly be accepted: that this being, when it is spoken of and heard of, cannot be conceived not to exist in the way in which even God can be conceived not to exist. For if this is impossible, what was the object of this argument against one who doubts or denies the existence of such a being? . . . I, so far as actual knowledge of the object, either from its specific or general character, is concerned, am as little able to conceive of this being when I hear of it, or to have it in my understanding, as I am to conceive of or understand God himself: whom, indeed, for this very reason I can conceive not to exist. For I do not know that reality itself which God is, nor can I form a conjecture of that reality from some other like reality. For you yourself assert that that reality is such that there can be nothing else like it.

For, suppose that I should hear something said of a man absolutely unknown to me, of whose very existence I was unaware. Through that special or general knowledge by which I know what man is, or what men are, I could conceive of him also, according to the reality itself, which man is. And yet it would be possible, if the person who told me of him deceived me, that the man himself, of whom I conceived, did not exist; since that reality according to which

I conceived of him, though a no less indisputable fact, was not that man, but any man.

Hence, I am not able, in the way in which I should have this unreal being in concept or in understanding, to have that being of which you speak in concept or in understanding, when I hear the word God or the words, *a being greater than all other beings*. For I can conceive of the man according to a fact that is real and familiar to me: but of God, or a being greater than all others, I could not conceive of at all, except merely according to the word. And an object can hardly or never be conceived according to the word alone.]

GAUNILO, POSING AS THE FOOL, THEN ARGUES CRAFTILY that before we can say that the being than which nothing greater can be thought necessarily exists, we must have evidence that He does, in fact, exist. Otherwise, we might imagine a most beautiful of all conceivable islands, and say that because we conceive it, it must exist. If, Gaunilo says,

[. . . someone should tell me that there is such an island, I should easily understand his words, in which there is no difficulty. But suppose that he went on to say, as if by a logical inference: "You can no longer doubt that this island which is more excellent than all lands exists somewhere, since you have no doubt that it is in your understanding. And since it is more excellent not to be in the understanding alone, but to exist both in the understanding and in reality, for this reason it must exist. For if it does not exist, any land which really exists will be more excellent than it; and so the island already understood by you to be more excellent will not be more excellent."

If a man should try to prove to me by such reasoning that this island truly exists, and that its existence should no longer be doubted, either I should believe that he was jesting, or I know not which I ought to regard as the greater fool: myself, supposing that I should allow this proof; or him, if he should suppose that he had established with any certainty the existence of this island. For he ought to show first that the hypothetical excellence of this island exists as a real and indubitable fact, and in no wise as any unreal object, or one whose existence is uncertain, in my understanding.

This, in the meantime, is the answer the fool could make to the arguments urged against him. When he is assured in the first place that this being is so great that its nonexistence is not even conceivable, and that this in turn is proved on no other ground than the fact that otherwise it will not be greater than all things, the fool may make the same answer, and say,

When did I say that any such being exists in reality, that is, a being greater than all others?—that on this ground it should be proved to me that it also exists in reality to such a degree that it cannot even be conceived not to exist? Whereas in the first place it should be in some way proved that a nature which is higher, that is, greater and better, than all other natures, exists; in order that from this we may then be able to prove all attributes which necessarily the being that is greater and better than all possesses.

Moreover, it is said that the nonexistence of this being is inconceivable. It might better be said, perhaps, that its nonexistence, or the possibility of its nonexistence, is unintelligible. For according to the true meaning of the word, unreal objects are unintelligible. Yet their existence is conceivable in the way in which the fool conceived of the nonexistence of God. I am most certainly aware of my own existence; but I know, nevertheless, that my nonexistence is possible. As to that supreme being, moreover, which God is, I understand without any doubt both his existence, and the impossibility of his nonexistence. Whether, however, so long as I am most positively aware of my existence, I can conceive of my nonexistence, I am not sure. But if I can, why can I not conceive of the nonexistence of whatever else I know with the same certainty? If, however, I cannot, God will not be the only being of which it can be said, it is impossible to conceive of his nonexistence.]

ST. ANSELM RETURNED TO THE FRAY, AND, INDEED, HIS
comeback was better than his first attack:

{ I say: if a being than which a greater is inconceivable is
not understood or conceived, and is not in the understanding or in concept, certainly either God is not a being than
which a greater is inconceivable, or else he is not understood or conceived, and is not in the understanding or in
concept. But I call on your faith and conscience to attest
that this is most false. Hence, that than which a greater cannot be conceived is truly understood and conceived, and is
in the understanding and in concept. Therefore either the
grounds on which you try to controvert me are not true, or
else the inference which you think to base logically on those
grounds is not justified.

But you hold, moreover, that supposing that a being
than which a greater cannot be conceived is understood, it
does not follow that this being is in the understanding;
nor, if it is in the understanding, does it therefore exist in
reality.

In answer to this, I maintain positively: if that being
can be even conceived to be, it must exist in reality. For
that than which a greater is inconceivable cannot be conceived except as without beginning. But whatever can be
conceived to exist, and does not exist, can be conceived to
exist through a beginning. Hence what can be conceived
to exist, but does not exist, is not the being than which a
greater cannot be conceived. Therefore, if such a being can
be conceived to exist, necessarily it does exist.

Furthermore: if it can be conceived at all, it must exist.
For no one who denies or doubts the existence of a being
than which a greater is inconceivable, denies or doubts that
if it did exist, its nonexistence, either in reality or in the
understanding, would be impossible. For otherwise it
would not be a being than which a greater cannot be conceived. But as to whatever can be conceived, but does not
exist: if there were such a thing, its nonexistence, either in
reality or in the understanding, would be possible. Therefore if a being than which a greater is inconceivable can
be even conceived, it cannot be nonexistent.

But, assuredly, in no understanding is a being than which a greater is conceivable a being than which a greater is inconceivable. Does it not follow, then, that if a being than which a greater cannot be conceived is in any understanding, it does not exist in the understanding alone? For if it is in the understanding alone, it is a being than which a greater can be conceived, which is inconsistent with the hypothesis.

But, you say, it is as if one should suppose an island in the ocean, which surpasses all lands in its fertility, and which, because of the difficulty, or rather the impossibility, of discovering what does not exist, is called a lost island; and should say that there can be no doubt that this island truly exists in reality, for this reason, that one who hears it described easily understands what he hears.

Now I promise confidently that if any man shall devise anything existing either in reality or in concept alone (except that than which a greater cannot be conceived) to which he can adapt the sequence of my reasoning, I will discover that thing, and will give him his lost island, not to be lost again.

But it now appears that this being than which a greater is inconceivable cannot be conceived not to be, because it exists on so assured a ground of truth; for otherwise it would not exist at all.

Hence, if anyone says that he conceives this being not to exist, I say that at the time when he conceives of this either he conceives of a being than which a greater is inconceivable or he does not conceive at all. If he does not conceive, he does not conceive of the nonexistence of that of which he does not conceive. But if he does conceive, he certainly conceives of a being which cannot be even conceived not to exist. For if it could be conceived not to exist, it could be conceived to have a beginning and an end. But this is impossible.

He, then, who conceives of this being conceives of a being which cannot be even conceived not to exist; but he who conceives of this being does not conceive that it does not exist; else he conceives what is inconceivable. The non-

existence, then, of that than which a greater cannot be
conceived is inconceivable.

You say, moreover, that whereas I assert that this supreme being cannot be *conceived* not to exist, it might better be said that its nonexistence cannot be *understood*.

But it was more proper to say, it cannot be conceived.
For if I had said that the object itself cannot be understood not to exist, possibly you yourself, who say that in
accordance with the true meaning of the term what is unreal cannot be understood, would offer the objection that
nothing which is can be understood not to be, for the nonexistence of what exists is unreal: hence God would not
be the only being of which it could be said, it is impossible
to understand its nonexistence.*]

AND SO ST. ANSELM CONCLUDES TRIUMPHANTLY:

[Whoever, then, denies the existence of a being than
which a greater cannot be conceived, at least understands
and conceives of the denial which he makes. But this denial
he cannot understand or conceive of without its component
terms; and a term of this statement is *a being than which
a greater cannot be conceived*. Whoever, then, makes this
denial, understands and conceives of that than which a
greater is inconceivable.

Moreover, it is evident that in the same way it is possible to conceive of and understand a being whose nonexistence is impossible; but he who conceives of this conceives of a greater being than one whose nonexistence is
possible. Hence, when a being than which a greater is inconceivable is conceived, if it is a being whose nonexistence
is possible that is conceived, it is not a being than which a
greater cannot be conceived. But an object cannot be at
once conceived and not conceived. Hence he who conceives
of a being than which a greater is inconceivable, does not
conceive of that whose nonexistence is possible, but of that
whose nonexistence is impossible. Therefore, what he con-

* *St. Anselm*, by Sidney Dean (The Open Court Publishing Co.,
1944).

ceives of must exist; for anything whose nonexistence is possible, is not that of which he conceives.]

ST. ANSELM'S CONCLUSIONS WERE ACCEPTED FOR A little over a hundred years. Then his argument was rejected by St. Thomas Aquinas, who said: "Even if it be granted that everyone understands this name *God* to signify what is said (namely, that than which a greater cannot be thought), it does not follow from this that he understands that which is signified by the name to be in the nature of things, but only in the apprehension of the understanding. Nor can it be argued that it is in reality, unless it be granted that there is in reality something than which a greater cannot be thought—which is not granted by those who maintain that God is not."*

But it was reaffirmed by René Descartes: "It is no less inconsistent to think of a God (that is, a being supremely perfect) to whom existence is lacking (that is, to whom any perfection is lacking) than to think of a mountain to which a valley is lacking."**

Rejected again by Immanuel Kant: "I simply ask you, whether the proposition, that *this or that thing . . . exists,* is an analytical or a synthetical proposition. If the former, then by its existence you add nothing to your thought of the thing. . . . If . . . you admit . . . that every proposition involving existence is synthetical, how can you say that the predicate of existence does not admit of removal without contradiction?"†

It was given a new look by Hegel (as pointed out by Dr. Burch in his *Early Medieval Philosophy*: "Undoubtedly God would be imperfect, if he were merely thought and did not also have the determination of Being. But in relation to God we must not take thought as merely subjective; thought here signifies the absolute pure thought, and thus we must ascribe to him the quality of Being."

* Reprinted from *Summa Theologica* 1, 2. 1 and 2, with the permission of Benziger Brothers, Inc., publisher and copyright owners.
**Meditationes de Prima Philosophia*, V.
† Kant, *Critique of Pure Reason*, trans. Müller, Vol. II, III (The Macmillan Company).

CHAPTER VI

Abelard and St. Bernard

ST. ANSELM SOLVED SATISFACTORILY, IF TEMPORARILY, the dichotomy of faith and reason. John Scotus Erigena had relied on reason alone. Anselm related and reverenced both faith and reason, both of which, he thought, provided circumstantial evidence of God's existence. The problem of Universals that Boethius had posited, flared into controversy with Roscelin of Compiègne (died after 1120). For St. Anselm, as he showed in his book on the Incarnation, called *Cur Deus Homo* (why God became man), the rational and the real were one. For Roscelin real things were all individuals. The *persons* of the Trinity alone were real, the idea of the Trinity was unreal. Universals, whiteness, the Trinity, were but words, but breaths of air blown from mouths, as Boethius had said all words were. Anselm disagreed violently with Roscelin and said logicians holding such views should be blown out from discussions. Roscelin was primarily a semanticist. According to Victor Cousin "he bequeathed to modern philosophy two great principles: first, that abstractions must not be reified, and second that the power of the human soul and the secret of its development are largely in language."

Peter Abelard, born in 1079 near Nantes, was a knight, but gave up his inheritance in order to study. A pupil of William of Champeaux, in Paris, he was so much more brilliant than his master that he soon set up a rival school at Melun, twenty-five miles away. Later he was able to make his old master admit that the essence theory he had been teaching was false, and William's students deserted him for Abelard. Abelard then set up his school in Paris itself, in what is now the Latin Quarter, and there he

criticized the nature of *genera* and *species* as universals.
Are Universals words or are they things? Abelard's theory,
called *Sententia Nominum* from the first two words of his
thesis, caused his disciples to be called *nominalists*. His ad-
versaries called themselves *realists*. Abelard insisted that
Socrates and Plato agree in both being men, but the fact
of being a man is not a thing. A thing can't be universal in
the sense of being predicated of many. The thing called
Socrates remains Socrates and not Plato, nor do all their
sharing of being man make that *being man* a third thing or
a third man. Abelard avoided both nominalist and realist
extremes "by maintaining that the universal is neither a
thing nor a concept but a logical term which is related
to both things and concepts." The astonishing genius of
Abelard was that before the translations of Aristotle made
by the Arabs had become available in the West, and with
only what had filtered down through Porphyry, he concluded that universals exist not before the thing nor after
the thing, but in the thing: *non ante rem, nec post rem, sed
in re.* They have a real existence, but only in particulars.

St. Bernard wrote angrily of Abelard that "he sees
nothing through a glass darkly but stares at everything
face to face," and Abelard got into trouble when he practiced his theories on the dogma of the Trinity. His affair
with Héloïse, the brilliant niece of Canon Fulbert of Chartres, made Abelard more famous than did his philosophy;
like Augustine, his autobiography and his letters have
brought him to us whole, so that he is more alive for us
and touches us more nearly than many greater philosophers. Abelard, beyond even Héloïse and the gelding her
uncle's friends performed on him, beyond Héloïse's greater
love, that moved even saints like Peter the Venerable,
remains in himself one of the greatest of medieval philosophers, because of his *status* theory (as Dr. Burch has
suggested it might be called), though it "is radically opposed to the Aristotelian doctrine that the specific form
is objectively the most essential and subjectively the most
intelligent aspect of things." Abelard succeeded in combin-
ing reason and faith; as he said to Héloïse, "I do not wish
to be a philosopher to the point of resisting Paul; I will

not be an Aristotelian to the point of rejecting Christ."
Abelard retired into a monastery after the friends and
servants of Héloïse's uncle, Canon Fulbert, had mutilated
him, and he obliged Héloïse to enter a convent. He continued to attract pupils, and to make enemies, wherever he
went. Even when, driven from one monastery to another
by envious rivals, he founded his own retreat in a remote
spot and called it the Paraclete, students flocked to him.
But his lack of judgment, that antagonized more people
than even his brilliantly logical mind convinced, twice
brought about the condemnation of his ideas, once at a
Council at Soissons in 1121, and again at another at Sens
in 1141. After the latter he took refuge with his loyal friend
Peter the Venerable and soon after died piously in 1142.
Peter the Venerable's letter to Héloïse on Abelard's death,
besides being, with Abelard's and Héloïse's own correspondence and Abelard's autobiography, among the most
pathetic documents that have come down to us from medieval times, also gives us some idea of how much Abelard impressed his contemporaries.

St. Bernard of Clairvaux was the most famous of Abelard's opponents, and he has had a bad press in the last
few centuries. Since Jean Jacques Rousseau made sexual
appetite not merely physically, sentimentally and emotionally but also intellectually and psychologically a crite-
rion of human value, Abelard has enjoyed a great vogue
because of his famous, or infamous, seduction of Canon
Fulbert's niece. St. Bernard, who, for quite other reasons,
very much objected to Abelard, has been regarded as lacking both in intelligence and in charity. Actually St. Bernard was both more of a thinker and more of a warm human
being than is currently supposed. Born of good family in
1091, he entered the Benedictine Order in 1112, at Cî-
teaux, where his prior was an Englishman, St. Stephen
Harding. Bernard arrived with thirty companions, and the
troop of young men must have taken the newly reformed
monastery (from which Cistercians, or Trappists, as we
call them today, take their name) rather by storm. Within
two years Bernard was sent out to found the abbey of Clairvaux. He had, at one time, 700 novices; one of his disciples

became Pope, six became cardinals, and thirty became
bishops. From 1131 to 1138 he spent his time healing
schisms in the Church; in 1120 at Soissons, and again in
1140 at Sens, he confounded Abelard and obtained his
condemnation by the Church; in 1146 Bernard preached a
crusade, and died in 1153. All this gives a totalitarian impression, of a sledge-hammer personality, ruthless and ty-
coonishly successful. Bernard was far from being thus, as
can be seen from what he wrote to the monk, Adam, whom
he accused of too much obedience to an unworthy superior:

[Was it willingly or unwillingly you went forth? If it was
willingly, then it was not from obedience. If unwillingly,
you would seem to have had some suspicion of the order
which you carried out with reluctance. But where there is
suspicion there consideration is necessary. But you, to dis-
play your obedience or to exercise it, obeyed without discussion and suffered yourself to be taken away, not only
without your volition, but even against your conscience.
O patience, worthy of all impatience! I cannot, I confess,
help being angry with this most questionable patience.
You saw that he was scattered, yet you followed him, you
heard him directing what was scandalous, yet you obeyed
him.]

IN HIS *Treatise Concerning Grace and Free Will,* WRITTEN
around 1128, when he was thirty-eight, which was ad-
dressed to William, Abbot of St. Thierry, near Reims,
Bernard set forth clearly and categorically the absolute
and complete freedom and responsibility of every individual soul. From the omnipotent state and the omnipotence of fate the Christian is by Christ set free. And the
revolutionary nature of that freedom is described by Bernard in terms that are philosophical but also social and
psychological.

[It happened once [he wrote] that, when I was publicly
commending the grace of God toward me . . . one of the
bystanders demanded, "what is then thine own work in

the matter, or what recompense or reward dost thou hope for, if so be that God doeth it all? Give," saith he, "the glory to God." "Thou counsellest well," say I, "provided only that thy counsel can be followed." "Where then, sayest thou, are our merits? Or where is our hope? What, therefore, thou askest, doth free-will do?" I answered in a word: "It is saved. Take away free-will and there remaineth nothing to be saved, take away grace and there is no means whereby it can be saved. This work of salvation cannot be wrought without two factors: the one, that by which it is wrought, and the other that for which or in which it is wrought. Salvation is given by God alone, and it is given only to the free-will: even as it cannot be wrought without the consent of the receiver it cannot be wrought without the grace of the giver. Accordingly free-will is said to co-operate with the grace which worketh salvation, when the free-will consenteth, that is to say, is saved, for to consent is to be saved. It followeth that the spirit of a brute can in no wise receive such salvation, for it lacketh the faculty of free consent whereby it may submissively obey the God that saveth it. But consent of the will is one thing, natural appetite is another. The latter is common to us with the irrational animals, nor hath it the power of giving consent to the spirit, being ensnared by the attractions of the flesh. Having this appetite in common with the brutes, it is voluntary consent which distinguisheth us from the same. It is a habit of the mind, self-determining. Voluntary consent is not under compulsion, nor can it be extorted. It is an act of the will, it is not subject to necessity, it neither denieth itself nor yieldeth itself to any, save only willingly. Otherwise, if it can be compelled to act where when it would not, it is subject to force and not voluntary. But where there is not an act of will, there is not consent, for consent cannot be other than an act of will. Where, therefore, there is consent, there is an act of will. Moreover, where there is an act of will, there is freedom. In this sense it is that I understand free-will . . . consent is spontaneous assent of the will, or indeed (as I remember that I have already said) it is a habit of the mind, self-determining. Further, will is a movement of reason, and rules over both sense

perception and appetite. In fact will, by whatever direction
it determine itself, always has reason as its companion, we
may say, as its follower. . . . For no creature can be intelligent, even in wrongdoing, save only by the aid of
reason.

But reason has been given to the will in order to instruct
it, not to destroy it. It would, however, destroy it, were it
to impose upon it such necessity that it could not freely
of its own choice determine itself, whether by wrongly
consenting either to the appetite or to some evil spirit. . . .
If, I say, the will were unable, owing to the prohibition of
reason, to take either of these courses, then it would cease
to be the will. For where necessity is, there is not free-will.

We possess, therefore, on the one hand, life in common
with the plants, and, on the other hand, as well as life,
sense perception and appetite in common with the beasts,
while that which distinguisheth us from both is what is
called will. And it is consent of the will, free, not necessitated, which, seeing that in it consisteth our righteousness
or unrighteousness, maketh us deservedly blessed or the
reverse. Such consent, then, on account both of the inalien-
able freedom of the will, and of the inevitable judgment
which reason everywhere and at all times exerciseth when
to be the will. For where necessity is, there is not free-will.
and self-judging on account of the reason. And rightly doth
judgment accompany freedom, seeing that he that is free
to determine himself, when he sinneth, judgeth himself.
Therefore, save only the will, all that belongeth to man,
seeing that it is incapable of self-determination, is a matter
neither for the award of merit nor for judgment. Life, sense
perception, appetite, memory, thought and anything else
there may be are subject to necessity, except in so far as
they are subject to the will. . . . The will can no more be
deprived of its freedom than it can be deprived of itself;
. . . were a man able to will anything unwillingly, then
and then only would the will be able to be deprived of
its freedom. Hence it is that to the insane, to infants, and
also to persons asleep, nothing which they may do, whether
it be good or bad, is imputed because, plainly, just as they
are not in possession of reason, so they do not possess

the use of their own wills, and therefore their freedom is not subject to judgment. Seeing, then, that the will hath nothing free save itself, it is only rightly judged as it is in itself. Indeed, neither slowness of intellect, nor lapse of memory, nor restlessness of appetite, nor obtuseness of sense of perception, nor feebleness of vitality, of themselves bring a man into condemnation, even as their contraries do not make him innocent, because these conditions are caused necessarily, and independently of the will.*]

ST. BERNARD DISTINGUISHES BETWEEN THREE ASPECTS OF freedom: freedom from sin, freedom from misery, and freedom from necessity. The first two cannot be complete here, they will exist fully only *in patria,* in the fatherland of heaven. But from fate, or necessity, the Christian must believe that every human being is free here and now. The fourth Christian freedom, from the state if it command evil, was asserted confidently by all the Church's representatives throughout the Middle Ages—and, indeed, from the time the letters A.U.C. (*ab urbe condita*—from the beginning of the city—the letters by which the Romans dated their era) were succeeded by the letters A.D.—Anno Domini, the year of our Lord. Opposition to the Church's concept of man's final freedom even from the State was challenged first by the pagans, for whom the State included all the Church was for Christians, and later by the inheritors of the idea of the Roman State—the advocates and partisans of the Holy Roman Empire. The Church itself, primed by the great Gospel command "Render unto Caesar the things that are Caesar's," believed in and taught the supremacy of the State over the "things that are Caesar's," but insisted that over and above the area the State controlled was an inviolable area, over which individual man alone was master. The State accepted this position, at first because it could not do otherwise, for it was the Church that hallowed and protected Charlemagne and his successors, who desperately needed the Church's help; later, because it was frankly beaten by the Church—at Canossa

* St. Bernard, *Treatise Concerning Grace and Free Will,* trans. Watkin Williams (SPCK, 1920).

in the person of the Emperor kneeling in the snow to apologize to the Pope for trespassing on the forbidden area; at Canterbury, in the person of Henry II doing penance for the murder of St. Thomas à Becket.

These collective freedoms, from necessity and from the ruler, if he command what be against God's will and law, belong indifferently to every creature, whether he be good or bad, Christian or pagan. So St. Bernard insisted; so the Church still insists. But, as Lord Acton pointed out, when Jesus Christ said "Render unto Caesar," He both gave the State an authority that was from God, and gave the individual a liberty that was no less from God. With the spread of Christianity the defense of that liberty ceased to be left to "a few ineffectual philosophers . . . and became the perpetual charge of the universal Church."

Freedom from necessity, St. Bernard insisted, is not lost either by our sin or our misery. For it is created in us, it is the divine image, which nothing and no one can destroy. But the freedoms lost by Adam in the Fall—the freedoms from sin and from misery—are the resemblance to God that man then forfeited.

This contrast, of man's grandeur and his misery, that was later to wring from Shakespeare's Hamlet his great cry "What a piece of work is a man . . . yet . . . what is this quintessence of dust?" and from Blaise Pascal (1623-1662) and Jacques Bossuet (1627-1704) their most splendid passages, brought St. Bernard to his knees before the mystery of Christ's incarnation, which provides the paradox of man restored and made whole by the passion of God. Here St. Bernard ceased philosophizing, and, as Henry Thoreau (1817-1862) says we all should, sang his love. "Love seeks no cause nor end but itself. Its fruit is its activity. I love because I love, I love that I may love. Love is a mighty thing, if so it return to its own principle and origin, if it flows back to its source and ever draws anew whence it may flow again. Love is the only one of all the sense movements and affections of the soul by which the creature can answer to its Creator and repay like with like."

CHAPTER VII

The Arabs

PETER ABELARD WAS TRULY A PHILOSOPHER, NOT A theologian with philosophical overtones. St. Anselm was both; St. Bernard, a theologian and mystic who occasionally wrote philosophy much as Molière's bourgeois wrote prose, without knowing he was doing it. By the beginning of the twelfth century, there were some philosophical students and a growing awareness of philosophy in many western European schools, that a century later developed into the universities or made way for them. Paris, where Abelard heckled and argued, was one such school; another was Chartres, whence came such reputable men of learning as the Platonists Bernard and Thierry of Chartres, and Gilbert de la Porrée (1070-1154), who was an Aristotelian, and wrote a classic crib of Aristotle's *Categories*, called the Book of Six Principles. But John of Salisbury (?1115-1180), an Englishman, was perhaps the most indestructible writer of the school of Chartres. His *Policraticus* is one of the first primers of political science, and is still today required reading for the schools of Oxford University.

John was, incidentally, an excellent example of the true internationalism of medieval learning. He was a pupil of Abelard's, and later went to Chartres, first as student, then as bishop. He was a friend of St. Bernard of Clairvaux, and for twenty years he lived at Canterbury as secretary first to Archbishop Theobald, and later to St. Thomas à Becket, with whom he went into exile, and whose death he witnessed. John of Salisbury visited Rome many times, and was an intimate friend of the only English Pope, Nicholas Breakspear, who in 1154 became Adrian IV. John wrote a *Metalogicon*, a plea for the study of logic, and 329 of his letters have survived.

The following quotation from Chapter 21 of the *Policraticus* shows him wrestling with the problem of whether God can know the unknown. In it John of Salisbury shows his indebtedness to Abelard very clearly.

[Behold the horns of another dilemma and wheresoever I turn I seem involved in error. For if things which are not nor will be, can be foretold, God can know what he does not know or something can occur without his knowledge. For a naval engagement which is not to be can be waged so it can be known by those who wage it. Can that not be known by God which can assuredly both be and be known by man? If therefore God can know what he does not know he can assuredly also not know what he knows, for the reason that there can be no knowledge of contradictories, since one of the two must be false because it lacks the substance of truth. Besides, there is no knowledge of what is not true. How therefore can there be unvarying knowledge which is subject to increase and decrease of fact, and which can be ignorant of what it knows or can know that of which it is ignorant? . . .

Hence the Stoic believes that all things are unavoidable for fear of bringing to naught immutable knowledge. On the contrary, Epicurus thinks that there are no events which are the result of the regulation of providence for fear of imposing necessity upon things subject to change.

They are both equally mistaken since the one subjects the universe to chance and the other to necessity. There is therefore a changeless disposition of changeable things. Since this providence cannot be moved from its state of eternity, it has freed the train of events from all bond of necessity . . .

For just as what I see is impending does not occur of necessity from the fact that I see it, so also what His eye contemplates is under no compulsion of coming to pass.

I know indeed that the stone or arrow which I have shot into the clouds will by nature's law fall back upon the earth as do all heavy bodies borne by their own weight;

yet there was no compulsion that they fall onto the earth
either naturally or because I know they do. For there is
the possibility of their falling or not falling; one or the
other, though not of necessity, is nevertheless true. That
which I know will, in any case, be. For if it is not to be,
though it is thought to be, it nevertheless is not known,
since there is no knowledge of that which is not, there is
merely opinion.*]

BY THE BEGINNING OF THE THIRTEENTH CENTURY, THE
functional organs of Christendom included the hierarchy
of the clergy, from the Pope to the humblest cleric in minor
orders; the Holy Roman Empire, which protected and
patronized both the Papacy and the priesthood; and the
Universities. Of these Paris was foremost, and it was Paris
to which all the greatest medieval thinkers came, and where
they stayed and taught, from Alexander of Hales (c.1175-
1245) to John Duns Scotus (1265-1308), although none
of them were Frenchmen by birth. The speed of medieval
communication and integration seems astonishing: twenty
years after St. Francis, an Italian, had founded the Franciscans, twenty years after St. Dominic, a Spaniard, had
founded the Dominicans, both orders were entrenched
in Paris and dominating its teaching. And much of what
was taught, the very texts that were commented on, of
Plato and even more of Aristotle, were available only in
translations made into Arabic from the original Greek,
and translated from the Arabic into Latin. These translations came to Western Europe through the Mohammedan
conquests, either from the Arabs themselves or from the
Spaniards. Greek disappeared early from the West, and
by St. Augustine's time even the educated were reading
Greek authors in Latin translations. Only the Irish, in their
settlements such as St. Gall in Switzerland, kept the study
of Greek alive, and in some cases they even spread the
knowledge of Greek again. But by 917 it was hard to find
anyone who knew Greek: Severus, Bishop of Ashmounein

* Salisbury's *Policraticus*, from *Frivolities of Courtiers and Footprints of Philosophers* by Joseph Pike (University of Minnesota
Press, 1938).

in Africa wrote, for example, "I asked among the Christian brothers for help in translating the document we found from Coptic and Greek into Arabic, which is the language of the people of Egypt, for most know neither Coptic nor Greek." (Quoted by A. Mallon, in *Mélanges de l'Université St. Joseph,* Beyrouth, 1906.) These "Christian brothers" were Syrians, and it was they who acted as the agents, transmitting ancient Greek culture to Christian Egypt and later also to the Muslims. The translations they made had the most tremendous influence on European thought. Indeed, so tremendous was it, that it is thanks to them that the greatest figure of the thirteenth century (the age above all others of great individuals) is not a man, but a ghost: the ghost of Aristotle whom both the Christian St. Thomas Aquinas and the Muslim Averroës were to call, simply "*The* Philosopher," as though there were none other. Nor was Aristotle only *the* Philosopher. He was also, for medieval man, *the* natural scientist, a sort of super Einstein-cum-Dewey, none the less alive for having been, at the time of his "recovery," dead for more than fifteen hundred years.

Aristotle's recovery, which brought his influence from East to West, was a direct consequence of the Mohammedan conquests. It must be remembered that all the time the scholars were puzzling over the universe in the monasteries, and the philosophers were teaching about grace and free-will in the schools and universities, Christendom was fighting a life-and-death battle with Islam, at first on its outskirts, in countries such as Armenia and Spain, but later in the heartland, in Sicily and northern Spain, at the very gates of Paris and Vienna.

And the most all the armies of Christendom could do, severally or together, beyond the frontiers of Arabia, for many centuries, was to contain the Muslim tide, so that the medieval world was divided into a rather larger Muslim half and a smaller Christian half. In fact, the situation for several centuries was rather like that in the early fifties of the twentieth century, when capitalist and communist powers exist side by side, with sporadic fighting between them in fringe areas, like Korea and Indo-China.

To realize the immense contribution of Islamic thought to medieval philosophy—and it is only recently that historians have begun to become aware of its extent—it is necessary to understand the contrast between Christianity and Islam; first as faiths, and then as philosophies.

Mohammed, born of poor parents at Mecca, in Arabia, in 570, received what he declared to be a revelation from God when he was already middle-aged, and preached his message, called by him the "Koran" and written down by his followers, to the polytheist tribes around him. He fled on July 16, 622, from the persecuting Koreish, his kinsmen, to Medina, and this date, of the Hegira, or flight, marks the beginning of their era for some 400,000,000 Mohammedans today. Mohammed called the religion he had founded "Islam," or the Surrender (to God); his followers he called "Muslims," or those who have surrendered. Islam is a straightforward, uncluttered creed, based on the statement "There is no God but God, and Mohammed is his prophet."

Islam included in its tenets the duty of almsgiving, a minimum of a tenth yearly of all income and possessions, and the obligation to make once in a lifetime the pilgrimage to Mecca. To die in battle for Islam was the best death, and Jihad, or Holy War—war against the enemies of Islam—was given high priority as a religious activity. A Muslim has to pray five times daily, after ritual ablutions, and he may not drink wine, eat the flesh of pigs, nor shellfish. He may have up to four wives simultaneously, but must treat all alike, and a Muslim is responsible for every child he begets, or any wife bears, legitimate or illegitimate. Already by the time of Mohammed's death, in 632, Islam had spread outside Arabia, and in its first two centuries the new faith had conquered Egypt, Syria, Mesopotamia, North Africa, Morocco and Spain. All Muslims are absolutely equal, and the conquered, whenever they accept Islam, are integrated completely. Islam declared Jews and Christians to be "people of the Book"—they, too, had sacred scriptures, and were allowed to live and to keep their religion, upon payment of indemnities and taxes.

Two of the conquered countries, Egypt and Syria, had

been profoundly Hellenized, with Greek-speaking schools,
and strong philosophical traditions. The Arabs found the
Syrians possessed of almost all of Aristotle, as we know
him today, and a thorough knowledge of Aristotle's
thought, as the late neo-Platonists understood it, is common to all Arabic philosophers from Al-Kindi (died after
870) to Ibn Rashid in the twelfth century.

The Arabs had found dualism in Persia, the country of
Zoroaster. His theory of good and evil as comparable
though conflicting powers, filtered through Manichaean-
ism, had strongly affected local Christianity. The Arabs
found the Syrian Christians divided into three main groups
(Mohammed himself never met a Catholic, nor learned
what was the Catholic faith): the orthodox; the Nestorians,
who divided Christ's nature so completely into two parts,
human and divine, that the human Being, Willing and Acting were separated from and contrasted with the divine;
and the Monophysites, who were most numerous in Syria,
and who believed Christ to have but one nature, and for
whom the Divinity absorbed the Humanity. The Sabaeans, or Harraneans, traced their beliefs back to Hermes
Trismegistus and other pagans and, although not Christians, were included by Mohammed as "people of the
Book" together with Jews and Christians. The Sabaeans
were interested in the mathematical and astronomical, as
well as the medical studies of the Neo-Pythagoreans and
the Neo-Platonists. They prized the medical works of Hip-
pocrates and Galen no less than the philosophical works
of Aristotle and helped to transmit these to the West. The
Syrian translations from the Greek extend from the fourth
to the eighth century, from the time of Probus "priest and
physician in Antioch" during the first half of the fifth century, to that of Jacob of Edessa (c. 633-708), who even
after the Muslim conquest translated Greek theological
writings, and insisted that it was permissible for Christian
priests to teach Muslim children. St. John Damascene
(700-754) was born into a Christian family which held
an important hereditary position under the Saracens in
Damascus. John's Arabic name was Mansur, the Ran-
somed. In 735 he entered the monastery of St. Sabas, near

Jerusalem, after ordination to the priesthood, and among
his works is a Dialogue between a Christian and a Saracen;
which is not the most original of his writings. But he is
important as an example of the close cooperation, almost
assimilation, possible between Christians and Muslims in
the eighth century.

One of the best translators from the Greek was Sergius
of Rasain, who died in Constantinople, aged about seventy,
around 536. Sergius recast into Christian language much
of what he translated, even turning Plato into a hermit,
dwelling in the wilderness. Aristotle he regarded first and
foremost as a logician. Sergius' contemporary, Paulus
Persa, who wrote in Syriac for Khosrau Anosharwan (521-
579), placed knowledge above faith, and defined philosophy as the process by which the soul becomes conscious
of its own inner essence.

The Arab translations of Aristotle began only in early
Abbasid times—about the same date as the coronation
of Charlemagne in the West (A.D. 800), and for the next
three hundred years, there can be no question that,
intellectually, Cairo and Baghdad far outshone any contemporary European city, including both Rome and Constantinople. Indeed they vied with one another as the
greatest centers of learning in the world, with Cordova in
Spain running a close third. The contacts and cooperation
within the vast Muslim world were extended to Christendom even though the confrontation of the two entailed a
struggle for the possession of Europe. To cite but one
example (given by Christopher Dawson): A manuscript
of the Greek Dioscorides was sent as a present by the
Byzantine emperor, Constantine Porphyrogenitus, to the
Spanish Caliph Abd ar Rahman III (891-961). It was
translated by a Jew called Hasday ibn Shapru, with the
assistance of a Greek monk who came for the purpose from
Constantinople to Cordova.

The Arab translators began with Ibn al-Moqaffa, a Persian, but none of his work has survived. During the reigns
of Al-Ma'mun (813-833) and Al-Mu'tasim (833-842),
Yakya ibn Bitrip is said to have translated the *Timaeus*
of Plato, and Abu Zaid Honain ibn Ishaq (809-873),

working together with his son and nephew, was a prolific translator. Dr. Richard Walzer, in a chapter in *The History of Philosophy Eastern and Western** notes that the Greek authors translated by the Arabic philosophers were those studied in the late Greek schools. In fact, the Greeks the Muslims studied were Aristotle and his commentators, and these were a splendid corrective to the Neo-Platonic texts almost exclusively used in early medieval Christendom. Dr. Walzer enumerates the Greek philosophic writers known to the Arabs, "Plato's *Timaeus, Republic* and *Laws,* which were textbooks of political theory in the school of Al-Farabi; Aristotle's treatises with the exception of the *Politics,* and the *Dialogues.*" The Christian translators also "smoothed the passage of Greek and Islamic thought to medieval Jewry, and eventually created in the eleventh and twelfth centuries, for the first time, a Jewish philosophy superior to Philo's unsuccessful attempt." For the Arabs, as for the early Fathers, Greek philosophy provided a "natural theology," and they accepted, at least as a starting point, from which to comment, argue and develop, the basic premise of Greek philosophy, that of the eternal order of the universe, with "the stars in their stations set, and every wandering star." But Islamic thought is not plagiaristic; it is a "productive assimilation" of Greek thought. Given the entirely different background of Arab and Christian theology, and of the actual philosophers, the degree of interpenetration is surprising.

Qosta ibn Luqa al-Balabakki (flourished about 835) wrote a brief treatise on the distinction between soul and spirit, which survives in a Latin translation. Spirit, *ruh,* is a subtle material, which animates the human frame and causes its movements and perceptions. But the soul is something else again; being incorporeal it is unchangeable, and does not, like the spirit, which acts as intermediary between body and soul, perish with the body.

By the tenth century, Islamic scholars divided the sciences into the Arab sciences, and the old, or non-Arab sciences: to the former belong grammar, ethics, history

* *The History of Philosophy Eastern and Western,* ed. Sir S. Radhakrishnan (George Allen & Unwin, Ltd.).

and literature; to the latter, philosophy, natural science and medicine. Arab philosophy stemmed partly from oriental Christian teachings, partly from gnostic and Zoroastrian sources, partly from Greek, Neo-Platonic elements. According to tradition, Mohammed said "the first thing which God created was reason." This was widely quoted by those who found the Koranic precepts, although excellent ethics, lacking in dialectics. For example, the same teasing problem of free-will, which caused so many Christian arguments, also split Muslims into various groups. The Mutazalites, and before them, the Qadarites, considered God had no property except essence, His essential nature could have no predicate; they declared that His holiness was incapable of causing man's sin, and also that, man is responsible for his actions. But the energy by which he acts, whether the action be good or evil, comes from God. Is this energy created previous to an action, or coincidentally and simultaneously therewith? God's omnipotence, it would seem, is limited by His goodness. Later, the Mutazalites went further and taught that God *could* not act in a way that was contrary to his nature. But the Traditionalists angrily maintained that God's might could not be limited, even by His nature. But the Mutazalites insisted on denying power, life, will, speech, sight and hearing to God, as they feared that He would become anthropomorphized if He were the possessor of attributes. Indeed, a God whose Word was Himself was already at least an approximation of the Christian Trinity.

Al-Nazzam, who died in 845, declared God can do nothing evil, nor, indeed, anything but what He actually does. He rejected the Greek theory of atoms, and instead, postulated accidents as the components of corporeal substances. He thought of accidents as the substance itself or as part of the substance. Thus in a log of wood, for example, "fire" or "warmth" exists latently; it becomes actual only when, by means of friction, its opposite "cold" disappears. He considered color, smells, even intellects and souls as types of matter; everything created, visible or invisible, is material.

Al-Muammar, who is thought to have flourished around

900, also denied the existence of any attribute in God,
Who cannot know himself or any other being, for knowing
would suppose a plurality in Him. In the problem of Universals, al-Muammar may be said to be a conceptualist:
for him whiteness, fatness, etc., have only an intellectual
existence. But so long as we discuss a white thing, the
whiteness exists in our minds.

The disciples of al-Ashari (873-935) elaborated the
Muslim doctrine of atoms. This, derived from the Greeks,
especially from Democritus (c.460 B.C.) via the Latin
Lucretius (?99-51 B.C.), was an explanation of creation
that did not detract from God's omnipotence, and was
favored by the later Mutazalites. All we perceive, al-Ashari
declared, is but accident, and all accidents are in continual
flux, according to the atomists. Since everything changes,
everything has come into being, and therefore has been
created by a necessary, and necessarily unchanging, God.
Accidents are divided into substances and qualities, which
are the categories by which reality is perceived. Matter
exists only in thought, and "time is nothing other than
the coexistence of different substances, a simultaneity of
accidents. Space, time and motion are atoms devoid of
extension, moments without duration. Between each individual 'now' of time, there is a rest, or void." Goethe
was to suggest some of these theories in his *Faust*:

> All that passes
> Is but a likeness.

Al-Kindi (who died after 870) wrote the preface to
the earliest metaphysical work in Arabic. "It is fitting to
acknowledge the utmost gratitude to those who have contributed even a little to truth, not to speak of those who
have contributed much. We should not be ashamed to
acknowledge truth and to assimilate it from whatever
source it comes to us, even if it is brought to us by former
generations and foreign peoples. For him who seeks the
truth there is nothing of higher value than truth itself: it
never cheapens or abases him who searches for it, but
ennobles and honors him." And he went on to describe

his aim: "My principle is first to record in complete quo-
tations all the Ancients have said on the subject, the
second, to complete what the Ancients have not fully expressed, and this according to the usage of our Arabic
language, the customs of our age, and our own ability."
But there was one exception to the general acceptance
by al-Kindi of the basic tenets of Greek philosophy: the
Greek "eternal creation" is denied and instead the Koranic
creation of the world from nothing "in a single moment of
time by the omnipotent will of God," is accepted.

A famous physician, Abu Bakr al-Razi (850-923), was
a courageous and original thinker. He disapproved of the
Jewish, Christian and Islamic religions, all of which he
considered to have brought more evil than good into the
world, and all of which he declared are to some extent self-
contradictory. For him it was only in the pursuit of philosophy that man could improve his lot: "whoever makes
an effort and busies himself with study and research has set
out on the way of truth. Indeed, the souls of men can be
purged from the mud and darkness of this world and saved
for the world to come only by the study of philosophy."
Al-Razi's medical knowledge was considerable and was
praised by Vesalius (1514-1564), and his autobiography
is impressive. Both he and al-Kindi wrote treatises on
popular ethics, now available in translation. Al-Kindi was
an Arab, al-Razi a Persian, Al-Farabi (died 950) a Turk.

Al-Farabi was a philosopher anxious to separate philosophy from its theological swaddling clothes and to establish it as supreme in its own sphere. Dr. Walzer says:
"Aristotle's logic of demonstration, according to Al-Farabi,
provides the key to the philosophical understanding of the
universe which springs from the study of physics and
metaphysics. . . . There is one universal religion, but many
forms of symbolic representation of ultimate truth, which
may differ from land to land and from nation to nation.
There exists only one true God for the philosophical mind,
but He has different names in different religions. Al-
Farabi's theory of human nature was fully and almost
exclusively based on Aristotelian psychology. The faculties of nutrition, of sense perception, of imagination and

intellect are described and their hierarchical order within the one and undivided soul is particularly stressed, as parallel to the order in the universe, and the order to be established in society."

Ibn-Sina (Avicenna)* (980-1037), born in Persia, passed all his life there, and held high political office at various times. He is the greatest of the early Muslim philosophers. He wrote 160 books and was besides a profound mystic. One of his best poems is a long account of the descent of the human soul into the body—an idea he got from the late Neo-Platonist pantheists. He is "a systematic thinker of the first order," wrote a medical and a philosophical encyclopedia, and was able to accept the Muslim belief in prophecy as the highest of God's gifts, by identifying it with sagacity, "the power of hitting the middle term of a syllogism in an imperceptible time . . . the power of infallibly guessing the truth without the help of imagination."

His proof of the unicity of God was later found useful by St. Thomas Aquinas. Avicenna wrote his autobiography, and described how "I read the *Metaphysica* of Aristotle, but did not understand its contents and was baffled by the author's intention; I read it over forty times, until I had the text by heart. Even then I did not understand it, or what the author meant, and I despaired within myself." Then one day he found at a bookseller's Al-Farabi's *On the Objects of the Metaphysics.* "I returned home and hastened to read it, and at once the objects of that book became clear to me, for I had it all by heart."

On the nature of God, Avicenna wrote:

[*That there Is a Necessary Being*

Whatever has being must either have a reason for its being, or have no reason for it. If it has a reason, then it is contingent, equally before it comes into being (if we make this mental hypothesis) and when it is in the state of being—for in the case of a thing whose being is contingent the mere fact of its entering upon being does not remove

* The names in parentheses are those by which the Muslim philosophers were phoneticized into medieval Latin.

from it the contingent nature of its being. If on the other
hand it has no reason for its being in any way whatsoever,
then it is necessary in its being. This rule having been confirmed, I shall now proceed to prove that there is in being
a being which has no reason for its being.

Such a being is either contingent or necessary. If it is
necessary, then the point we sought to prove is established.
If on the other hand it is contingent, that which is contingent cannot enter upon being except for some reason
which sways the scales in favour of its being and against
its not-being. If the reason is also contingent, there is then
a chain of contingents linked one to the other, and there
is no being at all; for this being which is the subject of our
hypothesis cannot enter into being so long as it is not preceded by an infinite succession of beings, which is absurd.
Therefore contingent beings end in a Necessary Being.

Of the Unicity of God

It is not possible in any way that the Necessary Being
should be two. Demonstration: Let us suppose that there
is another necessary being: one must be distinguishable
from the other, so that the terms "this" and "that" may be
used with reference to them. This distinction must be either
essential or accidental. If the distinction between them is
accidental, this accidental element cannot but be present
in each of them, or in one and not the other. If each of them
has an accidental element by which it is distinguished from
the other, both of them must be caused; for an accident
is what is adjoined to a thing after its essence is realized. If
the accidental element is regarded as adhering to its being,
and is present in one of the two and not in the other, then
the one which has no accidental element is a necessary
being and the other is not a necessary being. If, however,
the distinction is essential, the element of essentiality is
that whereby the essence as such subsists; and if this
element of essentiality is different in each and the two are
distinguishable by virtue of it, then each of the two must
be a compound; and compounds are caused; so that neither
of them will be a necessary being. If the element of essentiality belongs to one only, and the other is one in every

respect and there is no compounding of any kind in it, then the one which has no element of essentiality is a necessary being, and the other is not a necessary being. Since it is thus established that the Necessary Being cannot be two, but is All Truth, then by virtue of His Essential Reality, in respect of which He is a Truth, He is United and One, and no other shares with Him in that Unity: however the All-Truth attains existence, it is through Himself.

That God Is Without Cause

A necessary being has no cause whatsoever. Causes are of four kinds: that from which a thing has being, or the active cause; that on account of which a thing has being, or the final and completive cause; that in which a thing has being, or the material cause; and that through which a thing has being, or the formal cause.

The justification for limiting causes to these four varieties is that the reason for a thing is either internal in its subsistence, or a part of its being, or external to it. If it is internal, then it is either that part in which the thing is, potentially and not actually, that is to say its matter; or it is that part in which the thing becomes actually, that is to say its form. If it is external, then it can only be either that from which the thing has being, that is to say the agent, or that on account of which the thing has being, that is to say its purpose and end.

Since it is established that these are the roots and principles of this matter, let us rest on them and clarify the problems which are constructed upon them.

Demonstration that He has no active cause: This is self-evident: for if He had any reason for being, this would be adventitious and that would be a necessary being. Since it is established that He has no active cause, it follows on this line of reasoning that His Quiddity is not other than His Identity, that is to say, other than His Being; neither will He be a subsistence or an accident. There cannot be two, each of which derives its being from the other; nor can He be a necessary being in one respect, and a contingent being in another respect.

Proof that His Quiddity is not other than His Identity,

but rather that His Being is unified in His Reality: If His Being were not the same as His Reality, then His Being would be other than His Reality. Every accident is caused, and every thing caused requires a reason. Now this reason is either external to His Quiddity, or is itself His Quiddity: if it is external, then He is not a necessary being, and is not exempt from an active cause; while if the reason is itself the Quiddity, then the reason must necessarily be itself a complete being in order that the being of another may result from it. Quiddity before being has no being; and if it had being before this, it would not require a second being. The question therefore returns to the problem of being. If the Being of the Quiddity is accidental, whence did this Being supervene and adhere? It is therefore established that the Identity of the Necessary Being is His Quiddity, and that He has no active cause; the necessary nature of His Being is like the quiddity of all other things. From this it is evident that the Necessary Being does not resemble any other thing in any respect whatsoever; for with all other things their being is other than their quiddity.

Proof that He is not an accident: An accident is a being in a locus. The locus is precedent to it, and its being is not possible without the locus. But we have stated that a being which is necessary has no reason for its being.

Proof that there cannot be two necessary beings, each deriving its being from the other: Each of them, in as much as it derives its being from the other, would be subsequent to the other, while at the same time by virtue of supplying being to the other, each would be precedent to the other: but one and the same thing cannot be both precedent and subsequent in relation to its being. Moreover, if we assume for the sake of argument that the other is non-existent: would the first then be a necessary being, or not? If it were a necessary being, it would have no connection with the other: if it were not a necessary being, it would be a contingent being and would require another necessary being. Since the Necessary Being is One, and does not derive Its being from any one, it follows that He is a Necessary Being in every respect; while anything else derives its being from another.

Proof that He cannot be a Necessary Being in one respect and a contingent being in another respect: Such a
being, in as much as it is a contingent being, would be
connected in being with something else, and so it has a
reason; but in as much as it is a necessary being, it would
have no connections with anything else. In that case it
would both have being and not have being; and that is
absurd.

Demonstration that He has no material and receptive
cause: The receptive cause is the cause for the provision
of the place in which a thing is received; that is to say, the
place prepared for the reception of being, or the perfection
of being. Now the Necessary Being is a perfection in pure
actuality, and is not impaired by any deficiency; every perfection belongs to Him, derives from Him, and is preceded
by His Essence, while every deficiency, even if it be met-
aphorical, is negated to Him. All perfection and all beauty
are of His Being; indeed, these are the vestiges of the perfection of His Being; how then should He derive perfection
from any other? Since it is thus established that He has no
receptive cause, it follows that He does not possess anything
potentially, and that He has no attribute yet to be awaited;
on the contrary, His Perfection has been realized in actuality; and He has no material cause. We say "realized in
actuality," using this as a common term of expression,
meaning that every perfection belonging to any other is
non-existent and yet to be awaited, whereas all perfection
belonging to Him has being and is present. His Perfect
Essence, preceding all relations, is One. From this it is
manifest that His Attributes are not an augmentation of
His Essence; for if they were an augmentation of His
Essence, the Attributes would be potential with reference
to the Essence and the Essence would be the reason for
the Attributes. In that case the Attributes would be subsequent to a precedent, so that they would be in one respect
active and in another receptive; their being active would be
other than the aspect of their being receptive; and in consequence they would possess two mutually exclusive aspects. Now this is impossible in the case of anything what-

soever; when a body is in motion, the motivation is from one quarter and the movement from another.

If it were to be stated that His Attributes are not an augmentation of His Essence, but that they entered into the constitution of the Essence, and that the Essence cannot be conceived of as existing without these Attributes, then the Essence would be compound, and the Oneness would be destroyed. It is also evident, as a result of denying the existence of a receptive cause, that it is impossible for Him to change; for the meaning of change is the passing away of one attribute and the establishment of another; and if He were susceptible to change, He would possess potentially an element of passing-away and an element of establishment; and that is absurd. It is clear from this that He has no opposite and no contrary; for opposites are essences which succeed each other in the occupation of a single locus, there being between them the extreme of contrariety. But He is not receptive to accidents, much less to opposites. And if the term "opposite" is used to denote one who disputes with Him in His Rulership, it is clear too on this count that He has no opposite. It is further clear that it is impossible for Him not to be; for since it is established that His Being is necessary, it follows that it is impossible for Him not to be; because everything which exists potentially cannot exist actually, otherwise it would have two aspects. Anything which is receptive to a thing does not cease to be receptive when reception has actually taken place; if this were not so, it would result in the removal of both being and not-being, and that is untenable. This rule applies to every essence and every unified reality, such as angels and human spirits; they are not susceptible to not-being at all, since they are free from corporeal adjunctions.

Demonstration that He has no formal cause: A formal, corporeal cause only exists and is confirmed when a thing is possessed of matter: the matter has a share in the being of the form, in the same way that the form has a part in the disposition of the matter in being in actuality; such a thing is therefore caused. It is further evident as a result of denying this cause to Him, that He is also to be denied all corporeal attributes, such as time, space, direction, and being in one place to the exclusion of all other; in short, whatever is possible in relation to corporeal things is impossible in relation to Him.

Proof that He has no final cause: The final cause is that on account of which a thing has being; and the First Truth has not being for the sake of anything, rather does everything exist on account of the perfection of His Essence, being consequent to His Being and derived from His Being. Moreover the final cause, even if it be posterior in respect of being to all other causes, yet it is mentally prior to them all. It is the final cause which makes the active cause become a cause in actuality, that is to say in respect of its being a final cause.

Since it is established that He is exalted above this last kind of cause too, it is clear that there is no cause to His Attributes. It is also evident that He is Pure Benevolence and True Perfection; the meaning of His Self-Sufficiency likewise becomes manifest, namely that he approves of nothing and disapproves of nothing. For if He approved of anything, that thing would come into being and would continue to be; while if He disapproved of anything, that thing would be converted into not-being and would be annulled. The very divergency of these beings proves the nullity of such a proposition; for a thing which is one in every respect cannot approve of a thing and of its opposite. It is also not necessary for Him to observe the rule of greater expediency or of expediency, as certain Qualitarians have idly pretended; for if His acts of expediency were obligatory to Him, He would not merit gratitude and praise for such acts, since He would merely be fulfilling that which it is His obligation to perform, and He would be to all intents and purposes as one paying a debt; He would therefore deserve nothing at all for such benevolence. In fact His acts proceed on the contrary from Him and for Him, as we shall demonstrate later.

His Attributes as Interpreted According to the Foregoing Principles

Since it is established that God is a Necessary Being, that

He is One in every respect, that He is exalted above all
causes, and that He has no reason of any kind for His
Being; since it is further established that His Attributes
do not augment His Essence, and that He is qualified by the
Attributes of Praise and Perfection; it follows necessarily
that we must state that He is Knowing, Living, Willing, Omnipotent, Speaking, Seeing, Hearing, and Possessed of all
the other Loveliest Attributes. It is also necessary to recognize that His Attributes are to be classified as negative, positive, and a compound of the two: since His Attributes are of
this order, it follows that their multiplicity does not destroy
His Unity or contradict the necessary nature of His Being.
Pre-eternity for instance is essentially the negation of not-
being in the first place, and the denial of causality and of
primality in the second place; similarly the term One means
that He is indivisible in every respect, both verbally and
actually. When it is stated that He is a Necessary Being,
this means that He is a Being without a cause, and that He
is the Cause of other than Himself: this is a combination
of the negative and the positive. Examples of the positive
Attributes are His being Creator, Originator, Shaper, and
the entire Attributes of Action. As for the compound of
both, this kind is illustrated by His being Willing and
Omnipotent, for these Attributes are a compound of Knowledge with the addition of Creativeness.

God's Knowledge

God has knowledge of His Essence: His Knowledge, His
Being Known and His Knowing are one and the same thing.
He knows other than Himself, and all objects of knowledge.
He knows all things by virtue of one knowledge, and in
a single manner. His Knowledge does not change according
to whether the thing known has being or not-being.

Proof that God has knowledge of His Essence: We have
stated that God is One, and that He is exalted above all
causes. The meaning of knowledge is the supervention of
an idea divested of all corporeal coverings. Since it is established that He is One, and that He is divested of body,
and His Attributes also; and as this idea as just described
supervenes upon Him; and since whoever has an abstract

idea supervening upon him is possessed of knowledge, and it is immaterial whether it is his essence or other than himself; and as further His Essence is not absent from Himself; it follows from all this that He knows Himself.

Proof that He is Knowledge, Knowing and Known: Knowledge is another term for an abstract idea. Since this idea is abstract, it follows that He is Knowledge; since this abstract idea belongs to Him, is present with Him, and is not veiled from Him, it follows that He is Knowing; and since this abstract idea does not supervene save through Him, it follows that He is Known. The terms employed in each case are different; otherwise it might be said that Knowledge, Knowing and Known are, in relation to His Essence, one. Take your own experience as a parallel. If you know yourself, the object of your knowledge is either yourself or something else; if the object of your knowledge is something other than yourself, then you do not know yourself. But if the object of your knowledge is yourself, then both the one knowing and the thing known are your self. If the image of your self is impressed upon your self, then it is your self which is the knowledge. Now if you look back upon yourself reflectively, you will not find any impression of the idea and quiddity of your self in yourself a second time, so as to give rise within you to a sense that your self is more than one. Therefore since it is established that He has intelligence of His Essence, and since His Intelligence is His Essence and does not augment His Essence, it follows that He is Knowing, Knowledge and Known without any multiplicity attaching to Him through these Attributes; and there is no difference between "one who has knowledge" and "one who has intelligence," since both are terms for describing the negation of matter absolutely.

Proof that He has knowledge of other than Himself: Whoever knows himself, if thereafter he does not know other than himself this is due to some impediment. If the impediment is essential, this implies necessarily that he does not know himself either; while if the impediment is of an external nature, that which is external can be removed. Therefore it is possible—nay, necessary—that He should have knowledge of other than Himself, as you shall learn from this chapter.

Proof that He has knowledge of all objects of knowledge: Since it is established that He is a Necessary Being, that He is One, and that the universe is brought into being from Him and has resulted out of His Being; since it is established further that He has knowledge of His Own Essence, His Knowledge of His Essence being what it is, namely that He is the Origin of all realities and of all things that have being; it follows that nothing in heaven or earth is remote from His Knowledge—on the contrary, all that comes into being does so by reason of Him: He is the causer of all reasons, and He knows that of which He is the Reason, the Giver of being and the Originator.

Proof that He knows all things by virtue of one knowledge, in a manner which changes not according to the change in the thing known: It has been established that His Knowledge does not augment His Essence, and that He is the Origin of all things that have being, while being exalted above accident and changes; it therefore follows that He knows things in a manner unchanging. The objects of knowledge are a consequence of His Knowledge; His Knowledge is not a consequence of the things known, that it should change as they change; for His Knowledge of things is the reason for their having being. Hence it is manifest that Knowledge is itself Omnipotence. He knows all contingent things, even as He knows all things that have being, even though we know them not; for the contingent, in relation to us, is a thing whose being is possible and whose not-being is also possible; but in relation to Him one of the two alternatives is actually known. Therefore His Knowledge of genera, species, things with being, contingent things, manifest and secret things—this Knowledge is a single knowledge.

Acts Emanating from God

Since you now know that He is a Necessary Being, that He is One, and that He has no Attribute which augments His Essence (for that would imply a succession of various acts, whereas the Act of God is the vestiges of the Perfection of His Essence); this being so, it follows that His First Act is one.

For if there had emanated from Him two acts, the emanation would have been in two different manners, for duality in the act implies duality in the agent. He who acts by virtue of his own essence, if his essence is one only one act emanates from it.*]

IBN-RUSHD (AVERROËS) (1126-1198) WROTE COMmentaries on Aristotle, and "for more than three hundred years western scholars read Aristotle mainly with the help of these commentaries of Averroës." As for the medieval world in general, and for St. Thomas Aquinas in particular, Aristotle was *"The* Philosopher," for them Averroës was *The* Commentator. His most famous and original book is called *The Incoherence of Incoherence,* in which he defended philosophy against al-Ghazzali who wrote *The Incoherence of Philosophers.* Avicenna came from one extreme limit of the Islamic world, Central Asia (near Bokhara); Averroës came from another—Spain. Al-Ghazzali (Algazel) (1058-1111), as great a theologian as Averroës was a philosopher, was a Persian. Averroës used against him the whole "arsenal of Aristotelian philosophy to prove that only philosophy can give a satisfactory answer" to all those "questions that we do not know." Avicenna was a Neo-Platonist, while Averroës, the last of the Muslims who dared stand up for philosophy against orthodox theology, was Aristotelian to the core; "the last great representative of Greek philosophy in medieval Islam." For orthodox Islam did not hold with the pantheist inclination of some of the Muslim commentators of Aristotle any more than did Christian orthodoxy, and ibn-Hazm, who was to the West what al-Ghazzali was to the East, comments bravely but ruefully after trouble with the authorities: "Trouble me not regarding this burning of books and papers, but rather say 'now we shall see what he knows.' If they have burned the paper, they have not burned what the paper contained. That is in my breast, and

* Avicenna, *On Theology,* trans. A. J. Arberry (John Murray Ltd., Publishers, 1951).

I carry it whithersoever my horses take me. It stays where I halt, and it will only be buried in my tomb."

Averroës declared that philosophy was an investigation into the nature of the existent. But the existent is the created, and the created leads at once to the Creator. The entire problem of the eternity or newness of the world, he went on to say, resolved itself into a mere difference of words: essentially the philosophers agree. There were, for Averroës, three categories of existence, two extremes and a mean. The first existence is caused by an agent, composed of matter and form and generated in time, for example, the various bodies, water also and air. The other extreme is uncaused, made out of nothing, and not subject to time—i.e., God. The mean is made out of nothing, not preceded by time, yet created by an agent—i.e., the world in its totality, and it is this existent that has occasioned much strife and discussion. All men posit future time as endless, but there is a division of opinion with respect to past time. The school of Plato holds that past time is finite, while Aristotle and his school hold that it is infinite. Fundamentally, concluded Averroës, it is a question of terminology.

As in Europe, so also in Islam, side by side with the theoretical philosophers were to be found the mystics, who agreed with St. Augustine that "to Him Who is everywhere present, one comes by love and not by sail" nor even by thought. These *Sufis*, as they were called (from *suf*, the white woollen gown they wore), were persecuted generally by the more orthodox Muslims. It must be admitted that many of them used language that seemed blasphemous to their co-religionists: al-Hallaj (died 921), for example, cried out in ecstasy "I am the Truth! I am He" and was executed for his audacity. But al-Ghazzali was a philosopher as well as a sufi. Born at Tus in Khorassan in A.D. 1058 he studied at Nysabur, and later at Baghdad, where he acquired great renown as lawyer and theologian. Then suddenly, he experienced so great an onslaught of doubt that it caused a breakdown in his health: "the bond of blind conformity was loosed from me, and the beliefs I had inherited were broken away," he relates of himself.

In his initial process of doubt al-Ghazzali adumbrates
Descartes, but in his view of causality he anticipates the
Scotsman, David Hume (1711-1776): If God is the ultimate cause, al-Ghazzali asked, why should there be a
causal connection in the succession of events? Nothing, he
replies, causes anything. Antecedents have consequence.
God alone is the efficient cause. Al-Ghazzali turned the
tables on the Christians by using Aristotelian arguments
and methods when arguing against them. In the *Al Rad
al Jamil* a "refutation of the divinity of Jesus Christ from
the text of the Gospel," al-Ghazzali wrote that Christians
were divided into two kinds, those who blindly lean on
tradition, and clutch with tooth and nail to the literal sense,
and those who have a minimum of intelligence and of
scientific knowledge, and refer to the authority of the
Philosopher on the divine vision, and are impressed by
the consequences of this doctrine established by so many
authorities, so they are convinced that the Philosopher has
penetrated the darkest recesses and obscurities and has
made them as clear as day. These latter link up the question
of the divine union with the linking up of body and soul,
and make an analogy when referring to the essence of the
necessary Being. But how wrong they are! For the Philosopher insisted that for body and soul to be united there
must be a certain correspondence between them—but how
far from this is God. The Philosopher says the bond between body and soul is one of government, and the pleas-
ure-pain impressions are conveyed from the soul to the
body. But there can be no comparison between such a relationship, and that of the soul with its creator, for He
cannot experience sensible pleasure or pain.

Al-Ghazzali also came into conflict with Aristotle, as
taught by al-Farabi and Avicenna, for he insisted on the
principle of contradiction, to which, he declared, God Himself submits. He denied the eternity of the world, and his
theories of space and time much influenced those of the
Jewish thinker Moses Maimonides (1135-1204), who was
a physician at the court of Saladin in Alexandria. According to al-Ghazzali:

"He who believes in endless time must, to be consistent,

also assume the existence of infinite space. To say that
space answers to the external sense and time to the internal,
does not alter the case. For just as space bears a relation
to body, so does time to the movement of body. Both are
merely relations between our conceptions, which God
creates in us."*

Only God is limitless in His causative activity; He is
the only "willing" being. The philosophers who refuse to
believe that God made the world out of nothing by an absolute act of creation, because they recognize only an ex-
change of accidents in the one material, a passing of the
actual from possibility to possibility, do not recognize that
every apprehension of the sensible, and every spiritual
perception, is entirely new. For the definite, final existence,
that is necessary to causation, as to space and time, is God's
eternal will. "God has cognizance of the world because He
wills it." Like Augustine, al-Ghazzali insists that this
divine creative will is compatible with man's freedom, for
His foreknowledge is not distinguishable from His memory
—His knowledge is outside of time or space.

The Jewish philosopher Saadya of Fayum, an author
who lived early in the tenth century, also denied that God
was in space, to the point, indeed, of denying the divine
omnipresence, for if God is everywhere, then He must
be in space also. But for Saadya, God is in the universe as
conscience is in the body: "Cut off a limb from the living
body, and the soul is not lessened; annihilate half of the
universe, and the deity is unimpaired." This is positing an
"abstracted spatiality" which René Descartes would have
declared a nonsensical contradiction. For Descartes "space
is that attribute of things without which their existence is
impossible"; space is the one "absolute and unconditioned
reality." Immanuel Kant, however, returned to a position
nearer that of Saadya: for him space was not necessarily an
external reality, it is rather the mental condition of perception. Things-in-themselves are beyond the category of
space; things as we perceive them must be in space.

Besides the Arab Aristotelians, there were several great

* T. J. de Boer, *The History of Philosophy in Islam* (Luzac,
1903).

medieval Jewish philosophers, who, following upon the work of the early and not entirely convincing Philo, thought out a synthesis of Jewish and Greek thought. Of these ibn-Gabirol (Avencebrol), a Jewish philosopher living in Spain in the eleventh century and much quoted by St. Thomas Aquinas, had suggested that the intellect, like material things, was composed of matter and form, but that the form and matter both were spiritual and emanated from God, rather than were created by Him. God alone is active, all things are passive, and the divine will, the only active force in the universe, traverses bodies and performs all the actions bodies seem to perform. This was, of course, untenable for Christians, but Moses Maimonides suggested a compromise. Maimonides, commenting on Aristotle, wrote that "the twenty-five propositions which are employed in the proof of the existence of God, or in the arguments that God is neither corporeal nor a force connected with material being, or that He is one, have been fully established, and their correctness is beyond doubt. There is, however, one proposition which we do not accept, namely, that proposition which affirms the eternity of the universe." (*Moreh*, Book II, from the Introduction.)

The proofs so confidently adduced by Maimonides were finally reduced by him to three:

1. God's existence follows from the Aristotelian principle of motion.

2. If one component exists separately, the other must also. Therefore the "causing motion" must exist separately.

3. If there is a possible existence there must also be a necessary existence and therefore God's existence follows from the Aristotelian principles of potential and actual.

Motion, causality and contingency; these were to be accepted later by St. Thomas Aquinas as the first three of his famous "five proofs" of God's existence.

CHAPTER VIII

St. Bonaventura

THE ASSIMILATION OF ARISTOTLE AT DIFFERENT LEVELS by Christians, Muslims and Jews in the tenth to thirteenth centuries may be compared—all other things being unequal—with the assimilation, in the twentieth, by Christian and non-Christian philosophers, of such scientific systems as those of Karl Marx (1818-1883), Sigmund Freud (1856-1939), and Albert Einstein (1879-), in that it was not a single idea that had to be incorporated, but a whole system, a total view of God and the universe.

The Christian assimilation of Aristotle, which was gradual, cumulative, and total, was a process in which every medieval writer, consciously or unconsciously, took part, although of course the angles, attitudes and emphases varied greatly from country to country. There is as much difference, for example, between English Aristotelianism— as evinced by Robert Grosseteste (c. 1169-1253), the chancellor of Oxford University, and his even more brilliant student, the Dorsetshire Franciscan, Roger Bacon (?1214-1294)—and Belgian, as exemplified by, say, David of Dinant (flourished around 1200), as between a German existentialist of today, such as Karl Jaspers, and a French, such as Jean-Paul Sartre. Also, just as contemporary literature takes its tone and theme from the prevailing philosophic attitude (e.g., the novels of Albert Camus, André Malraux and John Hersey, the paintings of Picasso, Rivera or Rouault), so, too, in the Middle Ages, the poetry of Dante (1265-1321) and the later Chaucer (1340-1400) reflect the philosophic postulates and concerns of their time. In fact, Dante's *Divine Comedy* has been called the *Summa Theologica* in verse, as its divisions and descriptions can be traced to the *Secunda Secundae* of the *Summa*.

Robert Grosseteste affirmed that by praying that all might be one in Him, Jesus Christ had included all creatures, not men only, and that all derive from His one unity and return to It. In his *On Light or the Beginning of Forms* he discusses light as the very form of matter itself, whose function is to multiply, propagate, and diffuse itself.

[The first corporeal form which some call corporeity is in my opinion light. For light of its very nature diffuses itself in every direction in such a way that a point of light will produce instantaneously a sphere of light of any size whatsoever, unless some opaque object stands in the way. Now the extension of matter in three dimensions is a necessary concomitant of corporeity, and this despite the fact that both corporeity and matter are in themselves simple substances lacking all dimension. But a form that is in itself simple and without dimension could not introduce dimension in every direction into matter, which is likewise simple and without dimension, except by multiplying itself and diffusing itself instantaneously in every direction and thus extending matter in its own diffusion. For the form cannot desert matter, because it is inseparable from it, and matter itself cannot be deprived of form.——But I have proposed that it is light which possesses of its very nature the function of multiplying itself and diffusing itself instantaneously in all directions. Whatever performs this operation is either light or some other agent that acts in virtue of its participation in light to which this operation belongs essentially. Corporeity, therefore, is either light itself or the agent which performs the aforementioned operation and introduces dimensions into matter in virtue of its participation in light, and acts through the power of this same light. But the first form cannot introduce dimensions into matter through the power of a subsequent form. Therefore light is not a form subsequent to corporeity, but it is corporeity itself.

Furthermore, the first corporeal form is, in the opinion of the philosophers, more exalted and of a nobler and more excellent essence than all the forms that come after it. It

bears, also, a closer resemblance to the forms that exist
apart from matter. But light is more exalted and of a nobler
and more excellent essence than all corporeal things. It
has, moreover, greater similarity than all bodies to the
forms that exist apart from matter, namely, the intelligences. Light therefore is the first corporeal form.

Thus light, which is the first form created in first matter,
multiplied itself by its very nature an infinite number of
times on all sides and spread itself out uniformly in every
direction. In this way it proceeded in the beginning of time
to extend matter which it could not leave behind, by draw-
ing it out along with itself into a mass the size of the material universe. This extension of matter could not be
brought about through a finite multiplication of light, because the multiplication of a simple being a finite number
of times does not produce a quantity, as Aristotle shows
in the *De Caelo et Mundo*. However, the multiplication of
a simple being an infinite number of times must produce a
finite quantity, because a product which is the result of an
infinite multiplication exceeds infinitely that through the
multiplication of which it is produced. Now one simple
being cannot exceed another simple being infinitely, but
only a finite quantity infinitely exceeds a simple being. For
an infinite quantity exceeds a simple being by infinity times
infinity. Therefore, when light, which is in itself simple, is
multiplied an infinite number of times, it must extend matter, which is likewise simple, into finite dimensions.

It is possible, however, that an infinite sum of number
is related to an infinite sum in every proportion, numerical
and non-numerical. And some infinites are larger than
other infinites, and some are smaller. Thus the sum of all
numbers both even and odd is infinite. It is at the same time
greater than the sum of all the even numbers although this
is likewise infinite, for it exceeds it by the sum of all the
odd numbers. The sum, too, of all numbers starting with
one and continuing by doubling each successive number is
infinite, and similarly the sum of all the halves corresponding to the doubles is infinite. The sum of these halves must
be half of the sum of their doubles. In the same way the
sum of all numbers starting with one and multiplying by

three successively is three times the sum of all the thirds corresponding to these triples. It is likewise clear in regard to all kinds of numerical proportion that there can be a proportion of finite to infinite according to each of them.

But if we posit an infinite sum of all doubles starting with one, and an infinite sum of all the halves corresponding to these doubles, and if one, or some other finite number, be subtracted from the sum of the halves, then, as soon as this subtraction is made, there will no longer be a two to one proportion between the first sum and what is left of the second sum. Indeed there will not be any numerical proportion, because if a second numerical proportion is to be left from the first as the result of subtraction from the lesser member of the proportion, then what is subtracted must be an aliquot part or aliquot parts of an aliquot part of that from which it is subtracted. But a finite number cannot be an aliquot part or aliquot parts of an aliquot part of an infinite number. Therefore when we subtract a number from an infinite sum of halves there will not remain a numerical proportion between the infinite sum of doubles and what is left from the infinite sum of halves.

Since this is so, it is clear that light through the infinite multiplication of itself extends matter into finite dimensions that are smaller and larger according to certain proportions that they have to one another, namely, numerical and non-numerical. For if light through the infinite multiplication of itself extends matter into a dimension of two cubits, by the doubling of this same infinite multiplication it extends it into a dimension of four cubits, and by the dividing in half of this infinite multiplication, it extends it into a dimension of one cubit. Thus it proceeds according to numerical and non-numerical proportions.

It is my opinion that this was the meaning of the theory of those philosophers who held that everything is composed of atoms, and said that bodies are composed of surfaces, and sufaces of lines, and lines of points. This opinion does not contradict the theory that a magnitude is composed only of magnitudes, because for every meaning of the word whole, there is a corresponding meaning of the word part. Thus we say that a half is part of a whole, be-

cause two halves make a whole. We say, too, that a side is
part of a diameter, but in a different sense, because no matter how many times a side is taken it does not make a
diameter, but is always less than the diameter. Again we
say that an angle of contingence is part of a right angle
because there is an infinite number of angles of contingence
in a right angle, and yet when an angle of contingence is
subtracted from a right angle a finite number of times the
latter becomes smaller. It is in a different sense, however,
that a point is said to be part of a line in which it is contained an infinite number of times, for when a point is taken
away from a line a finite number of times this does not
shorten the line.

To return therefore to my theme, I say that light through
the infinite multiplication of itself equally in all directions
extends matter on all sides equally into the form of a sphere
and, as a necessary consequence of this extension, the
outermost parts of matter are more extended and more
rarefied than those within, which are close to the center.
And since the outermost parts will be rarefied to the highest
degree, the inner parts will have the possibility of further
rarefaction.

In this way light, by extending first matter into the form
of a sphere, and by rarefying its outermost parts to the highest degree, actualized completely in the outermost sphere
the potentiality of matter, and left this matter without any
potency to further impression: And thus the first body in
the outermost part of the sphere, the body which is called
the firmament, is perfect, because it has nothing in its composition but first matter and first form. It is therefore the
simplest of all bodies with respect to the parts that constitute its essence and with respect to its quantity which is
the greatest possible in extent. It differs from the genus
body only in this respect, that in it the matter is completely
actualized through the first form alone. But the genus body,
which is in this and in other bodies and has in its essence
first matter and first form, abstracts from the complete
actualization of matter through the first form and from the
diminution of matter through the first form.

When the first body, which is the firmament, has in this

way been completely actualized, it diffuses its light (*lumen*) from every part of itself to the center of the universe. For since light (*lux*) is the perfection of the first body and naturally multiplies itself from the first body, it is necessarily diffused to the center of the universe. And since this light (*lux*) is a form entirely inseparable from matter in its diffusion from the first body, it extends along with itself the spirituality of the matter of the first body. Thus there proceeds from the first body light (*lumen*), which is a spiritual body, or if you prefer, a bodily spirit. This light (*lumen*) in its passing does not divide the body through which it passes, and thus it passes instantaneously from the body of the first heaven to the center of the universe. Furthermore, its passing is not to be understood in the sense of something numerically one passing instantaneously from that heaven to the center of the universe, for this is perhaps impossible, but its passing takes place through the multiplication of itself and the infinite generation of light.*]

ROGER BACON, AN OMNIVOROUS NATURAL SCIENTIST, first "postulated a theory of science as a means of discovering reality and truth" (A. Crombie, *Grosseteste and the Origins of Experimental Science,* Oxford, 1953). Roger Bacon used both geometry and arithmetic in "some simple physics," and for him mathematics, or more simply numbers, rather than light, were the primal matter. Language, for men such as St. Anselm and Abelard the central mystery of the intellectual life, and logic, which for them was dependent on language, were for Roger Bacon subservient to mathematics. Observation, he insisted, was required for certification in mathematical physics, and, like Robert Grosseteste (of whose "circle" he was a member from 1249, and to whose manuscripts he had access), he begins from Aristotle's *Posterior Analytics.* In Part VI of his *Opus Majus* (translated by Robert Belle Burke for the University of Pennsylvania Press in 1928) he insists that he

* Grosseteste, *On Light,* trans. by Clare Riedl (Marquette University Press). Copyright, 1942, by Marquette University Press.

[. . . now wishes to unfold the principles of mathematical
science, since without experience nothing can be sufficiently known. For there are two modes of acquiring knowledge,
namely, by reasoning and experience. Reasoning draws a
conclusion and makes us grant the conclusion, but does
not make the conclusion certain, nor does it remove doubt
so that the mind may rest on the intuition of truth, unless
the mind discovers it by the method of experience; for
many have the arguments relating to what can be known,
but because they lack experience they neglect the arguments, and neither avoid what is harmful, nor follow what
is good. For if a man who has never seen fire should prove
by adequate reason that fire burns and injures things and
destroys them, his mind would not be satisfied thereby, nor
would he avoid fire, until he placed his hand or some com-
bustible substance in the fire, so that he might prove by
experience that which reasoning taught. But, when he has
had actual experience of combustion, his mind is made
certain and rests in the full light of truth. Therefore, reasoning does not suffice, but experience does . . . therefore all things must be verified by experience. . . . And,
if we turn our attention to the experiences that are particular and complete and certified or wholly in their own dis-
cipline, it is necessary to go by way of the principles of
this science which is called experimental.]

ROGER BACON WAS A FRANCISCAN, VERY MUCH
influenced by Avicenna, who for him was the greatest of
Aristotle's imitators. Bacon sets himself up against the
"moderns" who say that the intellect, which works in our
soul and illuminates it, is a part of that soul, so that the
soul is divided into two, an intellect that is agent, and an
intellect that is passive. The intellectual agent *must* be
distinct from the soul, must be God Himself, Roger Bacon
insisted, and all philosophy arises from a divine illumination. He too, praised the Ancients: "Nothing is better
calculated to invite us to live as we ought, we who are born
and raised in the life of grace, than to see men deprived of
grace reaching such incalculable dignity through the holiness of their lives."

Roger Bacon saw that in the proof of mathematical physics there was something beyond argument, i.e., experience. Arguments can bring us to concede their validity, but they cannot certify their own truth: the soul needs to rest in the intuition of truth, and for that, truth must be experienced. Christian truth is experienced in Christian society by behavior. In the Christian individual it is experienced by mystical illumination and proved by powers. Roger Bacon comes near to claiming for astrology, alchemy and magic a religious, even a divine, sanction. He is more completely convinced of the reality of individuals than of that of universals. "One individual has more reality than all the universals joined together," he said.

In Paris another great Franciscan, Alexander of Hales, was the first medieval philosopher actually to quote Aristotle as an authority. His *Summa Theologica* (which Roger Bacon rudely said would need more than one horse to carry it) was an early attempt to reconcile philosophically Aristotle and St. Augustine.

The greatest of all the Franciscans was St. Bonaventura, who, with the Dominican St. Thomas Aquinas, provides the perfect flowering of medieval philosophy. St. Francis (1182-1226) himself distrusted books and intellectual pursuits, and wished his followers to avoid them, to flee the schools and disputations. But his innocence of learning and ignorance of argument were as individual as Mohammed's and fared as badly; within twenty years of the foundation of his Order his followers were filling University chairs, and disputing with the best.

John of Fidenza, called Bonaventura, was born in 1221 at Bagnorea, became Minister General of the Franciscans in 1257, and died in 1274. His most famous book, the *Journey of the Mind to God,* is a philosophical whodunit, following the traces of God through the created universe, and ending with a proclamation of His evident existence. The natural human will to goodness present in each human being, the consciousness of each human being of and by itself, in turn, St. Bonaventura said, lead naturally to an awareness of God, who is present in every soul. These all are proofs of the Divine existence. The problem of the

active and the passive intellect, of love as both *eros* and
agape, has today been discussed at great length by such
eminent theologians as the Swedish Lutheran Bishop Ny-
gren, the English Jesuit Father M. C. D'Arcy, and the
Swiss Protestant Denis de Rougemont. It was a problem
also for the medieval philosophers, and is, of course, another aspect of the perennial dichotomy of grace and free
will. God is indeed the "light that lighteth every man" but
St. Bonaventura would not have the soul as merely passive, an object illuminated. For what is to know? To be
certain, to reach certainty. And such certainty supposes
immutability in the known, infallibility in the knower. Here
we have neither. For here all truth, being created, is relative, and the creature that knows, for the same reason, cannot be infallible. Only the Creator can give both infallibility to the knower and immutability to the known. And the
distinction between Creator and creature is one that must
at all times be kept clear.

Nicolas de Malebranche (1638-1715) accused St.
Bonaventura of ontologism. Ontologism is a theory which
claims that all intellectual ideas and principles are innate
in man, and that even the idea of God in man's mind is
antecedent to any experimental knowledge of Him. But St.
Bonaventura clearly stated that the Divine Light is inac-
cessible to the powers of every created nature on account
of its pre-eminence, and goes on to discuss the six illumina-
tions that man is given here below: the light of mechanical
art, the light of sensitive knowledge, the three lights of
natural, rational, and moral philosophy and the light of
Holy Writ (or revelation). The seventh illumination, which
will be only hereafter, is the light of glory.

In part he says:

[The first light is the light of mechanical art, which
illuminates artificial figures. The second light gives us
the illumination from the apprehension of natural forms
in the light of sensitive knowledge. It is rightly called
lower, because sensitive knowledge begins with the lower
and exists by the aid of the bodily light. And it is divided
according to the five senses. For the sensible spirit has

the nature of light, whenever it dwells in the nerves and it is multiplied in the five senses, according to the greater or less degree of its purity.

The third light which gives illumination from the examining of intelligible truths is the light of philosophic knowledge. It is accordingly called inward because it searches into the inward and hidden causes and does this through the principles and the disciplines of natural truth which are implanted naturally in man. And it is divided in three ways, into rational, natural, and moral. And its sufficiency can be shown thus. For there is the truth of speech, the truth of things and the truth of actions. The rational way considers the truth of speech; the natural the truth of things; and the moral the truth of action. Or, in another manner, as in the highest, in God Himself, there is to be considered the reason of the efficient, formal and final cause (because He is the cause of subsisting) the reason of understanding and the order of living, the case is the same in the illumination of philosophy, since it gives illumination either from knowing the cause of being, and then it is physics, or the reasons of understanding, and then it is logic, or the order of living, and then it is moral or practical. In the third way thus it is that the light of philosophical knowledge illuminates intellective reason. This, however, can take place in three ways, either in so far as it rules the motive of reason, and then it is moral, or in so far as it rules itself and then it is natural, or in so far as it rules the interpretative and then it is dialectical. And all this is to the end that man may be illuminated for the truth of life, the truth of science and the truth of doctrine.*]

ST. BONAVENTURA WAS ALSO CONCERNED WITH THE PROBlem of time. He denies the eternity of time by saying that being caused implies a beginning. If time—or any other matter—were eternal, God would not be the sole absolute being, for a process, such as God would be if He were creation, instead of creator, would not *be* being, it would only

* St. Bonaventura, *De Reductione Artium Ad Theologiam*, trans. Sister Emma T. Healy (Franciscan Institute).

have being from moment to moment. Further from St. Bonaventura's *On the Reduction of the Arts to Theology*.

【 A man's will is as simple or as composite as his love. By the will being simple we mean that its affective energies are without division or dissipation, because they are concentrated on one or a few objects. Now love is the principle of such simplicity, because with every act of love we unite ourselves with the object and with every union there comes about a further composition in the soul, and with that a further scattering of energy.】

IN HIS *Journey of the Mind to God,* WRITTEN ON MOUNT Avernia, where his master, St. Francis, had received the Stigmata, St. Bonaventura wrote:

【 For, inasmuch as, in our present condition, this universe of things is a ladder whereby we may ascend to God, since among these things some are God's footprints, some God's image, some corporeal, some spiritual, some temporal, some eternal, and, hence, some outside of us, and some inside, it follows that if we are to attain to the contemplation of the First Principle and Source of all things, in Himself altogether spiritual, eternal, and above us, we must begin with God's footprints which are corporeal, temporal and outside us and so enter on the Way that leads to God. We enter in within our own souls, which are images of the eternal God, spiritual and interior to us, and this is to enter into the Truth of God. Finally, we must reach out beyond and above ourselves to the region of the eternal and supereminently spiritual and look to the First Principle of all. . . .

In direct relation with this threefold progress of the soul to God, the human mind has three fundamental attitudes or outlooks. The first is towards corporeal things without, and in this respect it is designated as animal or simply sensual; the next is where it enters in within itself to contemplate itself, and here it ranks as spirit; the third is where its upward glance is beyond itself, and then it is designated 'mens' or mind. . . .

Unless we know, therefore, what Being as Being is, we are not in a position fully to understand the definition of any particular substance. Nor can Being as Being be known unless it is envisaged in its most general conditions, which are unity, truth, and goodness. Being may be considered in many ways: as complete and incomplete, perfect and imperfect, actual and potential, simple and conditioned, as a whole or in part, as static and dynamic, as from itself and as caused, as pure Being and as composite, as absolute and conditioned, as prior and posterior, as immutable and mutable, as simple and composite. But it is a general principle that the imperfect and that which is privative or negative may be understood only in terms of something positive. So the human reason cannot reach a full and final explanation of created things unless it is aided by an understanding of the most pure, actual, complete and absolute Being, in other words, unless it reaches out to the utterly simple and eternal Being of God in whose mind are to be found the ultimate ground and reason of all things. How indeed could the human mind surmise that the particular things with which it comes in contact are defective and incomplete did it not possess some knowledge of a Being who is utterly devoid of imperfection? And the same argument applies to the other conditions of created things above specified. The human intellect may be truly said to know the meaning of propositions when it knows with certainty that they are true. It may then be said really to know since in such an assent it cannot be deceived, and since the object of its affirmation cannot be conceived to be otherwise, the truth of its judgment must be something immutable.

Being so certainly exists that it cannot be conceived as not existing. Only in a perfect flight from nothingness is Being to be found in all its purity, for Being and nothingness are absolutely opposed. Even, therefore, as pure nothingness contains naught of Being or its conditions, so, on the contrary, Being contains naught of non-being, either actually or potentially, either ontologically or according to our modes of apprehension. Moreover, non-being must be regarded as a privation of Being, and as such it cannot be known except by reference to Being. Being, on the other

hand, is not dependent on anything outside it for its introduction to our minds, for everything that is known is known
either as non-being, or as potential being, or actual being.
If, therefore, non-being can be understood only in terms of
Being and potential being in terms of actual being, and if
Being moreover designates the pure act of that which is, it
follows that Being is that which first enters the human mind
and this Being is characterized by the qualities of Pure Act.
It cannot be identified with any particular being, for particular beings are limited and potential. Nor yet is it to be
equated with analogous being which has no reality since it
does not exist. It follows, therefore, that this Being in question is divine.*]

CHAPTER IX

St. Thomas Aquinas

ALTHOUGH ARISTOTLE, SIEVED THROUGH THE CHRISTIAN
minds and comments of Boethius or Abelard, had not
proved unacceptable to the Church, Aristotle, flavored by
Muslim commentators, though popular (St. Albert the
Great publicly discussed Averroës' doctrine of the intellect
in 1256) soon encountered official disapproval. Siger of
Brabant, the leader of the Averroists at the University of
Paris, maintained, as philosophical truth, that there was
only one Intellect, present in all intelligence, to whom was
the collective return after death; he maintained too that the
world was eternal, continuously and necessarily created by
God, who could no more stop creating than He could stop
existing, and that this same necessity of His nature, that
bound Him, bound our several natures to such an extent
that there was no possibility of human free-will. When

* Bonaventura, St., *The Franciscan Vision* (Burns, Oates & Washbourne).

challenged as to how these doctrines could be reconciled
with the Christian revelation, Siger of Brabant and the
other Christian Averroists took the line that what is true
philosophically bears no relation to what is true theologi-
cally. Revealed truths are not concerned with the same
problems as is philosophy. This line is often taken today by
Christians who find the truths of science at variance with
the Christian Revelation: their reply is that there is separate
truth for separate subjects. (The Muslim Averroists were
actually in exactly the same fix as Siger of Brabant and
the Christian Averroists, for the doctrines of the Koran
are as remote from Averroës' philosophy as is the Christian truth.) In 1277 Siger of Brabant's theories were
condemned by the Church, among them such statements as
"There is no more worth-while occupation in this world
than the study of philosophy. The only wise men are
philosophers." Aristotle himself came under suspicion: for
example, as early as 1215, Robert de Courçon, legate of
Pope Innocent III in Paris, forbade the reading of "Master
Aristotle on metaphysics and natural science" by the university students. (Later, Dante rehabilitated both Aristotle
and Averroës.) In 1231 Pope Gregory IX set up a com-
mission of three theologians to consider what corrections
were necessary to include Aristotle in the Christian fold,
and although St. Thomas Aquinas himself was to come
under a cloud at one point for his omnivorous acceptance
of Aristotle, Aristotle was generally taught and accepted
by the middle of the thirteenth century.

St. Albert the Great, born on the banks of the Upper
Danube in 1193, was the first medieval thinker of note, not
only to grasp the intrinsic value of Aristotle's scientific
writings, but also to see clearly the enormous importance
of his philosophy for the constitution of the Christian dogmatic system. St. Albert was well born and well educated.
He could read and write by the age of seven, then learned
Latin, and read Aesop's *Fables,* the *Sentences* of Cato,
Seneca, Aristotle, and Virgil. He kept up a lively interest
in the classics, and in his comments late in life on the Kyrie
of the Mass, he wrote: "The sublimest wisdom of which
the world could boast flourished in Greece. Even as the

Jews knew God by the Scriptures, so the pagan philosophers knew Him by the natural wisdom of reason, and were
debtors to Him for it by their homage." Elsewhere he wrote
"though shorn of the lights of the faith they have none the
less spoken in a wonderful manner of the Creator and His
creatures. Virtue and vice they knew, and a great number
of truths which faith as well as reason announce from
on high."

In 1223 St. Albert became a Dominican. "I had already
distinguished myself in science when I entered the Order,"
he wrote. He wrote admirably of animals—spiders, insects,
and indeed all animals being especially favorite subjects of
study. He taught at Hildesheim, then at Cologne. At that
time there were already over 30,000 Dominicans in
Europe. In 1244 St. Thomas Aquinas, then aged nineteen,
became St. Albert's student, and, when his fellows mocked
the "dumb ox" who sat so silent during St. Albert's lectures,
St. Albert prophesied "this dumb ox will fill the world with
his bellowing." Sts. Albert and Thomas shared lodgings in
the Stolkstrasse in Cologne, and when St. Albert was sent
to teach in Paris St. Thomas went with him. In 1248 both
were back in Cologne. St. Albert was twice provincial of
his order, and was also made Bishop of Ratisbon.

St. Albert taught that the Universal exists in a threefold
way: prior to things, in them, and posterior to them. As
prior, it is within the divine intelligence; in a thing, as that
by which that thing has its own nature; posterior, in the
human understanding, which arrives at it by abstraction
from things as the necessary and therefore proper object of
science. The Universal is *of* many things *in* many things,
but of all things God is the efficient, formal and final cause.
All earthly things are made of matter and form, and matter
is the substratum of all material things. Matter is an entity
needing no further determination; it is by reason of its form
that a thing is what it is. A thing is educed from matter by
the efficient cause, but it never is, and never becomes, that
cause. St. Albert thus avoids Siger of Brabant's pantheism,
and firmly insists that the substance of any person is his
free-will, and that man is wholly responsible for the first
movement of sensibility. Against Averroës (for whom mat-

ter was eternal, tending always to seek the forms it takes, which perish all, while the pure intellect "taking all shapes from Mah to Mahi," like Tennyson's river rolls on for ever), St. Albert maintained that although it could not be philosophically proven or demonstrated that matter was created, it must be accepted as revealed.

The thirteenth century is perhaps, more than any other, the century of outstanding personalities. One of the most outstanding was the Holy Roman Emperor, Frederick II (lived 1194-1250; emperor 1215-1250) known as the *Stupor Mundi,* the astonishment of the world, who was himself a scholar, and obtained Aristotle's works from Constantinople. His correspondence with the Arabic scholar ibn-Sabin has come down to us, and at his court in Sicily there were at least as many Muslims as there were Christians at the contemporary Moorish and Arabic courts. Two other great figures of the thirteenth century were St. Francis of Assisi and Pope Innocent III (1161-1216). The former represented contempt of self and of the earthly city carried to the supreme degree of absolute detachment required by Christian perfection. The latter was the individual, human embodiment of the concept of Christendom, the epitome and the concrete, physical expression of a society, indeed a world, belonging to God and faithful to Him. Together they represent the Church penitent and the Church politic. But neither had a philosophic thought in his head. St. Francis and Pope Innocent represent the Church as prayer and as power; St. Bonaventura and St. Thomas, on the other hand, represent the Church pensive, the Church as thought. St. Bonaventura, moreover, represents the Augustinian tradition within the Church; St. Thomas the Aristotelian. They complemented each other wonderfully, and were close friends. Both had been asked by the Pope (Gregory X) to compose a Mass for the newly prescribed Feast of Corpus Christi, which is celebrated on the Thursday after Trinity Sunday. St. Thomas' achievement is well known as one of the most magnificent of all Masses, filled with exquisite poetry and prayer. When St. Bonaventura heard it, in his humility he tore up the Mass he had himself just composed, judging it unworthy to compete. Some time before he died, St. Thomas himself stopped writing, leaving his greatest work, the *Summa Theologica,* forever unfinished, because he said it had been granted him to experience such things as made all he had ever written seem to him to be "of straw."

Experience, declared a necessary component of certainty by Roger Bacon, was for Sts. Albert the Great, Bonaventura, and Thomas Aquinas a gratuitous gift, obtainable by no effort on our part. The individual could only prepare to receive it, as these three saints did, by a combination of enormous intelligence with hardly less great personal holiness.

St. Thomas Aquinas, the greatest of medieval philosophers, and of Catholic theologians, was born in 1225 at the castle of Roccasecca, the son of a Count of Aquino. He studied first at Naples, later, under St. Albert the Great, in Cologne and Paris. In 1256 he became a Master of Theology and taught in Paris and elsewhere from then on, and died on March 7, 1274, at the Abbey of Fossanuova between Naples and Rome. He was on his way to the Council of Lyons.

Of his death his biographer wrote that he was "rather ravished to heaven by the force of his greater love than by that of his illness." Of his achievement a present day Dominican philosopher, Father Thomas Gilby, has written: "Christian thought henceforth was never to lose the temper of science, nor science the sensibility of matter. . . . The entire universe is all of a piece, the most fugitive phenomenon is not a metaphysical outcast: there are tensions, but not contradictions, in the order of being. . . . Contrasts are struck for the harmony of extremes in a higher principle, not as a prelude to the rejection of one or the blurring of both. . . . The systematic exploration of different branches of knowledge is called science, their arrangement into a unity is the work of wisdom, the knowledge of things by their ultimate cause. There are two wisdoms, St. Thomas held, natural and supernatural, the acquired knowledge of things in their highest rational causes, and the infused knowledge of things in the revelation of the divine mysteries."

ST. THOMAS WAS AN ARISTOTELIAN, WHOSE ATTITUDE to truth, however, compelled him to accept also much, in fact most, of the Neo-Platonic and Augustinian tradition. Three years after his death, when the Latin Averroists were condemned in 1277, some of St. Thomas' conclusions, e.g., that the spiritual soul is primarily the substantial form of the body, and that creation does not necessarily require a beginning in time, were also attacked, and St. Albert the Great rushed back from Cologne to Paris once more, this time to defend his pupil. Two Archbishops of Canterbury, one a Franciscan, John Peckham, the other a Dominican, Robert Kilwardby, also attacked St. Thomas' writings, but these soon won a preeminent place in the Church and all attacks ceased in 1323 when St. Thomas was canonized by the Church. His writings have been regarded as outstandingly orthodox ever since. St. Thomas died before he was fifty; sixty of his authentic books have survived.

St. Thomas' philosophy is based on the premise that knowledge and being are correlative. "In so far as a thing is, it is knowable, and in this resides its ontological truth." But he is not interested in the problem of whether we are capable of objective knowledge, or whether, as the idealists would contend, we produce all ideas out of ourselves, and they bear little or no relation to fact. As D. J. B. Hawkins points out in his admirable A Sketch of Medieval Philosophy, "St. Thomas is completely Aristotelian in finding the whole material of thought in sense-experience. Thomism is, therefore, a philosophy of experience, but it is not a mere empiricism, which stops short at sense-experience, and refuses to see in the development of thought anything but an elaboration of sensations and images."

When the philosophers William James and Henri Bergson met, on May 28, 1905, there were several instants of silence and then James asked Bergson straightway how he envisaged the problem of religion. It is good to believe, but is the experience of God or of oneself? Is the revela-

tion, James asked, our own revelation of God to ourselves,
or is it the revelation of God to us? This most central of
all questions—did God make us or we Him?—worried St.
Thomas not at all. He presented the Aristotelian view as
a mean between two extremes. One is the theory of Democritus, which reduces all knowledge to sensation and
imagination, the other is the Platonic outlook, according
to which sensation provides no more than the occasion
upon which the understanding climbs to contemplate the
spiritual world of forms. Aristotle, Aquinas says, finds the
happy mean by recognizing that all knowledge is derived
from sense experience, but at the same time he asserts that
thought has its proper activity, by which it can draw from
sense experience the materials of a knowledge which extends beyond the bounds of the world of sense. It is thinking that penetrates through the particular to the universal.
Particulars are, in fact, instances of universals. "In sense
experience we are acquainted with red things; by thinking we come to isolate the redness which these things
manifest."

This beginning St. Thomas owes to Abelard. But he goes
beyond Abelard when he sees the intellect both as active
and passive. As passive when it receives its material from
sense experience; as active when through the impressions
it receives it penetrates "through the unanalyzed super-
ficiality of sensation." St. Thomas did not accept that the
active intellect was God, or even a direct manifestation
of God. It is a real part of man, an essential part of his
make-up, and, once created, although it is sustained by
God, and continually assisted by the presence in the soul
of God himself, the active intellect, from the moment of its
creation, is on its own. It "drees its own weird" as the
Scots say, and has all it takes to fulfill of itself and by itself the purpose for which it was created.

The soul is the form of the body, the principle of
"bodily structure and organic life, of sensation and
thought." But in thinking, the human soul transcends its
form and is intrinsically independent of matter.

St. Thomas distinguishes between the notion of being as

a principle of identity and as a principle of difference:

[Being is in itself an identity in difference, while a genuine universal concept is merely an identity which connotes a difference.

That is why there is so close a connection between the notion of being and that of individuality. An excessive realism in the solution of the problem of universals falls before the Aristotelian principle that the individual alone exists in the proper sense of the term. We may now go farther and say that what in the individual corresponds with the universals which it verifies is not the intrinsic ground of its individuality; it is because it is an existent, and precisely through its substantial existence or subsistence, that it is this individual thing. While the principle of individuation of corporeal species is matter, the general principle of individuality is substantial existence or subsistence.

In this way we are led to distinguish between the order of essence and the order of existence. The order of essence represents in abstraction the ramification and interrelation of universal concepts; the order of existence runs parallel with it and lends to it individuality and reality. Existence, therefore, is proportional to essence, to that which exists. Existence is not a closed generic concept which is specified by the differences of essences; it is in itself different, and must be regarded as greater or less, according to the nature of that which it makes to exist. Here lies the fundamental significance of the analogy of being. Analogy, after all, means proportion, and the analogy of being means that the existence of each thing is proportionate to its essence.

If essence and existence are thus proportionate, there is in every finite thing between its essence and its existence a certain metaphysical tension, which in scholastic language is described as metaphysical composition. While existence realizes essence, essence provides the limits within which existence is circumscribed.*]

* *A Sketch of Medieval Philosophy*, by D. J. B. Hawkins, copyright 1947 by Sheed and Ward, Inc., New York.

SINCE THE PRIMARY OBJECT OF THE HUMAN INTELLECT IS
the being of sensible things, St. Thomas insists that we have
no direct knowledge of God. He rejects St. Anselm's ontological proof out of hand, and proceeds to demonstrate the
existence of God by his Five Ways (the first three of which,
as we have seen, he got from Maimonides).

In the *Summa Theologica* he writes:

[*Third Article: Whether God Exists?*
Objection 1. It seems that God does not exist; because
if one of two contraries be infinite, the other would be altogether destroyed. But the word "God" means that He
is infinite goodness. If, therefore, God existed, there would
be no evil discoverable; but there is evil in the world.
Therefore God does not exist.

Obj. 2. Further, it is superfluous to suppose that what
can be accounted for by a few principles has been produced by many. But it seems that everything we see in the
world can be accounted for by other principles, supposing
God did not exist. For all natural things can be reduced to
one principle, which is nature; and all voluntary things can
be reduced to one principle, which is human reason, or will.
Therefore there is no need to suppose God's existence.

On the contrary, It is said in the person of God: *I am
Who am* (Exod. iii. 14).

I answer that, The existence of God can be proved in
five ways.

The first and more manifest way is the argument from
motion. It is certain, and evident to our senses, that in the
world some things are in motion. Now whatever is in motion is put in motion by another, for nothing can be in motion except it is in potentiality to that towards which it is
in motion; whereas a thing moves inasmuch as it is in act.
For motion is nothing else than the reduction of something
from potentiality to actuality. But nothing can be reduced
from potentiality to actuality, except by something in a
state of actuality. Thus that which is actually hot, as fire,
makes wood, which is potentially hot, to be actually hot,
and thereby moves and changes it. Now it is not possible

that the same thing should be at once in actuality and potentiality in the same respect, but only in different respects. For what is actually hot cannot simultaneously be potentially hot; but it is simultaneously potentially cold. It is therefore impossible that in the same respect and in the same way a thing should be both mover and moved, *i.e.*, that it should move itself. Therefore, whatever is in motion must be put in motion by another. If that by which it is put in motion be itself put in motion, then this also must needs be put in motion by another, and that by another again. But this cannot go on to infinity, because then there would be no first mover, and, consequently, no other mover; seeing that subsequent movers move only inasmuch as they are put in motion by the first mover; as the staff moves only because it is put in motion by the hand. Therefore it is necessary to arrive at a first mover, put in motion by no other; and this everyone understands to be God.

The second way is from the nature of the efficient cause. In the world of sense we find there is an order of efficient causes. There is no case known (neither is it, indeed, possible) in which a thing is found to be the efficient cause of itself; for so it would be prior to itself, which is impossible. Now in efficient causes it is not possible to go on to infinity, because in all efficient causes following in order, the first is the cause of the intermediate cause, and the intermediate is the cause of the ultimate cause, whether the intermediate cause be several, or one only. Now to take away the cause is to take away the effect. Therefore, if there be no first cause among efficient causes, there will be no ultimate, nor any intermediate cause. But if in efficient causes it is possible to go on to infinity, there will be no first efficient cause, neither will there be an ultimate effect, nor any intermediate efficient causes; all of which is plainly false. Therefore it is necessary to admit a first efficient cause, to which everyone gives the name of God.

The third way is taken from possibility and necessity, and runs thus. We find in nature things that are possible to be and not to be, since they are found to be generated, and to corrupt, and consequently, they are possible to be and not to be. But it is impossible for these always to exist, for that which is possible not to be at some time is not. Therefore, if everything is possible not to be, then at one time there could have been nothing in existence. Now if this were true, even now there would be nothing in existence, because that which does not exist only begins to exist by something already existing. Therefore, if at one time nothing was in existence, it would have been impossible for anything to have begun to exist; and thus even now nothing would be in existence—which is absurd. Therefore, not all beings are merely possible, but there must exist something the existence of which is necessary. But every necessary thing either has its necessity caused by another, or not. Now it is impossible to go on to infinity in necessary things which have their necessity caused by another, as has been already proved in regard to efficient causes. Therefore we cannot but postulate the existence of some being having of itself its own necessity, and not receiving it from another, but rather causing in others their necessity. This all men speak of as God.

The fourth way is taken from the gradation to be found in things. Among beings there are some more and some less good, true, noble, and the like. But "more" and "less" are predicated of different things, according as they resemble in their different ways something which is the maximum, as a thing is said to be hotter according as it more nearly resembles that which is hottest; so that there is something which is truest, something best, something noblest, and, consequently, something which is uttermost being; for those things that are greatest in truth are greatest in being, as it is written in *Metaph*. ii. Now the maximum in any genus is the cause of all in that genus; as fire, which is the maximum of heat, is the cause of all hot things. Therefore there must also be something which is to all beings the cause of their being, goodness, and every other perfection; and this we call God.

The fifth way is taken from the governance of the world. We see that things which lack intelligence, such as natural bodies, act for an end, and this is evident from their acting always, or nearly always, in the same way, so

as to obtain the best result. Hence it is plain that not for-
tuitously, but designedly, do they achieve their end. Now
whatever lacks intelligence cannot move towards an end,
unless it be directed by some being endowed with knowledge and intelligence; as the arrow is shot to its mark by
the archer. Therefore some intelligent being exists by whom
all natural things are directed to their end; and this being
we call God.*]

SO ST. THOMAS CONCLUDES THAT THE ONE NECESSARY
being is being itself and pure act: *ipsum esse, actus purus.*
And all finite beings derive from Him, but whether they
derive eternally or temporally is known only to Him.

But if God is real, is He not the only reality? If *I am
Who am,* as given in Exodus iii. 14, is God's own authentic
description of Himself and the most reliable one we have,
is true, is not all other reality but the image of His? Are
we not, as the Red Queen told Alice in Lewis Carroll's
Through the Looking-Glass, only figures in the Red King's
dream, dissolved when he wakes? St. Thomas denies emphatically this position, and dubs Platonist all who "remove from natural things their own actions." Aristotle
maintained, and Aquinas cleaves to him here, that although
God *can* of Himself produce all natural effects, yet by His
goodness He willed to give to creatures His resemblance,
to the extent that in their turn they can be, and are, causes.
"To deny to creatures creativity is to misunderstand the
creator." As M. Etienne Gilson has put it, "a world of
secondary efficacious causes alone is worthy of a God
whose causality is essentially goodness." God's generosity
has endowed the creature with the power to co-operate
with Him, in creation as in Redemption. The generosity
of the Creator is total, and human history is the "working
out of the plan of the creative mind of God," while time is
the measure of the duration of that particular plan and the
law of the universe is the divine wisdom as it develops its
own plan. In man, reason is the faculty by which man apprehends that plan. "In relation to human nature an ac-

* Aquinas, *Summa Theologica* Q. 2 (Reprinted with the permission of Benziger Brothers, Inc. publishers and copyright owners).

tion is right because it is reasonable," and the highest
activity of man's intellect is philosophy, which is wholly
ordered to God as its final end.

When St. Thomas speaks as a philosopher, M. Gilson
points out, he is careful to proceed only by demonstrations.
"It does not matter if the thesis he is defending appears in
the context given it by faith, for he never brings faith, nor
expects it brought, into any proof which he considers ra-
tionally demonstrable." Where reason is, faith has no place;
it is impossible to know and to believe a thing at the same
time.

[*Fifth Article: Whether Those Things that Are of Faith
Can Be an Object of Science?*

Objection 1. It would seem that those things that are of
faith can be an object of science. For where science is lacking there is ignorance, since ignorance is the opposite of
science. Now we are not in ignorance of those things we
have to believe, since ignorance of such things belongs to
unbelief, according to I Tim. i. 13: *I did it ignorantly in
unbelief.* Therefore things that are of faith can be an object
of science.

Obj. 2. Further, Science is acquired by arguments. Now
sacred writers employ arguments to inculcate things that
are of faith. Therefore such things can be an object of
science.

Obj. 3. Further, Things which are demonstrated are an
object of science, since a *demonstration is a syllogism that
produces science.* Now certain matters of faith have been
demonstrated by the philosophers, such as the existence
and unity of God, and so forth. Therefore things that are
of faith can be an object of science.

Obj. 4. Further, Opinion is further from science than
faith is, since faith is said to stand between opinion and
science. Now opinion and science can, in a way, be about
the same object, as is stated in *Posterior Analytics* i.
Therefore faith and science can be about the same object
also.

On the contrary, Gregory says that *when a thing is manifest, it is the object, not of faith, but of perception.* There-

fore things that are of faith are not the object of perception, whereas what is an object of science is the object of perception. Therefore there can be no faith about things which are an object of science.

I answer that, All science is derived from self-evident and therefore *seen* principles; and so all objects of science must needs be, in a fashion, seen.

Now, as was stated above, it is impossible that one and the same thing should be believed and seen by the same person. Hence it is equally impossible for one and the same thing to be an object of science and of belief for the same person. It may happen, however, that a thing which is an object of vision or science for one, is believed by another; for we hope to see some day what we now believe about the Trinity, according to I Cor. xiii. 12: *We see now through a glass in a dark manner; but then face to face.* And this vision the angels possess already, so that what we believe, they see. In like manner, it may also happen that what is an object of vision or scientific knowledge for one man, even in the state of a wayfarer, is, for another man, an object of faith, because he does not know it by demonstration. Nevertheless, that which is proposed to be believed equally by all is equally unknown by all as an object of science . . . Consequently, faith and science are not about the same things.

Reply. Obj. 4. As the Philosopher says, science and opinion about the same object can certainly be in different men: yet it is possible for one and the same man to have science and faith about the same thing relatively, *i.e.,* in relation to the object, but not in the same respect. For it is possible for the same person, about one and the same object, to know one thing and to have an opinion about another. On the other hand, in one and the same man, about the same object, and in the same respect, science is incompatible with either opinion or faith, but for different reasons. For science is incompatible with opinion about the same object absolutely, for the reason that science demands that its object should be deemed impossible to be otherwise, whereas it is essential to opinion that its object should be deemed possible to be otherwise. But that

which is the object of faith, because of the certainty of
faith, is also deemed impossible to be otherwise, and the
reason why science and faith cannot be about the same
object, and in the same respect, is because the object of
science is something seen, whereas the object of faith is the
unseen.*]

IN THE *Questiones Disputatae* ST. THOMAS DISCUSSES
both the Trinity and the Creation in order to give the complete Christian answer to the emanationism of Avicenna,
who saw creation as the necessitated flux of the many from
the one through a series of intermediaries. The Christian
answer is creation and procession. In twenty-nine of his
texts St. Thomas mentions Avicenna and frequently agrees
with him. "As Avicenna said," he often quotes approvingly. For example, he saw no philosophic incompatibility
between the eternity of the world and the creation *ex
nihilo*, nor, said St. Thomas, can the noneternity of the
world be proved. But where St. Thomas and Avicenna most
emphatically part is that St. Thomas absolutely denies
necessity in God. For Avicenna, God *must* create, as a
stone must fall, or boiling water evaporate into steam. St.
Thomas, on the contrary, said that though God is a necessary being it by no means followed that what proceeded
from Him proceeded of necessity.

"God does not produce creatures from natural necessity as though the power of God were determined to the
existence of the creature. God does not act through natural
necessity but through will, whence he can make simple
things and composite things, things mutable and things
immutable. So therefore it should be said from the One
first thing the multitude and diversity of creatures proceeds,
not on account of the necessity of matter, not on account
of a limitation of His power, not on account of goodness,
not on account of an obligation of goodness, but from the
order of wisdom so that the perfection of the universe
might be realized in the diversity of creatures." In other
words, God is like a woman knitting a patterned sweater—

* *Summa Theologica*, Q. 1; from *Basic Writings of St. Thomas
  Aquinas*, Vol. 2, ed. Anton C. Pegis (Random House). Copyright, 1945, by Random House, Inc.

she could make the sweater any way she chose, or not make
it at all, but she has freely chosen a certain pattern, de-
signed by herself, and she chooses to make her sweater that
way and no other, to follow through her own pattern and
design.

Another way Avicenna put the question was: Can God
do what He does not do? Avicenna held that what God
does is the only possible order and that the only order must
be the best possible (centuries later, Voltaire in his *Candide,* a satire, written in 1759, on the optimism of Leibniz,
mocked this view and disagreed with Avicenna on this
point). Avicenna held, moreover, that everything except
God had in itself a possibility of being and of not being.
As Father G. Smith puts it, "Everything else is stiff and
spiky with reality; the possible is thus set over against God,
for God wills the possible necessarily." God's action is not
limited by any agent, replies St. Thomas, nor is it limited
by any recipient. "If we regard the possible as waiting in a
sort of pen of possibility ready to be turned out into the
pastures of existence, then the only pen is God; and the
pen is the uncreated power of God to create, it is not the
potency of creatures to be created," Father Smith concludes. In final analysis, it would appear that Avicenna's
God is causative, Aquinas' God is creative. St. Thomas
denied that this is the best of all *possible* worlds, even if he
agreed with Candide that it was the best of all *actual*
worlds. God is always able to do otherwise, although this
universe is the best with respect to things which actually
exist. With respect to others which God can think up, this
universe is not the best possible.

St. Thomas wrote many purely philosophic books, the
commentaries on Boethius, for example, and on the
Pseudo-Dionysius the Areopagite (*On the Divine Names*)
and on Aristotle. He kept much closer to the latter's text
than other commentators had done, and got his friend William of Moerbeke (flourished 1240) to devote himself to
revising existing translations and making new ones. He
used the Neo-Platonist writer Proclus (410-485) too, in
William of Moerbeke's translation, and Avicenna, Avencebrol, Maimonides and Averroës. He was an outstanding

teacher, and the *Summa contra Gentiles* and the *Summa Theologica* both were composed for the benefit of students.

St. Thomas commented in several of his books on the problem of the *nunc fluens* (now flowing) of time (a modern art critic, Roger Fry, has called it the "only now") and the *tunc simul,* or *tota simul* (then simultaneous) of eternity. Here is what he included in the *Summa Theologica* (Q. 10) on the subject:

[*Obj. 4.* Many days cannot occur together, nor can many times exist all at once. But in eternity days and times are in the plural, for it is said, *His going forth is from the beginning, from the days of eternity* (Mic. v. 2); and also it is said, *According to the revelation of the mystery hidden from eternity* (Rom. xvi. 25). Therefore eternity is not omnisimultaneous.

Obj. 5. Further, the whole and the perfect are the same thing. Supposing, therefore, that it is *whole,* it is superfluously described as *perfect.*

Obj. 6. Further, duration does not imply *possession.* But eternity is a kind of duration. Therefore eternity is not possession.

I answer that, As we attain to the knowledge of simple things by way of compound things, so we must reach to the knowledge of eternity by means of time, which is nothing but the numbering of movement by *before* and *after.* For since succession occurs in every movement, and one part comes after another, the fact that we reckon before and after in movement, makes us apprehend time, which is nothing else but the measure of before and after in movement. Now in a thing bereft of movement, which is always the same, there is no before and after. As therefore the idea of time consists in the numbering of before and after in movement, so likewise in the apprehension of the uniformity of what is outside of movement, consists the idea of eternity.

Further, those things are said to be measured by time which have a beginning and an end in time, because in everything which is moved there is a beginning, and there is an end. But as whatever is wholly immutable can have no succession, so it has no beginning, and no end.

Thus eternity is known from two sources: first, because what is eternal is interminable—that is, has no beginning nor end (that is, no term either way); secondly, because eternity has no succession, being simultaneously whole.

Reply Obj. 1. Simple things are usually defined by way of negation; as "a point is that which has no parts." Yet this is not to be taken as if the negation belonged to their essence, but because our intellect which first apprehends compound things, cannot attain to the knowlege of simple things except by removing the composite.

Reply Obj. 2. What is truly eternal, is not only being, but also living; and life extends to operation, which is not true of being. Now the protraction of duration seems to belong to operation rather than to being; hence time is the numbering of movement.

Reply Obj. 3. Eternity is called whole, not because it has parts, but because it is wanting in nothing.

Reply Obj. 4. As God, although incorporeal, is named in Scripture metaphorically by corporeal names, so eternity though simultaneously whole, is called by names implying time and succession.

Reply Obj. 5. Two things are to be considered in time: time itself, which is successive; and the *now* of time, which is imperfect. Hence the expression *simultaneously-whole* is used to remove the idea of time, and the word *perfect* is used to exclude the *now* of time.

Reply Obj. 6. Whatever is possessed, is held firmly and quietly; therefore to designate the immutability and permanence of eternity, we use the word *possession.*]

BUT, GIVEN TIME AND ETERNITY, IS GOD ETERNAL? ST. Thomas discusses the problem:

[*Second Article: Whether God Is Eternal?*

Objection 1. It seems that God is not eternal. For nothing made can be predicated of God. But eternity is a thing made; for Boethius says (*De Trin.* iv.) that, *The now that flows away makes time, the now that stands still makes eternity;* and Augustine says (*Octog. Tri. Quast. qu.* 28) that *God is the author of eternity.* Therefore God is not eternal.

Obj. 2. Further, what is before eternity, and after eternity, is not measured by eternity. But, as Aristotle says *(De Caus.), God is before eternity and He is after eternity:* for it is written that *the Lord shall reign for eternity, and beyond** (Exod. xv. 18). Therefore to be eternal does not belong to God.

Obj. 3. Further, eternity is a kind of measure. But to be measured belongs not to God. Therefore it does not belong to Him to be eternal.

Obj. 4. Further, in eternity there is no present, past, nor future, since it is simultaneously whole; as was said in the preceding article. But words denoting present, past, and future time are applied to God in Scripture. Therefore God is not eternal.

I answer that, The idea of eternity follows immutability, as the idea of time follows movement, as appears from the preceding article. Hence, as God is supremely immutable, it supremely belongs to Him to be eternal. Nor is He eternal only; but He is His own eternity; whereas, no other being is its own duration, as no other is its own being. Now God is His own uniform being; and hence, as He is His own essence, so He is His own eternity.

Reply Obj. 1. The *now* that stands still, is said to make eternity according to our apprehension. As the apprehension of time is caused in us by the fact that we apprehend the flow of the *now;* so the apprehension of eternity is caused in us by our apprehending the *now* standing still. When Augustine says that *God is the author of eternity,* this is to be understood of participated eternity. For God communicates His eternity to some in the same way as He communicates His immutability.]

AND IS ANYTHING BESIDES GOD ETERNAL? ASKS ST. THOMAS, and answers:

* Douay,—*for ever and ever.*

[Necessary means a certain mode of truth: and truth, according to the Philosopher (*Metaph.* vi), is in the mind. Therefore in this sense the true and necessary are eternal, because they are in the eternal mind, which is the divine intellect alone; hence it does not follow that anything beside God is eternal.]

ST. THOMAS THEN PROCEEDS TO THE FOURTH ARTICLE:

[*Whether Eternity Differs from Time?*

Objection 1. It seems that eternity does not differ from time. For two measures of duration cannot exist together, unless one is part of the other; for instance two days or two hours cannot be together; nevertheless, we may say that a day and an hour are together, considering an hour as part of a day. But eternity and time occur together, each of which imports a certain measure of duration. Since therefore eternity is not a part of time, forasmuch as eternity exceeds time, and includes it, it seems that time is a part of eternity, and is not a different thing from eternity.

Obj. 2. Further, according to the Philosopher (*Physic.* iv.), the *now* of time remains the same in the whole of time. But the nature of eternity seems to be that it is the same indivisible thing in the whole space of time. Therefore eternity is the *now* of time. But the *now* of time is not substantially different from time. Therefore eternity is not substantially different from time.

Obj. 3. Further, as the measure of the first movement is the measure of every movement, as said in *Physic.* iv., it thus appears that the measure of the first being is that of every being. But eternity is the measure of the first being— that is, of the divine being. Therefore eternity is the measure of every being. But the being of things corruptible is measured by time. Time therefore is either eternity, or is a part of eternity.

On the contrary, Eternity is simultaneously whole. But time has a before and an after. Therefore time and eternity are not the same thing.

I answer that, It is manifest that time and eternity are not the same. Some have founded this difference on the fact

that eternity has neither beginning nor an end; whereas
time has a beginning and an end. This, however, makes a
merely accidental, and not an absolute difference; because,
granted that time always was and always will be, according
to the idea of those who think the movement of the heavens
goes on forever, there would yet remain a difference between eternity and time, as Boethius says (*De Consol.* v.),
arising from the fact that eternity is simultaneously whole;
which cannot be applied to time: for eternity is the measure of a permanent being; while time is the measure of
movement. Supposing, however, that the aforesaid difference be considered on the part of the things measured, and
not as regards the measures, then there is some reason for
it, inasmuch as that alone is measured by time which has
beginning and end in time. Hence, if the movement of the
heavens lasted always, time would not be its measure as
regards the whole of its duration, since the infinite is not
measurable; but it would be the measure of that part of its
revolution which has beginning and end in time.

Another reason for the same can be taken from these
measures in themselves, if we consider the end and the
beginning as potentialities; because, granted also that time
always goes on, yet it is possible to note in time both the
beginning and the end, by considering its parts:—thus we
speak of the beginning and the end of a day, or of a year;
which cannot be applied to eternity. Still these differences
follow upon the essential and primary differences, that
eternity is simultaneously whole, but that time is not so.

Reply Obj. 1. Such a reason would be a valid one if time
and eternity were the same kind of measure; but this is seen
not to be the case when we consider those things of which
the respective measures are time and eternity.

Reply Obj. 2. The *now* of time is the same as regards its
subject in the whole course of time, but it differs in aspect;
for inasmuch as time corresponds to movement, its *now*
corresponds to what is movable; and the thing movable has
the same one subject in all time, but differs in aspect as
being here and there; and such alternation is movement.
Likewise the flow of the *now* as alternating in aspect, is
time. But eternity remains the same according to both sub-

ject and aspect; and hence eternity is not the same as the
now of time.

Reply Obj. 3. As eternity is the proper measure of permanent being, so time is the proper measure of movement;
and hence, according as any being recedes from permanence of being, and is subject to change, it recedes from
eternity, and is subject to time. Therefore the being of
things corruptible, because it is changeable, is not measured
by eternity, but by time; for time measures not things
only.*]

ST. THOMAS WROTE A LITTLE TREATISE ON THE PROBLEM
of essence and existence. *Concerning Being and Essence* is
one of the most astonishingly lucid of all St. Thomas's
works and is today still one of the most apposite; it is given
here** in part.

[INTRODUCTION:

Because a small error in the beginning is a great one in
the end, according to the Philosopher in the first book of
the *De Caelo et Mundo,* and since being and essence are
what are first conceived by the intellect, as Avicenna says
in the first book of his *Metaphysics,* therefore, lest error
befall from ignorance of them (being and essence), in
order to reveal their difficulty it should be said what is
signified by the names being and essence, and how they are
found in diverse things and how they are disposed with
respect to logical intentions, namely, genus, species, and
difference.

CHAPTER ONE:

Because indeed we must receive knowledge of the simple
from the composite and arrive at what is prior from what
is posterior, in order that beginning with the less difficult

* Reprinted from the *Summa Theologica* with the permission of
  Benziger Brothers, Inc., publisher and copyright owners.
**From: St. Thomas Aquinas' *Concerning Being and Essence*
  trans. George C. Leckie (Copyright 1937, D. Appleton-Century
  Co., Inc. Reprinted by permission of the publishers, Appleton-
  Century Crofts, Inc.).

instruction may be made more suitably, we should proceed from the meaning of being to the meaning of essence.

Therefore one should know, as the Philosopher says in the fifth of the *Metaphysics,* that being by itself is said to be taken in two modes: in the one mode, that it is divided into ten genera; in the other, that it signifies the truth of propositions. Moreover the difference between these is that in the second mode everything can be called being concerning which an affirmative proposition can be formed, even if it posits nothing in the thing, by virtue of this mode privations and negations are likewise called beings, for we say that affirmation is the opposite of negation, and that blindness is in the eye. But in the first mode only what posits something in the thing can be called being; consequently, according to the first mode blindness and such are not beings. The name essence, therefore, is not taken from being in the second mode, for in this mode some things are said to have essence which have not being, as is evident in privations. But essence is taken from being only in the first mode; whence the Commentator says in the same place that "being in the first mode is said to be what signifies the essence of the thing." And because, as has been said, being in this mode is divided into ten genera, it follows that essence signifies something common to all natures by which diverse beings are disposed in different genera and species, as for instance humanity is the essence of man and so for others. And because that by means of which the thing is constituted in its proper genus or species is that which is signified by the definition indicating what the thing is, hence it is that the name essence has been changed by philosophers into the name quiddity. And this is what the Philosopher frequently calls *"quod quid erat esse,"* that is, that by virtue of which a thing (anything) has to be what it is (something). And indeed it is called form according as by means of form the certitude of any single thing is signified, as Avicenna remarks in the second part of his *Metaphysics.* This is called by another name, nature, accepting nature according to the first of the four modes assigned by Boethius in his book *De Duabus Naturis,* namely, according as nature is said to be all that which can be comprehended by the intellect in any mode whatsoever; for a thing is not intelligible except by virtue of its definition and essence. And thus also the Philosopher in the Fourth book of his *Metaphysics* says that every substance is a nature. But the name nature taken in this sense is seen to signify the essence of a thing inasmuch as it has a disposition towards an operation proper to the thing, since no thing is lacking in its proper operation. Indeed the name quiddity is taken from that which signifies the definition; but it is called essence according as by virtue of it and in it being has existence.

But because being is asserted absolutely and primarily of substances and secondarily and as if in a certain respect of accidents, hence it is that essence also exists truly and properly in substances, but exists in accidents in a certain mode and in a certain respect. Some substances indeed are simple and others are composite, and in both there is an essence. But essence is possessed by simple substances in a truer and more noble mode according as simple substances have a more exalted existence, for they are the cause of those which are composite,—at least the primary substance, which is God, is. But since the essences of these substances are more concealed from us, therefore we must begin from the essences of composite substances in order that instruction may be made more suitably from what is easier.

CHAPTER TWO:

In composite substances, therefore, matter and form are noted, as for instance in man soul and body are noted. Moreover it cannot be said that either of these alone is called essence. For it is evident that matter alone is not the essence of the thing, because it is by means of its essence that the thing is both known and ordered in its species and genus. But matter is not the principle of cognition, nor is anything determined as regards genus and species according to it (matter), but according to that by means of which something is in act. And furthermore neither can form alone be called the essence of composite substance, however much some attempt to assert this. From what has been said it is clear that essence is what is signi-

fied by the definition of the thing. But the definition of
natural substances contains not only form but also matter;
for otherwise natural definitions and mathematical definitions would not differ. Nor can it be said that matter is
posited in the definition of a natural substance as an addition to its essence or as a being outside of its essence,
since this mode of definition is more proper to accidents
which do not have a perfect essence; whence it follows
that they must admit the subject into their definition, which
(subject) is outside of their genus. It is clear, therefore,
that essence comprehends matter and form. But it cannot
be said that essence signifies a relation which is between
matter and form, or that it is something superadded to
them, since something superadded would of necessity be
accidental or extraneous to the thing, nor could the thing
be conceived by means of it, for everything is appropriate
to its essence. For by the form, which is the actuality of
matter, matter is made being in act and a this somewhat.
Whence that which is superadded does not give existence
in act simply to matter, but existence in act of such sort as
likewise accidents make, as for instance whiteness makes
something white in act. Wherefore whenever such form is
acquired it is not said to be generated simply but in a certain respect. . . . Whence it follows that the essence by
virtue of which a thing is called being is not form alone,
nor matter alone, but both; although in its mode the form is
the cause of its existence. We discover it indeed thus in
other things which are constituted from more than one
principle, since a thing is not named from one of those
principles alone, but from that which unites both. . . .

But because the principle of individuation is matter, it
perhaps seems to follow from this that essence which unites
in itself both matter and form would be only particular and
not universal. From this it would follow that universals do
not have definition, if essence is what is signified by means
of the definition. One should therefore understand that
matter in any mode whatsoever is not taken to be the principle of individuation, but only signated matter. . . . Accordingly, it is clear that the essence of Socrates and the
essence of man do not differ except according to signate

and non-signate. Whence the Commentator remarks upon the seventh of the *Metaphysics:* "Socrates is nothing other than animality and rationality which are his quiddity." Thus also the essence of genus and of species differ according to signate and non-signate, although there is a different mode of designation for each of them, because the designation of the individual with respect to species is by means of matter determined by dimensions, whereas the designation of species in respect to genus is by means of the constitutive difference which is taken from the form of the thing. . . .

And . . . the nature of species is indeterminate in respect to the individual, just as the nature of genus is indeterminate with respect to species, hence it is that, just as that which is genus according as it is predicated concerning species implies in its signification, although indistinctly, all that is determinate in species, thus likewise it follows that what is species, according as it is predicated of the individual, signifies all that which is in the individual essentially although indistinctly. And in this mode the essence of Socrates is signified by the name of man, and as a consequence man is predicated of Socrates. But if the nature of the species be signified with the exclusion of designated matter, which is the principle of individuation, it will thus be disposed as a part (by means of the partitive mode). And in this mode it is signified by the name humanity, for humanity signifies that in virtue of which man is man. But designated matter is not that in virtue of which man is man; and, therefore, in no mode is it contained among those things from which man possesses manness. Since therefore humanity includes in its concept only those things from which man possesses manness, it is clear that designated matter is excluded from or cut off from its signification. And since the part is not predicated of the whole, hence it is that humanity is not predicated either of man or of Socrates. . . . Since, as has been said, the designation of species in respect to genus is by virtue of form, whereas the designation of the individual in respect to species is by virtue of matter, it follows therefore that the name signifying that whence the nature of genus is taken, with the ex-

clusion of the determinate form perfecting the species,
should signify the material part of the whole itself, as the
body is the material part of man. But the name signifying
that whence the nature of species is taken, with the exclusion of designated matter, signifies the formal part. And
therefore humanity is signified as a certain form, and is
spoken of as that which is the form of the whole; not indeed as if it were superadded to the essential parts, namely,
to form and matter, as for instance the form of a house is
superadded to its integral parts; but rather it is form that
is the whole, that is, embracing form and matter, yet with
the exclusion of those things by means of which matter is
found to be designated. So, therefore, it is clear that the
name man and the name humanity signify the essence of
man, but in different modes, as has been said, since the
name man signifies it as a whole, inasmuch as it does not
exclude the designation of matter but contains it implicitly
and indistinctly, as for instance it has been said that the
genus contains the difference. And therefore the name man
is predicated of individuals. But the name humanity signifies the essence as a part, since it does not contain in its
signification anything except what is of man inasmuch as
he is man, and because it excludes all designation of matter; whence it is not predicated of individual man. And
for this reason likewise the name essence sometimes is
found predicated of a thing, for Socrates is said to be an
essence, and sometimes it is denied, as for instance it is
said that the essence of Socrates is not Socrates.

CHAPTER THREE:

Having seen, therefore, what is signified by the name of
essence in composite substances, we should see in what
mode it is disposed towards the ratio of genus, species,
and difference. . . . The ratio of species applies to human
nature according to that existence which it has in the intellect. For human nature itself has an existence in the
intellect abstracted from all individuations, and therefore
it has a uniform ratio to all individuals which are outside
the soul, according as it is equally the likeness of all and

leads to the understanding of all inasmuch as they are men. And because, it has such a relation to all individuals, the intellect discovers the ratio of species and attributes it to it (human nature). Whence the Commentator observes in the first book of the *De Anima* that intellect is what actuates universality in things. Avicenna also says this in his *Metaphysics*. Whence, although this intellectual nature has the ratio of universal according as it is compared to things which are outside of the soul because it is a single likeness of all, nevertheless according as it has existence in *this* intellect or that it is a certain particular intellected species. . . . To be predicated applies to genus by virtue of itself since it is posited in its definition. For predication is a certain thing which is perfected by means of the action of the intellect composing and dividing, having in the very thing as its foundation the unity of those things of which one is asserted of the other. Whence the ratio of predicability can be included in the ratio of this mode of intention which is genus, which, similarly, is perfected by means of an act of the intellect. Yet, nevertheless, that to which the intellect attributes the intention of predication, composing the one with the other, is not the very intention of genus but rather that to which the intellect attributes the intention of genus, as for instance what is signified by the name animal. Thus, therefore, it is clear how essence or nature is disposed towards the ratio of species, because the ratio of species does not belong to those things which are appropriate to it according to its absolute consideration, nor likewise does it belong to the accidents which issue from it according to the existence which it has outside the soul, as whiteness or blackness. But it does belong to the accidents which issue from it according to the existence which it has in the intellect. And it is according to this mode that the ratio of genus and of difference also applies to it.

CHAPTER FOUR:

Now it remains to see through what mode essence exists in separate substances, namely, in the soul, in intelligences and in the first cause. . . .

All that belongs to anything is either caused from principles of its nature, as for instance risibility in man, or accrues to it through some extrinsic principle, as for instance light in air from the influence of the sun. But it cannot be that existence itself should be caused by the form or quiddity of the thing, caused, I say, as by means of an efficient cause, because thus something would be the cause of itself and would bring its very self into existence, which is impossible. Therefore it follows that everything such that its existence is other than its nature has existence from another. And because everything which exists by virtue of another is reduced to that which exists in virtue of itself, as to its first cause, it follows that there must be something which is the cause of the existence of all things, because it is very existence alone; otherwise the causes would proceed to infinity, since everything which is not existence alone would have a cause of its existence, as has been said. It is clear, therefore, that an intelligence is form and existence, and that it has its existence from the first being which is existence alone, and this is the first cause which is God. But everything which receives something from something is in potency in respect to that, and what is received in it is its act. Therefore it follows that the very quiddity or form which is the intelligence is in potency in respect to the existence which it receives from God, and that existence is received according to the mode of act. And thus potency and act are found in intelligences, yet not form and matter, except equivocally. Whence, too, to suffer, to receive, to be a subject and all things of this kind which are seen to belong to things by reason of matter, belong equivocally to intellectual substances and to corporeal substances, as the Commentator says in the third book of the *De Anima*. . . .]

ST. THOMAS WAS ALSO CONCERNED WITH THE QUESTION that had so preoccupied St. Augustine: what the memory is, and where? In his *Truth** he discussed the problem in

* St. Thomas, *Truth,* trans. J. McGlynn (Henry Regnery Company).

ARTICLE 11:

〔 *Secondly, We Ask: Is There Memory in the Mind?*

Difficulties:

It seems that there is not, for

1. According to Augustine, that which we share with brute animals does not belong to the mind. But memory is common to us and to brute animals, as is also clear from Augustine. Therefore, memory is not in the mind.

2. The Philosopher says that memory does not belong to the intellective but to the primary sensitive faculty. Therefore, since mind is the same as understanding, as is clear from what has been said above, memory does not seem to be part of the mind.

3. Understanding and all that belong to understanding abstract from space and time. Memory, however, does not so abstract, for it deals with a definite time, the past. For memory concerns things past, as Cicero says. Therefore, memory does not pertain to mind or understanding.

4. Since in memory we retain things that are not being actually apprehended, it follows that, wherever there is memory, there must be a difference between apprehension and retention. But it is in sense only, and not in understanding, that we find this difference. The two can differ in sense because sense makes use of a bodily organ. But not everything that is retained in the body is apprehended. But understanding does not make use of a bodily organ, and so retains things only according to the mode of understanding. So, these things have to be actually understood. Therefore, memory is not part of understanding or mind.

5. The soul does not remember until it has retained something. But before it receives from the senses, which are the source of all our knowledge, any species which it can retain, it already has the character of image (of the Trinity). Since memory is part of that image, it does not seem possible for memory to be in the mind.

6. In so far as mind has the character of image of God, it is directed toward God. But memory is not directed toward God, since it deals with things that belong to time.

But God is entirely beyond time. Therefore, memory is not in the mind.

7. If memory were part of the mind, the intelligible species would be maintained in the mind as they are in the angelic mind. But the angels can understand by turning their attention to the species which they have within them. Therefore, the human mind should be able to understand by turning its attention to the species it retains, without referring to phantasms. But this is obviously false. For, no matter to what degree one has scientific knowledge as a habit, if the organ of the power of imagination or memory is injured, this knowledge cannot be made actual. This would not result if the mind could actually understand without referring to powers which use organs. So, memory is not part of the mind.

To the Contrary:

1. The Philosopher says that the intellective soul, not the whole soul, is the place of the species. But it belongs to place to preserve what is kept in it. Therefore, since the preservation of the species belongs to memory, memory seems to be part of understanding.

2. That which has a uniform relation to all time is not concerned with any particular time. But memory, even in its proper acceptation, has a uniform relation to all time, as Augustine says and proves with the words of Virgil, who used the names memory and forgetfulness in their proper sense. Therefore, memory is not concerned with any particular time, but with all time. So it belongs to understanding.

3. Strictly speaking, memory refers to things past. But understanding deals not only with what is present, but also with what is past. For the understanding judges about any time, understanding man to have existed, to exist in the future, and to exist now, as is clear from *The Soul.* Therefore, memory, properly speaking, can belong to understanding.

4. As memory concerns what is past, so foresight concerns what is in the future, according to Cicero. But fore-

sight, properly speaking, belongs to the intellectual part. For the same reason memory does, too.

Reply:

According to the common usage, memory means a knowledge of things past. But to know the past as past belongs to that which has the power of knowing the now as now. Sense is this power. For understanding does not know the singular as singular, but according to some common character, as it is man or white or even particular, but not in so far as it is this man or this particular thing. In a similar way, understanding does not know a present and a past thing as this present and this past thing.

Since memory, taken strictly, looks to what is past with reference to the present, it is clear that memory, properly speaking, does not belong to the intellectual part, but only to the sensitive, as the Philosopher shows. But, since intellect not only understands the intelligible thing, but also understands that it understands such an intelligible thing, the term memory can be broadened to include the knowledge by which one knows the object previously known in so far as he knows he knew it earlier, although he does not know the object as in the past in the manner earlier explained. In this way all knowledge not received for the first time can be called memory.

This can take place in two ways, either when there is continuous study based on acquired knowledge without interruption, or when the study is interrupted. The latter has more of the character of past, and so it more properly participates in the nature of memory. We have an example of this when we say that we remember a thing which previously we knew habitually but not actually. Thus, memory belongs to the intellective part of our soul. It is in this sense that Augustine seems to understand memory, when he makes it part of the image of the Trinity. For he intends to assign to memory everything in the mind which is stored there habitually without passing into act.

There are various explanations of the manner in which this can take place. Avicenna holds that the fact that the soul has habitual knowledge of anything which it does not

actually consider does not come from this, that certain
species are retained in the intellectual part. Rather, he
understands that it is impossible for the species not actually
considered to be kept anywhere except in the sensitive
part, either in the imagination, which is the storehouse of
forms received by the senses, or in the memory, for particular apprehensions not received from the senses. The
species stays in the understanding only when it is actually
being considered. But, after the consideration, it ceases to
be there. Thus, when one wants actually to consider something again, it is necessary for new intelligible species to
flow from the agent intelligence into the possible intellect.

However, it does not follow, according to Avicenna,
that the new consideration of what was known previously
necessarily entails learning or discovering all over again,
for one retains a certain aptitude through which he turns
more easily to the agent intellect to receive the species
flowing from it than he did before. In us, this aptitude is
the habit of scientific knowledge. According to this opinion,
memory is not part of the mind because it preserves certain
species, but because it has an aptitude for receiving them
anew.

But this does not seem to be a reasonable explanation.
In the first place, since the possible intellect has a more
stable nature than sense, it must receive its species more
securely. Thus, the species can be better preserved in it
than in the sensitive part. In the second place, the agent
intelligence is equally disposed to communicate species
suitable for all the sciences. As a consequence, if some
species were not conserved in the possible intellect, but
there were in it only the aptitude of turning to the agent
intellect, man would have an equal aptitude for any intelligible thing. Therefore, from the fact that a man had
learned one science he would not know it better than other
sciences. Besides, this seems openly opposed to the opinion
of the Philosopher, who commends the ancients for holding
that the intellective part of the soul is the place of the
species.

Therefore, others say that the intelligible species remain
in the possible intellect after actual consideration, and that

the ordered arrangement of these is the habit of knowledge. In this classification the power by which our minds retain these intelligible species after actual consideration will be called memory. This comes closer to the proper meaning of memory.

Answers to Difficulties:

1. The memory which we have in common with brute animals is that in which particular intentions are preserved. This is not in the mind; only the memory in which intelligible species are kept is there.

2. The Philosopher is speaking of the memory which deals with the past as related to a particular present in so far as particular. This is not in the mind.

3. The answer to the third difficulty is clear from what has just been said.

4. Actual apprehension and retention differ in the possible intellect, not because the species are there somehow in a bodily manner, but only in an intelligible way. However, it does not follow that one understands according to that species all the time, but only when the possible intellect becomes that species perfectly in act. Sometimes it has the act of this species incompletely, that is, in some way between pure potency and pure act. This is habitual knowledge. The reduction from this to complete act takes place through the will, which, according to Anselm, is the mover of all the powers.

5. Mind has the character of image (of the Trinity) especially in so far as it is directed to God and to itself. It is present to itself and God is present to it before any species are received from sensible things. Furthermore, mind is not said to have the power of memory to preserve something.

6. The answer to the sixth difficulty is clear from what has been said.

7. No power can know anything without turning to its object, as sight knows nothing unless it turns to color. Now, since phantasms are related to the possible intellect in the way that sensible things are related to sense, as the Philosopher points out, no matter to what extent an in-

telligible species is present to the understanding, understanding does not actually consider anything according to that species without referring to a phantasm. Therefore, just as our understanding in its present state needs phantasm actually to consider anything before it acquires a habit, so it needs them, too, after it has acquired a habit. The situation is different with angels, for phantasms are not the object of their understanding.

Answers to Contrary Difficulties:

1. The authority cited can prove only that memory is in the mind in the way we have mentioned, not that it is there properly.

2. We must understand Augustine's statement to mean that memory can deal with present objects. However, it can never be called memory unless something past is considered, at least past with reference to cognition itself. It is in this way that we say someone, who is present to himself, forgets or remembers himself because he retains or does not retain the past knowledge about himself.

3. In so far as understanding knows temporal differences through common characters, it can thus make judgments according to any difference of time.

4. Foresight is in the understanding only according to general considerations about the future. It is applied to particular things through the mediation of particular reason which must act as the medium between general reason, which is the source of movement, and the movement which follows in particular things, as is clear from what the Philosopher says.]

THE DIVINE FORESIGHT NEVER CONSTRAINS US TO EVIL, for God "creates our choice and the freedom of our choice" and no one is deprived of grace unless they place in themselves an obstacle to grace. Thus, when the sun is shining, if any one shuts his eyes and falls over a precipice, it is his own fault, even though the sunlight is necessary for him to see; and the first revealing truth is both that which is believed and that by which one believes, as light is that which is seen, and that by which one sees.

St. Thomas was not only an admirable disputant (even such opponents as Archbishop John Peckham admitted how calm and collected he remained in the midst of the fiercest argument), he was also a careful and accurate historian, and his use of history is remarkable. Because he always accepted things "just as they were" and never "expected them to conform themselves to his own definitions of them—quite the reverse" (Gilson, *Reason and Revelation in the Middle Ages,* Scribner, 1938) he made possible the creation by Robert Grosseteste and "his thirteenth and fourteenth century successors" of "modern experimental science, by uniting the experimental habit of the practical arts with the rationalism of twelfth century philosophy" (A. Crombie, *Robert Grosseteste and the Origins of Experimental Science,* Oxford, 1953).

The distinguishing marks of St. Thomas' philosophy are its emphasis on contingent being (every real and complete being is distinct from every other: any being which becomes is necessarily limited); on the duality of potency and act; and on the distinction between the constituent reality and the actuality of every existent being except God, Who exists by His very essence. Only infinite Actuality is all existence.

St. Thomas' new theories have been summarized by Maurice de Wulf: "To the plurality of forms he opposed the unity of the substantial principle: to the hylomorphic composition of spiritual substances the doctrine of subsistent forms: to the Augustinian theory of the identity of the soul with its faculties, that of the real distinction between a limited substance and its operative powers: to the confusion of existence and essence, that of their real distinction: to the theory of a special illumination, that of the normal power of the intellect within its natural limits: to the theory of the light form, that of the accidental reality of every quality and action."*

* Maurice de Wulf, *History of Medieval Philosophy,* Vol. II, trans. Ernest Messenger (Longmans, Green, 1926).

CHAPTER X

Duns Scotus

GREGORY X SUMMONED TO THE FRENCH CITY OF LYONS, in 1274, the greatest of the medieval councils. The chief item on the council's agenda was the reunion of East and West, the ending of the Photian schism. St. Albert attended the Council, St. Thomas Aquinas died on his way there, and St. Bonaventura died during the Council. But the last had already taken part in the final negotiations with the ambassador of the Byzantine emperor and had preached at the bilingual mass which celebrated the reunion of East and West. It seemed the apotheosis of the idea of Christendom, the restoration of the seamless robe of Christ, the beginning of an Augustan age.

However, "the old order changeth, giving place to new, and God fulfills himself in many ways, lest one good custom should corrupt the world," as the Victorian poet Lord Tennyson pointed out, and what seemed a beginning was instead an end; indeed 1274 is as final a date as 1603 or 1902, and the death of St. Thomas Aquinas marks the end of an era as surely as did the death of Queen Elizabeth I or Queen Victoria.

One of the unsolved—and possibly insoluble—historical mysteries is why St. Thomas Aquinas suffered such an immediate and complete eclipse. The chief opponents of Thomism were the Franciscans. Although St. Bonaventura was himself such a close friend of St. Thomas, by 1282 the Franciscan Order as such had already officially adopted an antagonistic attitude to St. Thomas, and the study of the *Summa Theologica* was discouraged, while the contemporary William de la Mare published a "formal criticism of a hundred and seventeen points of doctrine found in Thomas' works." This constituted the Franciscan mani-

festo, as it were. After the condemnation by Stephe.
Tempier, Bishop of Paris, in 1277, of Averroës and his
opponent Aquinas in one breath, the Dominicans rallied
around their greatest writer, and by 1278, through the
decision of the General Chapter at Milan, Thomism became the official doctrine of the Dominicans.

While the Dominicans had no outstanding philosopher
after St. Thomas, the Franciscan John Duns Scotus,
born in Scotland around 1265, was to prove St. Thomas'
greatest rival. John Duns Scotus studied in Oxford and
Paris, was teaching at Oxford from 1300 to 1302, then
taught in Paris, then again in Oxford, and finally died in
Cologne in 1308. His great commentary on Peter Lombard's *Sentences,* and his treatise *On the First Principle*
were written in Oxford. He was a brilliant and "fair argumentative" man, like most of his race, and he attacked
"the majority of his contemporaries, Roger Bacon, Thomas
Aquinas, the Averroists, Richard of Middleton (a fellow
Franciscan) and Henry of Ghent." "This critical attitude,"
comments Maurice de Wulf, "though courteous, was bound
to make his teaching lively and popular. It makes his
works a repertory of contemporary philosophy of incom-
parable doctrinal value . . . At the same time he had a
sense of tradition. He appealed to St. Bonaventura. He
did not criticize for the sake of criticizing, but in order
to construct."

Father Christopher Devlin, S. J., has made a brilliant
comparison between St. Thomas and Duns Scotus:

[I would therefore compare the mind, as St. Thomas represents it [he told the London Aquinas Society on March
15, 1950], to a limpid and motionless pool in which both
the nature of the surrounding objects and the movements
of the heavens can be clearly discerned. Everything is
reflected in a two-dimensional surface, and yet there is
no mistaking the differences of depth and distance, there
is no confusion between earth and heaven. Yet when Duns
Scotus arrives, he complains that the pool fails to represent two things of vital importance without which it could
not long exist. These things are the secret entrance and

181

by which there is a continual influx and a .wing-off of the water without which it could fresh and sweet . . . the pool is the rational Scotus complains that if it is regarded as a closed cle sufficient unto itself, it does not adequately represent the human soul. The human soul is not co-extensive with reason or understanding . . . it is a mistake to regard the other powers of the soul simply as functions or adjuncts to understanding. There is a power of the soul which is below understanding, but which has better evidence of the soul's origin, and there is a power of the soul which is above understanding and which is more in touch with the soul's destiny. The secret entrance to the pool is the point where the unconscious begins to influence the conscious mind. The secret exit is the point where the soul finds that its intellectual powers extended to their fullest have still failed to satisfy it, and that it must bring a higher faculty into play. In this way he returns to, and hopes to reinstate St. Augustine's hierarchy of memory, understanding and will. He sees these powers as the one soul operating on different levels of consciousness.]

ON MANY POINTS, DUNS SCOTUS ABANDONS ARISTOTLE and goes back to Plato. Where Thomas and the Thomists said that God commands good because it is good, Duns Scotus said good is good only because God commands it. Thomas Aquinas had insisted that existence (*esse*) was more fundamental than essence (*essentia*), and had insisted on the higher dignity of the intellect than of the will. John Duns Scotus challenges these positions. He has been opposed to Thomas Aquinas as Immanuel Kant to Gottfried Leibniz; John Duns Scotus, the critic, has been assumed to be the destroyer of Thomas, the dogmatic. But the subtlety, the complexity, the feeling-after-and-finding technique of the former is at least as constructive as it is critical, and D. J. B. Hawkins goes so far as to say that "he is a systematic thinker in the grand manner, second only to St. Thomas in the middle age, and presenting another synthesis of Augustine and Aristotle."

For Duns Scotus, the will is superior to the intellect,

Scotus = will superior to intellect

and, for him, philosophy does not give man *enough* dignity: Christianity provides man with a greater *natural* dignity (upon which the supernatural is laid) than ever philosophy found. "God who so wonderfully didst constitute the dignity of the human substance," says the priest in the Mass, and this naturally constituted dignity is at the heart of medieval humanism. Although "every intellect as such is capable of apprehending the whole range of being," as Duns Scotus said, that tremendous quality of being *capax Dei,* capable of (the vision of) God, is what made man as seen by Duns Scotus the *whole* man of the Renaissance, of whom Pico della Mirandola was to cry *"L'anima mi s'aggrandisce"* (my soul swells).

Duns Scotus took up the problem of universals from where Abelard had left it. When the mind separates redness from things red, the mental activity isolates elements which do not exist apart in isolation. Yet redness exists *in* each red thing, but only in the mind *apart* from all things red. This distinction, though unreal, has a foundation in fact: what, asked Duns Scotus, is this foundation in fact? Duns Scotus "drew up a list of varying kinds of unity and the corresponding degrees of distinction." There was the unity of aggregation, the unity of order, the unity of qualification, the unity of essential principles, the unity of simplicity, and "the most absolute kind of unity which is formal identity." So, according to the Scotist school, humanity in Peter and humanity in Paul are *formally* identified, although not *really.*

Duns Scotus denied the distinction between essence and existence, because neither accounted for the individuality of real things. "Hence, beyond all that in reality corresponds to universals . . . he claims that things exhibit a principle of individuality, a *thisness,* which is not reducible to any other factor. The singular adds an entity over and above the entity of the universal. Consequently the apprehension of the universal is not the complete ground of an apprehension of the singular adequate to the whole knowability of the singular."* *Thisness* is not a universal like

* *A Sketch of Medieval Philosophy,* by D. J. B. Hawkins, copyright 1947 by Sheed and Ward, Inc., New York.

other universals like redness or fatness, for it is the very
principle by which I am I, you are you. And we cannot
understand anything until we have understood its *thisness*,
and the difference between *thisness* and *thatness*. Actually,
as Dr. Hawkins points out, Duns Scotus' *thisness* (*haec-
ceitas*, as he calls it) is much the same as St. Thomas'
existence. Both great philosophers refused to remain
among airy abstractions. The one by his *thisness*, the
other by his *existence*, brought philosophy down from the
thin speculative skies to the workaday world, by empha-
sizing the realness of what exists. In fact, for Duns Scotus,
the individual is the *only* existing thing, and it is not the
being of *being* but the being of the individual which is
investigated by philosophy. God is God because He is
more fully individual, more fully himself, than anyone
else is himself, and He is Pascal's God, the God of Abra-
ham, not of the philosophers.

It is in his theory of form that Duns Scotus most obviously clashes with St. Thomas Aquinas. The formal perfection of man for Duns Scotus, for example, is *humanitas*.
Either, in extramental existence, this is identified with
life, or with specific elements, such as rationality. In either
case, each one is not the other, and the individual *humanitas,* apart from its ideal existence, has a reality in each
individual, apart from its conceptual reality. Every essence
has its own existential being, according to Duns Scotus,
and "the generic and specific concepts utilized by the mind
in its scientific constructions attain to univocal realities
and have the same value in the indefinitely numerous
being to which these concepts apply. Even the notion of
being, which we apply to substance and accident, to creatures and to God, is characterized by univocity, and corresponds, in the measure in which it signifies opposition, to
a homogenous determination in all that is or can be."*

God, for Duns Scotus, is demonstrable in physics, which
arrives at an unmoved mover, and in metaphysics, which
arrives at a first being.

"It is because we find that the things around us are

* Maurice de Wulf, *History of Medieval Philosophy,* Vol. ii
(Longmans, Green).

manifold, contingent and composite that we are able to
see that they must have an ultimate cause which is one,
necessary and metaphysically simple." The most obvious
attribute of contingency is finitude. And infinity is the
"most essential characteristic which thought must attribute
to the necessary being." For St. Thomas, therefore, God
is the infinite *being,* for Duns Scotus, He is the *infinite*
being. Only in God is the will in total harmony with the
intelligence, and God's first motion is toward Himself. But
for Duns Scotus "the second motion of God's will is towards the creation of persons who will be able to love him
in their degree, and the third towards the creation of the
means which those persons will require."

In his *De Primo Principio* (Of the First Principle) Duns
Scotus works out clearly and completely his own proof
of the existence of God. This work, probably a late one,
is generally regarded as genuine.

[CHAPTER I:
May the First Principle of things grant me to believe,
understand, and make known those things which may
please His Majesty and elevate our minds to the contemplation of Him.

O Lord our God, when Moses thy servant asked Thee,
the most true teacher, about thy Name, so that he might
tell it to the Children of Israel, Thou, knowing what the
intellect of mortals could conceive of Thee, didst answer:
I AM WHO AM, thus disclosing thy Blessed Name. Thou
art true Being, Thou art total Being. This, if it be possible
for me, I should like to know. Help me, O Lord, in my
inquiry as to how much knowledge our natural reason can
attain concerning the true Being, which Thou art, beginning with "being," which Thou hast predicated of Thyself.

There are many properties of "being," the consideration
of which would be valid for the pursuit of our purpose.
However, from the essential order as from a more fruitful
means, I shall first proceed in the following manner: In
this first chapter I shall set forth the four divisions of
order; from these divisions it will be gathered how many
essential orders there are.

For the manifestation of a division this much is required: first, that the resultants be made known and be shown to be thus contained under that which is divided; secondly, that the resultants be shown to be mutually exclusive; thirdly, that it be proved that the resultants exhaust the content of that which is divided. The first requirement will be met in this chapter, the others in the second chapter. Here then I shall simply set down the divisions and assign the meanings of the resultants.

I do not take essential order in the strict sense, as some do who say that the posterior is in an order but that the prior or first is above order. Rather, I take it in its common meaning, in so far as order is a relation of mutual comparison predicated of the prior with regard to the posterior, and conversely—that is, in so far as that which is ordered is sufficiently divided into that which is prior and that which is posterior. Hence at times there will be mention of order and at others of priority or posteriority.

First Division. I say then first that essential order seems to be divided by a primary division, as an equivocal term into its equivocates, namely, into the order of eminence and the order of dependence.

In the first mode the prior is called the eminent, and the posterior is called that which is exceeded. To put it briefly, whatever is more perfect and noble according to essence is thus prior. In this manner of priority Aristotle proves in the ninth book of the *Metaphysics* that act is prior to potency, when he calls the former prior according to substance and species. For he says that those things which are posterior in generation are prior in species and substance.

In the second mode the prior is called that upon which something depends, and the posterior is called that which depends. With regard to this prior I understand the following meaning (which Aristotle likewise shows in the fifth book of the *Metaphysics,* using the testimony of Plato): The prior according to nature and essence is that which is able to exist without the posterior, but not conversely. I take this in the following sense: Even if the prior necessarily causes the posterior and therefore cannot exist without it, still this is not because it needs the posterior for its own being, but conversely. For if it be assumed that the posterior does not exist, the prior will nevertheless exist without the inclusion of a contradiction. The converse will not be true, because the posterior needs the prior; this need we can call dependence. Thus we can say that everything which is essentially posterior depends necessarily upon its prior, but not conversely, even though sometimes the posterior necessarily follows it. These can be called the prior and the posterior according to substance and species, as the others were called above. However, for the purpose of speaking clearly, let them be called the prior and the posterior according to dependence.

Second Division. Leaving the order according to eminence undivided, I subdivide the order of dependence. For, either the dependent is an effect and that upon which it depends is its cause, or the dependent is a more remote effect of some cause and that upon which it depends is a more proximate effect of the same cause.

With regard to this second division the meaning of the first member is sufficiently known, as well as the fact that it is contained under what is divided. For it is clear what a cause is and what an effect is, likewise that an effect essentially depends upon a cause and that the cause is that upon which it depends, according to the above meaning of the first member of that which is divided here.

But the second member of this second division is not evident in itself, nor is it clear how it is contained under what is divided.

The first part is explained thus: If of the same cause there are two effects, one of which is by its nature fit to be caused by that cause in a prior and more immediate way, and the other only through that more immediate effect already caused, I say that this other is a posterior effect with regard to the same cause, and the more immediate one is a prior effect. This is the meaning of this member.

From this I show, secondly, that this member is contained under that which is divided, that is, that the more remote effect depends essentially upon the more proximate effect. For first, it cannot exist if the more proximate effect does not exist; secondly, the causality of the cause is related to them within an order; therefore . . .; and conversely, they have an essential order between each other, being compared to a third, which is the cause of both of them; therefore, they also have an essential order between each other in an absolute way; thirdly, such a cause of itself is understood only as the proximate cause of the proximate effect alone; and if that one is not caused, the cause is understood as somehow remote with regard to the others; but if that one is already caused, the cause is understood as proximate with regard to the second effect. However, from the remote cause only in so far as it is remote, no effect follows. Therefore the second effect depends upon the cause which has brought the more proximate effect into being; consequently it depends also upon the more proximate being.

Third Division. Each member of this second division is subdivided, and I subdivide the second member first, because this is in harmony with what has already been said. For the prior, which is the more immediate effect of the cause, is declared to be the more immediate effect not only of a proximate cause of both but of a remote cause as well. Take for example: The proximate cause of one effect— let it (viz. the proximate cause) be A—is in no way the cause of the other effect, B. But some other prior cause is the proximate cause of this B and is the remote cause of that effect of which the other (viz. A) is the proximate cause. Nevertheless, between these effects there will be an essential order as of a prior effect to a posterior effect, and this is true if the causality of the common cause of both according to an essential order is related to them as to its effect.

It is not so apparent that the second member of this division is under that which is divided. However, it is proved in this way: Since each effect is in an essential order with reference to a third, which is the cause of both of them, it follows that they are in an essential order with reference to each other. Besides, the common cause is understood as if it were a remote cause with regard to posterior, if the prior is not caused. Moreover, the posterior cannot exist without the prior . . .

In summing up I gather together the fruit of this chapter. The essential order is exhausted through six orders which divide it; viz., four orders of cause to effect; and one of effect to effect, by including here under the same order the two members of the third division; and one of eminent to that which is exceeded.]

FROM THE NATURE OF THE CREATOR, DUNS SCOTUS GOES on to the nature of the created.

[CHAPTER III: The three-fold primacy in the First Principle.

First conclusion: It is possible that among beings there is some nature which effects.

This is shown: It is possible that there is some nature which is effected; therefore, it is possible that there is some nature which effects. The consequence is evident from the nature of correlatives. The antecedent is proved: Some nature is contingent; therefore it is possible for it to be after not being; therefore not from itself, nor from nothing —in both these cases being would be from non-being. Therefore it is possible that there is a nature which is effected by another. The antecedent is proved furthermore: It is possible for some nature to move or change, for it is possible for it to lack some perfection that is possible to be in it. Therefore, the term of motion can begin, and so be effected.

In this conclusion and certain following ones, I could propose the actual thus: Some nature is an efficient cause, because some nature is effected, because some nature begins to be, because some nature is the term of motion and contingent. But I prefer to submit conclusions and premises about the possible, for if those about the actual are conceded, those about the possible are conceded, but not conversely. Also, those about the actual are contingent, though manifest enough; those about the possible are necessary. The former pertain to existing being, the latter can properly pertain also to being quidditatively taken. And later on there will be shown the existence of that quiddity about which there is now shown the efficiency.

Second conclusion: It is possible that something which effects is simply first; that is, it is not possible that it is effected or that it effects in virtue of another.

It is proved from the first conclusion: It is possible that there is something which effects. Let it be A. If it is first, in this manner expounded, our purpose is soon attained. If it is not, then it is a posterior possible efficient cause, because it is possible that it is effected by another or that it effects in virtue of another. If the negation is denied, the affirmation is posited. Let that other be given; let it be B, and about that let it be argued as it was argued about A. Either there will be an infinite process in possible efficient causes, of which everyone will be second with respect to a prior, or there will be a stop in some one not having a prior. Infinity is impossible in ascent. Consequently a primacy is necessary, because that which does not have a prior is not posterior to anything posterior to itself, for the second conclusion of the second chapter destroys a circle in causes.

Here it is objected that according to those who philosophize an infinity is possible in ascent, as they posited about infinite generating beings, of which none would be first but every one would be second; and nevertheless this would be posited by them without a circle. In excluding this instance I say that the philosophers did not posit an infinity as possible in causes essentially ordered, but only in causes accidentally ordered, as is clear from Avicenna— in the sixth book of the *Metaphysics,* chapter 5—where he speaks of the infinity of individuals in a species.

In order to show forth our purpose I explain what essentially ordered causes are, and what accidentally ordered causes are. Hence it must be known that it is one thing to speak of causes by themselves (per se) and incidental causes; and it is another thing to speak of causes per se or essentially ordered, and causes accidentally ordered. For in the first case there is only a comparison of one to one, of cause, namely, to effect; and that is a cause per se which causes according to its own nature and not according to something accidental to it. In the second there is a comparison of two causes with each other, in so far as there is an effect from them.

Essentially and per se ordered causes differ from accidentally ordered causes in three respects. The first difference is that in essentially ordered causes the second, in so far as it causes, depends upon the first; in accidentally ordered causes it does not, although in its being or in some other way it does depend. The second difference is that in essentially ordered causes there is a causality of another nature and order, because the higher is more perfect; in accidentally ordered causes there is not. This difference follows from the first. For no cause depends essentially in causing upon a cause of the same nature, because in the causation of anything, one of one nature suffices. The third difference follows, that all essentially ordered causes are necessarily required simultaneously for causing. Otherwise some proper causality would be lacking to the effect. Accidentally ordered causes are not required simultaneously.

From these considerations our purpose is shown thus: An infinity of essentially ordered causes is impossible, and an infinity of accidentally ordered causes is impossible unless it be posited that it is based on essentially ordered causes. Therefore, an infinity in essentially ordered causes is altogether impossible. And even if an essential order is denied, infinity is impossible. Therefore, it is altogether possible that something which causes is simply first.

Here there are three propositions assumed. For the sake of brevity let the first be called A, the second B, the third C.

The proof of these. First A is proved: The totality of essentially ordered effects is caused; consequently by some cause which is nothing of that totality; for then it would be the cause of itself; for the whole totality of dependents depends, and upon nothing of that totality. Furthermore, infinite causes essentially ordered would be simultaneously in act—from the third difference above—a consequent no philosopher posits. Thirdly, the prior is nearer the beginning—from the fifth book of the *Metaphysics;* consequently, where there is no beginning, there is nothing essentially prior. Fourthly, the higher is more perfect in causing—from the second difference; consequently what is infinitely higher is infinitely more perfect and thus of infinite perfection in causing; it is therefore not causing in virtue of another, since every such a one causes imperfectly because it is dependent in causing. Fifthly, that which is able to effect does not necessarily posit any imperfection—this is evident in the eighth conclusion of the second chapter; consequently it can be in some nature without imperfection, but if it is in none without dependency upon a prior, it is in none without imperfection; therefore, independent efficient causality can belong to some nature; that nature is simply first; consequently an efficient causality simply first is possible; this suffices, because later it will be concluded from this, that it exists in reality. Thus by five reasons A is evident.

B is proved: For if an accidental infinity is posited, this evidently occurs not simultaneously, but successively only, one member after the other; so that the second, although in some way it will be from the prior, nevertheless does not depend upon it in causing. For it can cause when the former does not exist, as, for instance, a son generates when his father is dead just as when he is living. For such an infinity of succession is impossible, unless it depends upon some nature of infinite duration, upon which the whole succession and everything of it depends. For no difformity is perpetuated, unless in virtue of something permanent which is nothing of the succession, because all the members of the succession are of the same nature; but it is something essentially prior because every member of the succession depends upon it, and this in a different order than that in which a member depends upon the proximate cause, which is something of that succession; therefore B is evident.

C is proved: Since from the first conclusion of this chapter it is possible that there is some nature which effects, if the essential order of possible efficient causes be denied, then that nature causes in virtue of no other; and even if it be posited as caused in some singular, nevertheless in some one singular it is uncaused, and this is the goal regarding the first nature. For if in every one it be posited as caused, a contradiction is already implied in denying the essential order. The reason is that no nature can be posited as caused in every one, so that there is an accidental order under it, without there being an essential order to another nature—from B.

Third conclusion: It is possible that the simply first efficient is uncausable, because it is not effected and it effects independently.

This is evident from the second conclusion. For if it is possible that it is caused by another or that it causes in virtue of another, then there will be an infinite process, or a circle, or there is a stop in something uncausable and capable of causing independently; I say that that is first and the other, as is clear from your admissions, is not first. It is concluded further: If the first is ineffectible, then it is uncausable, because it cannot be ordered to an end—from the fifth conclusion of the second chapter; and it cannot be caused from the matter—from the sixth conclusion of the same chapter; and it cannot be caused through the form—from the seventh conclusion there; and it cannot be caused from the matter and form together—from the eighth conclusion of the same chapter.

Fourth conclusion: The simply first efficient in the possible order is actually existing, and some nature actually existing is effective in this way.

It is proved: That to the definition of which it is repugnant to be able to be from another, if it can be, can be by itself. It is simply repugnant to the definition of that which can be the first efficient to be able to be from another—from the third conclusion; and it can be—from the second conclusion. Indeed, in that place the fifth proof of A, which does not seem conclusive, concludes this. Other proofs can be treated with regard to existence, and they are about contingent facts, though manifest; or with regard to nature and quiddity and possibility, and they are from necessary facts. Consequently that which can be the simply first efficient can be by itself. That which is not by itself cannot be by itself, because then non-being would bring something to being, and this is impossible; and besides, then it would cause itself and so would not be altogether uncausable. This fourth conclusion is declared in another way because it is inconvenient for the universe to be lacking the highest degree possible in being.

According to this fourth conclusion, note a corollary, that that which can be the first efficient is not only that which is prior to others, but that to be prior to which includes a contradiction; thus, in so far as it is first, it exists. This is proved as the fourth conclusion was proved. For in the definition of this there is especially included the uncausable. Therefore, if it can be because it does not contradict being, it can be by itself, and so it is by itself.

Fifth conclusion: The uncausable is a being which is necessary of itself.

It is proved: For by excluding every cause different from itself, both intrinsic and extrinsic, with regard to its being, of itself it is impossible not to be. Proof: Nothing is able not to be unless something positively or privatively incompatible with it can be, because in any case one of two contradictories is always true. Nothing incompatible with the uncausable can be, either positively or privatively, because it would be either of itself or from another; not in the first manner, because then it would be so of itself— from the fourth conclusion—and so incompatibles would exist simultaneously; and for a like reason neither would be, because you concede by that incompatible that the uncausable does not exist; and so it follows conversely; not in the second manner because no effect has more intense or more powerful being from a cause than the uncausable has by itself, because an effect is dependent in its being, whereas the uncausable is not. Also the possibility of the causable to exist does not necessarily posit its actual being, as is the case with the uncausable. However, nothing incompatible with an already existing being can be from a cause, unless it receive from that cause a being more intense or more powerful than is the being of that which is incompatible with it.

Sixth conclusion: The necessity of being of itself belongs to only one nature.

It is proved thus: If two natures can be necessary of themselves, their necessity of being is common; therefore also some quidditative entity according to which the necessity is common to them and from which is taken, as it were, their genus; and besides this they are distinguished by their ultimate actual formalities.

From this there follow two incompatibles. First, each will be a necessary being first of all through the common nature, which is of lesser actuality, and not through the distinguishing nature, which is of greater actuality. For if it is formally a necessary being through that distinguishing nature also, then it will be a necessary being twice, because that distinguishing nature does not formally include the common nature, just as a difference does not include the genus. However, it seems impossible that a lesser actuality is that by which something is first of all necessary, and that by a greater actuality it is necessary neither first of all nor per se.

The second impossible consequence is that through the common nature, by which it is posited that each is first of all a necessary being, neither one is a necessary being, because neither is sufficiently through that nature. For every nature is what it is through the ultimate formal element. However, through whatever something is a necessary being, through that same element it is in effect regardless of every other thing.

If you say that the common nature suffices for its being, besides the distant natures, then it follows that that common nature itself is of itself actual and not distinguished, and consequently cannot be distinguished, because the necessary being already existing is not in potency to being in an unqualified sense; the being of a genus in a species is simply being with regard to it.

Besides, two natures under the same common class are not of the same degree. This is proved through the differences dividing a genus; if they are unequal, then the being of one will be more perfect than the being of the other; no being is more perfect than a being which is necessary of itself.

Moreover, if two natures were necessary of themselves

one would have no dependence upon the other in being; consequently neither would it have any essential order to the other. Therefore one of them would be nothing of this universe, for there is nothing in the universe which does not have an essential order among beings, because the unity of the universe derives from the order of the parts.

Here it is objected that because each has an order of eminence to the parts of the universe, that order suffices for unity. Against this objection: The one does not have that order to the other, because the more perfect being is of a more eminent nature; but none is more perfect than that very being which is necessary of itself. Likewise, one of them has no order to the parts of the universe; because of one universe there is one order, there is one order to one first. The proof: To two first natures, if they are posited, the nature next to the first does not have only one order or only one dependence, but two, as there are two *termini ad quem,* and so with regard to every lower nature. Therefore, there will accordingly be in the whole universe two first orders, and so two universes, or there will be an order to only one necessary being and no order to the other.

However, because in proceeding reasonably it seems that nothing must be posited in the universe unless some necessity for it is apparent and some order towards other beings manifestly shows its entity, since plural beings are not to be posited without necessity—from the first book of the Physics—a necessary being shown in the universe from the uncausable; and that (viz., the uncausable) is shown from the first being causing, and that, in turn, is shown from the effects. It is not apparent from the effects that there is a necessity of positing more than one first nature causing; nay, it is impossible, as will be shown later in the fifteenth conclusion of this third chapter. Therefore it is not necessary to posit more than one uncaused or necessary being according to the nature. Consequently with reason they are not posited.

According to the first four conclusions of this chapter concerning the possible efficient cause, I submit . . . similar conclusions about a final cause, and these conclusions will be shown in a similar manner.

The first is:

Seventh conclusion: It is possible that among beings there is some nature which is an end.

It is proved: It is possible that there is something which is ordered to an end. Proof: It is possible that there is something which is effected—from the proof of the first conclusion of this chapter; therefore, it is also possible that there is something which is ordered to an end. The consequence is evident from the fourth conclusion of the second chapter. This is more manifest with regard to the essential order—from the sixteenth conclusion of the second chapter—than it was with regard to the possible efficient.

Eighth conclusion: It is possible that something which is an end is simply first; that is, it is not possible that it is ordered to another or that it is fit to be an end for others in virtue of another.

It is proved by five proofs similar to those of the second conclusion of this third chapter.

Ninth conclusion: It is possible that the first end is uncausable.

It is proved: because it cannot be ordered to an end; otherwise it would be first; and further, it is therefore ineffectible—from the fourth conclusion of the second chapter; further, as above in the proof of the third conclusion of this third chapter.*]

* Duns Scotus, *De Primo Principio*, trans. by Father Evan Roche (Franciscan Institute).

CHAPTER XI

William of Ockham

WITH THE CLOSE OF THE THIRTEENTH CENTURY, THE ERA of the great medieval philosophical systems is over. This age of synthesis was marvelously also the age of criticism; the fourteenth century is very different, an age of disassociation, of dissolution, of fragmentation. The wheel turns slowly at first, but as the century progresses the angle grows steeper, until Reformation and Renaissance both appear at the Council of Constance in 1415. There the grave scandal of the Great Schism of the West (which had lasted from 1378 to 1417) led to the proclamation of the superiority of a General Council over the Pope. The Great Schism, during which the rival Popes, at Rome and Avignon, had each been supported by whole nations and by separate saints, greatly weakened the power of the Papacy, while the burning of the Czech heretic, John Huss, by the Council of Constance, after he had been given a safe-conduct to attend it and state his case, gave the cause of Reform its most sincere martyr.

The rise of the mendicant orders, of friars and preachers, Franciscan and Dominican, was but an ecclesiastical expression of the rise of the people. The Dominican Order was the first institution in Europe to be run on truly democratic lines: the more than 50,000 Dominicans had from their foundation representative government, with the Master-General elected by a simple majority. This may have come from the fact that St. Dominic was a Spaniard, for, on the Continent of Europe, the Spaniards had, in their Cortes, the nearest thing to a parliament of any country.

The strong tide of mysticism which arose in the fourteenth century was partly caused by the miseries of the

Hundred Years War, which decimated Europe, and caused people to turn more and more to an increasingly interior life as a refuge from exterior misery, and partly by the undermining of ecclesiastical authority, due to the Great Schism, which led individuals to seek each his own separate, entirely personal and intimate individual relationship with God, without benefit of clergy. The famines and plagues all over Europe, and the extended outbreak of the Black Death in England and in Germany, led to great discontent among the poor, and also to a scarcity of laborers, who thus became more important and valuable and were able to escape their feudal obligations, through the deaths of their masters from wars or plague, and through commerce, which helped establish a middle class. The rise of nationalism, the growth of lay claims, the multiplication of universities (all national or local in character, unlike Paris or even Oxford in their heyday) led to an entirely different emphasis in philosophy.

Perhaps the best known of all the fourteenth century mystics is Meister (Master) Eckhart of Hochheim, near Gotha. Born about 1260, he taught in Paris at the turn of the century, was called by Boniface VIII to Rome, and given the title of Doctor by the Pope himself. Later he returned to Cologne, but got into trouble with the Archbishop, who took proceedings against his doctrines, in 1326. Eckhart appealed to the Pope in 1327, and died in that year. In 1329 Pope John XXII condemned some of Meister Eckhart's statements, and later Martin Luther was warmly to commend him. In Eckhart's great *Threepartite Work,* published at the end of the thirteenth century, mysticism and metaphysics mingle. He is an orthodox Thomist in that he agrees that in God alone essence and existence are identical, but he goes on to say that God is pure affirmation, and that all negation is distasteful to him. God is the only existence, says Eckhart, and as God is all existence, nothing can exist apart from Him.

Another Dominican, Durandus of St. Pourçain (flourished 1312-died 1332) abandoned Thomism in spite of the instruction of the General Chapter of Saragossa, which in 1309 declared it to be the official doctrine of the Dominican Order. Durandus said relationship was a real form of existence, and three forms of being must be admitted: being in itself, being in another, being becoming another. Durandus' view of relative reality brought him to a theory of knowing by which the soul and the intellect, far from being illuminated passively, are, on the contrary, very active. The soul's perfection is such that it need receive nothing from outside, it spontaneously adapts itself to whatever it encounters. Durandus died as Bishop of Meaux, after having been called upon to judge William of Ockham's orthodoxy.

One of the most interesting and original figures of the early fourteenth century is Raymond Lully, a layman and a Franciscan tertiary. Born in Palma, Majorca, about 1235, he was "converted" in 1266, and thereafter devoted his life to the study of Arabic and to opposing the ideas of Averroës. He traveled to Tartary, to Armenia, to Africa, seeking the salvation of the Muslims by bringing them to Christ. He was a mystic, philosopher, linguist, poet and religious troubadour. Towards the end of the century he taught at Montpellier and Paris (1297-99, and 1309-1311) and died in 1315. He founded the first European school of Oriental languages at Miramar, in Majorca, to train men for the conversion of the paynim, and he claimed to have discovered a logical method, the *Great Art*, by which all knowledge was reduced to certain combinations of principles. "Since every science has its own principles," he wrote, "different from the principles of other sciences, the intellect longs and needs a general, universal science, which would contain and embrace all the principles of the other sciences, as the particular is contained in the universal." He also wrote "the Friend was asked 'what is the world?' and He replied 'for those who know how to read, it is the book where one may learn of my Beloved.'" To prove the Muslims wrong, Lully says it is only necessary to prove Catholicism true, and he set heroically about "proving" the Trinity, so much to his own satisfaction that he could write "I have proved the divine Trinity in such a manner that the human intellect cannot now reasonably suppose that it does not exist."

Whatever happens in history is temporal, and must follow the same sequence of birth, through growth, to death. This is as true of philosophical systems as it is of individuals, and the particular expression of each idea has its decline as it had its heyday or its incipience. The beginning of the end came for scholastic philosophy around 1320, when many theologians began to fear for the future of religion itself amidst the complications of the conflicting systems. Duns Scotus had corrected Bonaventura, Aquinas had straightened out Albert, but then along came a flurry of minor clerics: of the Dominicans, some were Thomists, some more or less avowed Averroists; some Franciscans were Scotists, but each was bent upon demolishing the other's theories.

One of the reactions to the aggravated fragmentation, to the constant sharpening and whittling of truth that went on, was a "back to the Gospel" movement that wished to divorce finally faith from reason, and to separate completely mind and soul. Nicolas of Autrecourt, for example, who was condemned in 1346 and fled, as did many others, from the Papal jurisdiction to the court of Emperor Lewis of Bavaria, said that in so far as the evidence is concerned, these propositions, that God exists, and that God does not exist, signify absolutely the same thing. Another Nicolas, of Cusa, writing about a hundred years later (in 1433, at the height of the Great Schism) found the world in great danger of becoming as unthinkable as God.

And with the atomization of philosophy and theology went a breakdown of the principle of the single emperor, that relic of Roman times, into that of a plethora of nation-states. The various fourteenth century thinkers each propounded their own varieties of attack on the given scholastic positions, but it is William of Ockham who stands, if any single man can claim such a position, at the end of the Middle Ages as the great iconoclast, clearing the encumbered ground and preparing a beach-head for the philosophers of the Renaissance, for such men as Francis Bacon and Thomas Hobbes.

A great deal of work has recently been done on William of Ockham, and many of the "facts" hitherto believed

venerable
bachelor

about him have been proved false, thanks to the researches of Messrs. Hofer, Etienne Gilson and Léon Baudry. Ockham was born in the Surrey village of that name about 1300, and the first certain historical mention of him was in 1324. In 1322 Pope John XXII declared the Franciscan doctrine of absolute poverty to be heretical. William of Ockham was suspected of having written in favor of this heresy; other of his writings, too, fell under suspicion, and he was called from Oxford to Avignon, where Pope John XXII was in exile, to plead his cause. At that time he was a bachelor of the University of Oxford, and a Franciscan. As he never went further with his studies, he was known as *inceptor venerabilis* or the "venerable bachelor" by his admirers. It has been proved that he never was a pupil of Duns Scotus, as had been thought. But he did say, in his *Dialogue,* that the innovations of St. Thomas Aquinas, the theory especially of the unity of form, caused "an almost infinite scandal" at Oxford. He began early to write logic, and was very "antimodern." He wrote a commentary on Aristotle's *Physics,* of which several manuscripts remain, but his most famous work is the *Quodlibets.* After a bachelor at Oxford had finished commenting on the *Sentences* of Peter Lombard, he might not teach for two years, but might take part in the *Quodlibet* discussions, and might preach. These *Quodlibets* were sort of free-for-all discussions and Ockham's seven *Quodlibets* show us something of his razorlike mind. Indeed, a razor is the name applied to his most famous principle, that "entities are not to be multiplied without necessity." This principle, which Robert Grosseteste had assumed as the *lex parsimoniae,* or law of economy, was derived from Aristotle, who stated it as a pragmatic principle. "That is better and more valuable," wrote Grosseteste, "which requires fewer, other circumstances being equal; which necessitates the answering of a smaller number of questions for a perfect demonstration . . . As Aristotle says in Book V of the *Physics,* nature operates in the shortest way possible." The Franciscans after Grosseteste had leaned heavily on this "principle," which was quoted by Duns Scotus, Durandus of St. Pourcain and William of Ockham's contemporary, Peter Aurioli (d. 1322).

Among Ockham's early works, composed at Oxford, was an *Exposition* on Aristotle's *Physics,* in which several of Ockham's most original and famous ideas appear. It served as a sketch for the *Commentary on the Sentences* which got him into so much trouble later. In this *Exposition* Ockham explains that some authors have said that things possess a common nature, and that the idea of such a common nature plus some new concept *individualizes* in creatures, and this makes them universals, or rather *universalizes* them in the intellect. Intelligence cannot perceive this common quality or nature; indeed intelligence cannot know an individual directly, as an object, but only by reflection, by a reflex action, at second bounce, as it were. This, Ockham said, is nonsense: by no twist of the intellect can a man be a goat, or Socrates at home when he is walking on the street. No more can the intellect make the mobile immobile; the perishable, the eternal; or the singular, universal. *Only* individuals are real, singly; there is no such thing as an individual universalized. The object of scientific enquiry or research is always the individual, never the universal, and the object perceived exists before the act of perceiving it. Nothing, Ockham says, exists before knowledge of an object except the object that is known; and the object of the senses and of the intelligence must be the same.

Matter, Ockham continues, and form, cannot be known by us in themselves. We can only know them in the relations and oppositions they have with each other. We are unable ever to form simple concepts, *propter sibi,* as such, but only composite concepts. And if this is so with regard to sensible objects, to things whose reality we can ascertain from their properties, and whose nature we can infer, how much more so with regard to God, none of whose attributes we can experience, none of whose attributes can be the object of our experiment? God, it will be argued, is in relation to the world as a cause to its effect, and by knowing the effect, we can know the cause. This is an error. For actions are caused by individual agents. All causes are individualized realities, and differ each from the other, as knowledge of Plato from that of Socrates, and we can never arrive at a knowledge of the cause by an analysis of the effect, unless we have grasped the cause by a previous intuition. Divine nature is thus unintelligible to us. Indeed, we cannot know certainly that God is, and all the customary proofs are only arguments as to the probability of His existence, and nothing more. (Averroës for this reason blamed Avicenna for having said that the metaphysician can prove the existence of isolated substances.)

This theory, of course, flatly contradicted St. Thomas, who insisted that man can arrive at a certain proof of the existence of one God by reason alone without the help of revelation. And if that position of St. Thomas' is denied, we arrive, as Bertrand Russell has emphasized in all his writings, at agnosticism: we cannot *know* God exists. Either we can assume His existence, and incline to theism, or we can assume His nonexistence and incline to atheism; but in either case, we are agnostics; we cannot know, we can *never* know.

As Frederick Copleston has pointed out, in his *A History of Philosophy,* Vol. III (Burns, Oates, 1953),

"If by 'God' one means the absolutely supreme, perfect, unique and infinite being, Ockham did not think that the existence of such a being can be strictly proved by the philosopher. If, on the other hand, one means by 'God' the first conserving causes of this world, without any certain knowledge about the nature of that cause, Ockham did think that the existence of such a being can be philosophically proved. But as this second understanding of the term 'God' is not all that is usually understood by the term, one might just as well say, without further ado, that Ockham did not admit the demonstrability of God's existence."

This position of Ockham follows naturally and logically from that of Peter Abelard, and although we do not know how much Ockham was aware of his debt, or how consciously he derived from his tenth-century predecessor, the sequence is absolutely clear, and the Church, threatened in its basic assumption by both, was well aware of its danger. For if reason cannot, unaided by revelation, arrive at a knowledge of the existence of God, but only at belief in Him, then, since (as Aquinas proved) the object of science and that of faith can never be the same, all we can have of God is faith. It follows then, since there is no evident necessity for belief in God that you "pays your penny and you takes your choice," for faith is something you can take or leave.

It is probable that the boldness of Ockham's views was the reason he never got his doctorate, for, since he constantly repeated himself, it may be said that by 1324, when the Papacy took alarm at his theories, his fundamental position was already clear, and the future development of his thought obviously adumbrated. In 1324 Ockham was summoned to Avignon to defend his views before John XXII, and it is particularly interesting that Durandus of St. Pourçain, one of the men to whom he is nearest in thought, was one of the men to whom his writings were given after John Lutterell had brought them from Oxford to Avignon in 1323.

John Lutterell denounced the *Commentary on the Sentences* in which Ockham referred approvingly to Peter Aurioli. Peter was a papal nominee, who had attended the lectures of Duns Scotus, and was a disciple of St. Augustine, and a refuter of St. Thomas Aquinas, whom he regarded as an innovator. Peter was a special favorite of John XXII, who had made him Bishop of Aix, the next See to Avignon. Like Ockham, Peter Aurioli said that the notion of species had no other content than "the qualitative resemblances between various beings." The multiplicity of beings in the same species is "meaningless." And Peter Aurioli goes almost as far as Ockham in denying any "extramental value to abstract knowledge; normally intuitive knowledge, sensible or intellectual, presents us with a real and existing object." But Peter does admit that God could "in the absence of real beings, create in sensation and intellectual intuition a content which would give us the illusion of its existence." Both Durandus and Peter Aurioli denied the distinction between essence and existence.

Ockham was not, however, then condemned. He remained four years at Avignon, and, it must be supposed, there continued to develop the two major principles of his philosophy: that beings must not be multiplied without necessity, and that there is no real distinction between material substances.

Ockham was very careful to protect his audacious theories with constantly recurring phrases such as "I believe everything that the Church explicitly believes and nothing else"; "I am ready to submit my reason to the authority of the Church, and to believe with my heart and teach with my tongue all that the Church teaches." He probably would have escaped formal condemnation of his theories successfully all his life, in view of the similarity of his views with those of two such highly placed and regarded men as Durandus and Peter Aurioli, had it not been for his actions.

In 1322, John XXII had declared the Franciscan doctrine of absolute poverty, and in 1328 Michael of Cesena, the General of the Order, heretical. Ockham fled to the Emperor Louis of Bavaria in Pisa, where another Franciscan, Marsilius of Padua, had taken refuge earlier. In 1328 Marsilius, Michael and Ockham were all excommunicated. Ockham, who had declared in the most famous of his works, *On the Sacrament of the Altar,* that whenever there was a dispute between theologians, "recourse was to be had to the Pope," and indeed, seemed to maintain that the Pope was above even a General Council (a dogma not defined by the Church until the nineteenth century) now said the Pope was a heretic—a position taken, under somewhat similar circumstances, in the 1950's by the Jesuit Father Feeney. Ockham's writings after his flight were largely political: he and Marsilius of Padua are the two major political theorists of the later Middle Ages, but Ockham's greatest philosophical works were written in the peace of Oxford before his stormy political career began. He went with Louis of Bavaria to Munich and stayed there. His tone then became very shrill against the Pope, and although his antipapal views were never as extreme as those of Marsilius of Padua, they reached a climax in 1334. After the death of Louis of Bavaria, in 1348, he asked to be reinstated in his order, and begged the Pope's pardon but hoped he would not be required to come to Avignon to make his submission in person "as it was not easy for him to come"—an understatement, as his political opinions would have probably made it impossible for him to travel safely. On June 8, 1349, the Pope gave authority for the absolution of William of Ockham and his companions, though it is not known whether he received this pardon before his death. But as he is buried in the Franciscan chapel in Munich, next to Michael of Cesena, it is likely that he perished in the Black Death in 1349, after being released from the excommunication.

Pierre Duhem, writing in 1909 (*Etudes sur Leonardo da Vinci*) regards Ockham's "natural philosophy" as a forerunner of the mathematico-mechanical world-view of Descartes and Newton. Of Ockham's theory of motion he says "the affirmation that the continuation of the local motion does not need any moving cause is the law of inertia itself, formulated by Descartes and at the time of Ockham too new to be admitted."

Herewith follow some definitions from Stephen Chak Tornay's translations from William of Ockham (contained in his *Studies and Sentences*, published by the Open Court Publishing Co., 1938).

From the *Expositio Aurea:*
〔 Any imaginable thing which exists by itself without any addition is singular and numerically one. Every science begins with individuals. From sensation, which gives only singular things, arises memory, from memory experience, and through experience, we obtain the universal which is the basis of art and science.〕

From *The Sentences of Peter Lombard:*
〔 It is possible to have intuitive knowledge, both sensitive and intellectual, of a thing which does not exist . . . This intuitive vision, whether sensitive or intellectual, is an absolute thing, distant in place and subject from the seen thing object, therefore vision can remain after, say, the star has been destroyed . . .

It is clear too, that our intellect, in our present state,

does not know merely sensory things, but particularly and intuitively knows some intelligible things too, which by no means are objects of the senses. To these belong acts of intellect, acts of will, pleasure, sorrow and the like, which one can experience as internal without their being sensory or objects of the senses.]

From the *Quodlibets:*
[Every universal is one singular thing and is universal only by the signification of many things.]

From the *Sentences* once more:
[I am enquiring now, whether this universal . . . is something real from the part of the thing which is outside of the soul. All whom I meet agree by saying that the entity which is somehow universal is really in the individual, although some say that it is distinguished only formally, and some that it is not distinguished at all according to the nature of the thing, but only according to reason. All these opinions coincide in that the universals are allowed to exist somehow away from the thing, so that their universality is held to be really present in the singular objects themselves. This latter opinion is simply false and absurd. Against it this is my case. There is no unitary, unvaried or simple thing in a multiplicity of singular things, nor in any kind of created individuals, together and at the same time. If such a thing were allowed, it would be numerically one, therefore it would not be in many singular objects nor would it be of their essence. But the singular and the universal thing are by themselves two things, really distinct and equally simple, therefore if the singular thing is numerically one, the universal thing will be numerically one also . . .

If humanity were different from particular individuals and a part of their essence, one and the same invariable thing would be in many individuals, and so this same numerically one and invariable thing would be at different places, which is false. In the same way, that same invariable thing would, say, be condemned in Judas and saved in Christ, and hence, there would be something condemned and miserable in Christ, which is absurd.

To conclude, I say that there is no such thing as a universal, intrinsically present in the things to which it is common. No universal, except that is such by voluntary agreement, is existent in any way outside of the soul, but everything that can be predicated of many things, is by its nature in the mind either psychologically or logically.]

CHAPTER XII

Conclusion

FOR A THOUSAND YEARS, THROUGHOUT THE MIDDLE AGES, the medieval philosophers had been concerned with certain static problems such as the nature of being, the relationship of essence to existence, the dichotomy of fate and free-will, the pluralist and monist views of ultimate reality and the question of the existence or non-existence of universals. Certain dynamic problems concerned them no less; for example, the distinction between matter and form, knowledge and experience; the relations between the mind and its object; the causal intervention of sense in the production of thought; and the change from non-being to being —these matters were hotly debated in the schools, the cloisters, the universities, and even the courts of Europe, by men of all nations and several creeds. And each thinker added something to the content of scholastic philosophy, which was born from the union of Greek philosophy and Christian revelation, and grew by gradual accumulation of detail accompanied, as Hawkins says, "by criticism and emendation as the occasion called for them." With the beginnings of experimental science, with Robert Grosseteste, St. Albert the Great and Roger Bacon, the questions changed. Men were no longer as anxious to know *Why?* as *How?* No longer was there passionate enquiry into such problems as *why* God became man (*Cur Deus*

Homo), but rather men wanted to know how the rainbow is put together, and how it is colored. Men such as Durandus of St. Pourçain and William of Ockham, and Ockham's many followers, criticized realism and conceptualism in a radical fashion. Dr. Tornay writes:

{ The universal concept, discovered by Socrates as the rock of knowledge, extended by Plato to metaphysical dimensions, and developed by Aristotle as the indwelling principle of all actuality, was accepted by both the Augustinian and Thomistic lines of thought as the surety to guarantee the solidity of science and of life. The stubborn facts of human defeat were bound to open the eyes sooner or later to the futility of such anthropocentrism. Realism, which had been dominant through the centuries of the Middle Ages, received its first serious blow under the onslaughts of Roscelin and Abelard in the middle of the twelfth century. The historical role however, of undermining its foundations in a fatal manner, was reserved to William of Ockham.}

ST. AUGUSTINE HAS SAID *"Virtus est ordo amoris,"* VIRTUE is the setting in order of love, and the whole of medieval thought appears as a huge, protracted effort to arrange all human knowledge tidily in a great system, whose motor and creator was the Love that, as Dante put it, moves the sun and other stars. Every detail, whether in physics or chemistry, astronomy or psychology as then apprehended, must be arranged and accounted for, fitted into its place in that giant jigsaw puzzle, the created universe. The Gothic cathedrals, with their astonishing universality, are each an explanation of theology, history and revelation; they are "frozen music" and art besides. Intentionally to the last detail they were concrete expressions of philosophy, for the instruction of the illiterate, recapitulations of a total and inclusive attitude to all things visible and invisible. The effect, in thought as in art, is sometimes crowded as are the catalogues of symbolic figures on the porches of Wells Cathedral or Chartres, the profusion of ornament in an illuminated manuscript, the relentless symmetry of structure in the writing of Dante or St. Thomas. But the cumulative effect was an enduring, and, as human philosophies go, a solid structure, that weathered the external attacks of the pagan and of the paynim and the internal threats of Avicenna and Averroës, incorporating and digesting what could be used from all external or alien substances because all good belonged to the giver of all good and must be returned to Him, as all truth must be greedily accepted and assimilated as His gift.

When Ockham declared that all our conceptions are mental signs which signify the external things, and that "a sign is anything, that, as apprehended, presents something else to cognition," he disassociated logic and metaphysics, philosophy and theology. For Ockham "the essence of the self is the power of self-determination" and "God is a supreme and arbitrary will, contingently decreeing." What is a mental sign? A concept of the soul, according to Ockham, "the act of intellect itself," according to Durandus, which Ockham accepts as "the most probable of all opinions." Universals are not real things, "their being is their being understood . . ." (Tornay, op. cit.)

Some of Ockham's contemporaries, for example Nicolas of Autrecourt (flourished 1340), said that "the existence of the external world cannot be demonstrated, and the only substance which a man can know with certitude is that of his own soul." Down with causality, cried the anti-scholastics of the fourteenth century, men must convert their intellect to the observation of phenomena, and forget Aristotle and his commentators. After their critical efforts had been expended, nothing was left but a succession of mental phenomena, and the reality of any human existence became a figment of some Red King's dream, as in *Alice Through the Looking-Glass*.

Ockham did not go so far. Repeated impressions of exterior reality, he said, produce a similarity of experience, and "such repeated experiences are molded into an exemplar, a logical fictum" (Tornay, op. cit.). "With his theory of signs, he inserted a medium between the knowing mind and the knowable world in such a way that what had been for ages a means of knowledge became with him the immediate object of knowledge." Meanwhile the scholastics gradually made themselves absurd by arguing more and more etiolated problems—of which a favorite (though fictitious) example is how many angels could stand on the point of a needle. The anti-scholastics (as the Ockhamists were called) could also rise to pretty ridiculous heights. To John Buridan (d. shortly after 1358) a leading Paris Ockhamist, is ascribed the dilemma (which is not, however, to be found in his writings) of the donkey dying of hunger between two equidistant bundles of hay, unable to choose between two equal goods. According to Buridan, every good "set before us by the intellect, exercises on the will, which is undetermined of itself, a natural attraction, and we necessarily choose what appears to us to be the better." Buridan, a French physicist, defined motion as a concept, having no reality apart from moving bodies.

"I say therefore that the moving thing in such a motion, after the separation of the moving body from the first projector, is the moved thing itself, not by reason of any power in it, for this moving thing and the moved thing cannot be distinguished."

While many of the best philosophical minds of the fourteenth century thus moved in the direction of experimental science, others were directed toward another experimental field—that of mysticism. Meister Eckhart is one example; Jan Ruysbroek (1293-?1350) and Gerard of Groot are others. Nicolas of Cusa (1401-1464), the busy bishop of Brixen, had studied at Deventer, and been influenced by the spirituality taught there: his *De Docta Ignorantia* (of the wise ignorance) is a continuation of the Anselmian-Aquinian tradition of philosophy, yet is based on a theory of knowledge which is expressed according to the principle of contradiction, and above it, on a spiritual vision "which grasps the coincidence of the contraries which reason regards as incompatible . . . A curved line becomes identical with a straight line when its curvature is infinitely diminished, and the hypotenuse of a triangle coincides with the two other sides when the angle becomes infinitely great," wrote Nicolas, who in the practical sphere worked long and hard to reconcile the Greek church with the Pope. In 1450 union seemed near, and the humanist Pope, another Nicolas (the Fifth), made Nicolas of Cusa a Cardinal and encouraged his efforts to promote peace and unity in Christendom. These seemed crowned by the Concordat of the Princes, and the successful culmination and close of the Council of Basle.

Nicolas, in his philosophy, returned to a platonist, and almost to a pantheist, position: God, the absolute Maximum, is at the same time identical with the lowest possible or Minimum. To say He is, is the same as to say He is not: to exist and not to exist coincide in Him as do all contraries. This is as obviously an end of philosophy as terminology is the end of logic: semantics and mysticism, theology and dialectic are all exits from philosophy proper: they are doors opening or closing, dead-ends or runways according to the attitude taken towards them.

Philosophy proper, however, marked time between William of Ockham and René Descartes, while the old structure of scholasticism was being torn down by the Reformation. Yet the full "epistemological approach" of Descartes depended on an analytical geometry which looks back to Nicolas of Cusa and to Roger Bacon.

The Age of Belief ended, to use T. S. Eliot's phrase, "not with a bang but a whimper."

Recommended Further Reading

BOER, Dr. Tzitze de. *History of Philosophy in Islam.* Luzac Publishers, 1903. A classic.

BURCH, G. B. *Early Medieval Philosophy.* Columbia University Press, 1951. A most useful book making free use of original texts.

COPLESTONE, Frederick. *A History of Philosophy.* Burns, Oates & Washbourne, 1953. An up-to-the-minute account of western philosophy by a hard-hitting writer.

CROMBIE, Alistair. *Robert Grosseteste and the Origins of Experimental Science: 1100-1700.* Oxford University Press, 1953. A very helpful study with a superlative bibliography.

GILSON, Etienne. *The Spirit of Medieval Philosophy.* Scribners, 1936. This is perhaps the best book ever written on this subject by its foremost living authority. This author has written recommended books on St. Thomas, Duns Scotus, and St. Bonaventura, among many.

HAWKINS, D. J. B. *A Sketch of Medieval Philosophy.* Sheed & Ward, 1947. A slight but useful outline.

HODGKIN, Thomas. *Italy and Her Invaders.* Oxford University Press, 1931. Excellent for background on the Dark Ages.

HUIZINGA, Johan. *The Waning of the Middle Ages.* E. Arnold, 1937. Excellent reference though a bit over-written.

HUSIK, I. *History of Jewish Medieval Philosophy.* Macmillan, 1916. An old book but one of the best in a sparse field.

MARGOLIOUTH, D. S. *The Early Development of Mohammedanism*. Williams & Norgate, 1914. A good introduction to the complicated study of Islamic thought.

MARITAIN, Jacques. *An Introduction to Philosophy*. Sheed & Ward, 1947. A useful outline of the Thomist viewpoint by a great living Catholic philosopher.

NICHOLSON, Reynold. *Mystics of Islam*. G. Bell & Sons, 1914. A fascinating account of the early Persian and Arab mystics.

PEGIS, Anton (ed.). *Basic Writings of St. Thomas Aquinas*. Random House, 1945. An excellent anthology in two volumes.

POWER, Eileen. *Medieval People*. Methuen, 1924. A vividly told day-to-day life story of people in the medieval period.

RAND, E. K. *Founders of the Middle Ages*. Harvard University Press, 1928. A comprehensive study by one of the great American scholars in this field.

TAYLOR, Henry Osborn. *The Medieval Mind: A History of the Development of Thought and Emotion in the Middle Ages*. Macmillan, 1927. Two of the best known volumes in this field; they wear well.

THOMAS AQUINAS, Saint. *Philosophical Texts*. Translated by Thomas Gilby, Oxford University Press, 1951. A stimulating collection with an excellent introduction.

VERNET, Felix. *Medieval Spirituality*. Herder, 1930. Good expression of the Catholic viewpoint.

WADDELL, Helen. *The Wandering Scholars*. Constable, 1927. An alive account of the "goliardes" who sang their way across Europe in medieval times.

WULF, Maurice de. *History of Medieval Philosophy*. Longmans, Green, 1938. An indispensable aid for students in two volumes.

Index of Names

Abelard, Peter, 98ff, 144, 150, 183, 204, 210
Abu Bakr al-Razi, 116
Al-Ashari, 115
Albert the Great, St., 144ff, 180, 201, 209
Alcuin, 78-79
Alexander of Hales, 108, 139
Al-Farabi, 116-17, 129
Algazel. *See* Al-Ghazzali.
Al-Ghazzali, 127ff
Al-Hallaj, 128
Al-Kindi, 111, 115
Al-Muammar, 114-15
Al-Nazzam, 114
Ambrose, St., 24, 25
Anselm, St., 88-97, 98, 152, 212
Aquinas, St. Thomas, 19, 20, 80, 88, 97, 109, 117, 127, 131, 139, 145-79, 180ff, 199, 201, 202, 210, 211, 212
Arians, 54, 61
Aristotle, 14, 19, 20, 54, 66, 99, 100, 106, 109, 111, 112, 116, 127, 129, 131, 132, 137, 139, 144, 145, 147, 149ff, 159, 165ff, 182, 202, 203, 210, 211
Augustine of Canterbury, St., 77

Augustine of Hippo, St., 14, 19, 23-53, 128, 130, 139, 172ff, 182, 210
Aurioli, Peter, 203, 205-06
Avencebrol. *See* Ibn-Gabirol.
Averroës (Ibn-Rushd), 109, 127ff, 144ff, 149, 152, 159, 181, 201, 204, 211
Avicenna (Ibn-Sina), 117ff, 129, 138, 158-59, 165ff, 190, 204, 211
Bacon, Sir Francis, 201
Bacon, Roger, 132, 137ff, 148, 181, 209, 213
Becket, St. Thomas à, 104, 107
Bérenger of Tours, 87
Bernard of Clairvaux, St., 18-19, 99ff
Boethius, Anicius Manlius Severinus, 19, 53-71, 98, 144, 159
Bonaventura, St., 19, 139-44, 147, 180, 201
Bossuet, Jacques, 105
Breakspear, Nicholas, 106
Buridan, John, 212
Calvin, John, 23
Capella, Martianus, 78
Cassiodorus, Flavius Magnus Aurelius, 70-71
Charlemagne, 78, 104

GREAT MINDS

☐ **EXISTENTIALISM FROM DOSTOEVSKY TO SARTRE, Selected and Introduced by Walter Kaufmann.** This volume provides basic writings, many never before translated, of Dostoevsky, Kierkegaard, Nietzsche, Rilke, Kafka, Ortega, Jaspers, Heidegger, Sartre, and Camus, along with an invaluable introductory essay by Walter Kaufmann. (009308—$10.95)

☐ **THE AGE OF IDEOLOGY: The 19th Century Philosophers. Edited by Henry D. Aiken.** A new interpretation of the conflicts of 19th-century philosophy with selections from the major works of Kant, Fichte, Schopenauer, Comte, Mill, Spencer, Marx, Mach, Nietzsche, Kierkegaard and Hegal. Includes recommended further reading and index. (009650—$6.00)

☐ **THE ESSENTIAL ROUSSEAU newly translated by Lowell Bair; with an Introduction by Matthew Josephson.** The major contributions of the great 18th-century social philosopher whose ideas helped spark a revolution that still has not ended. Included are: The Social Contract, Discourse on Inequality, Discourse on the Arts and Sciences, and The Creed of a Savouard priest (from *Emile*). (010314—$5.95)

☐ **THE ESSENTIAL ERASMUS. Selected and Translated with an Introduction and Commentary by John P. Dolan.** The first single volume in English to show the full range of thought of one of the great Catholic minds of the Renaissance. Includes the complete text of *The Praise of Folly*. (009723—$5.95)

Prices slightly higher in Canada.

WORLD MASTERPIECES

☐ **THE DECAMERON by Giovanni Boccaccio translated by Mark Musa and Peter Bondanella.** Introduction by Thomas C. Bergin. In this exuberant new translation, two scholars present a *Decameron* that speaks in contemporary *American* English, yet remains "remarkably faithful to the original in both letter and spirit ... The reader may be assured that he is, though in another tongue, truly reading *The Decameron*."—from Thomas Bergin's Introduction.   (627466—$6.99)

☐ **THE PRINCE by Niccolo Machiavelli.** Translated by Luigi Ricci and with an Introduction by Christian Gauss. Relates Machiavelli's 15th century masterpiece to the political and scholarly developments within the past hundred years.   (627555—$2.50)

☐ **THE SONG OF ROLAND translated by Robert Harrison.** This first and foremost example of the heroic epic in French literature stands out as one of the greatest achievements of the medieval artistic genius.   (628225—$4.50)

☐ **THE CANTERBURY TALES, A Selection, by Geoffrey Chaucer.** Edited and with an Introduction by Donald R. Howard. A group of stories told by an oddly assorted band of pilgrims en route to the shrine of Thomas à Becket in Canterbury Cathedral. Includes a Glossary of basic Middle English words.   (524004—$3.50)

☐ **DON QUIXOTE by Miguel Cervantes, translated by Walter Starkie.** Abridged. The entertaining misadventures of the dreamy knight-errant who tried to revive chivalry in Spain.   (626842—$4.95)

Prices slightly higher in Canada

There's an epidemic with 27 million victims. And no visible symptoms.

It's an epidemic of people who can't read.

Believe it or not, 27 million Americans are functionally illiterate, about one adult in five.

The solution to this problem is you... when you join the fight against illiteracy. So call the Coalition for Literacy at toll-free **1-800-228-8813** and volunteer.

Volunteer Against Illiteracy. The only degree you need is a degree of caring.

64 trees down